직독직해로 읽는

성경 이야기 - 구약편

The Story of the Bible

직독직해로 읽는
성경 이야기 – 구약편
The Story of the Bible

개정판 1쇄 발행 2020년 10월 30일
초판 1쇄 발행 2012년 5월 20일

역주	더 콜링(김정희, 박윤수, 이성진)
디자인	DX
일러스트	정은수
발행인	조경아
발행처	랭귀지북스
주소	서울시 마포구 포은로2나길 31 벨라비스타 208호
전화	02.406.0047 **팩스** 02.406.0042
이메일	languagebooks@hanmail.net
MP3 다운로드	blog.naver.com/languagebook
등록번호	101-90-85278 **등록일자** 2008년 7월 10일
ISBN	979-11-5635-143-6 (13740)
가격	13,000원

ⓒ LanguageBooks 2012

직독직해로 읽는

성경 이야기 - 구약편
The Story of the Bible

더 콜링 역주

Language Books

머리말

"어렸을 때 누구나 갖고 있던 세계명작 한 질.
그리고 TV에서 하던 세계명작 만화에 대한 추억이 있습니다."

"친숙한 이야기를 영어 원문으로 읽어 봐야겠다고 마음 먹고 샀던 원서들은
이제 애물단지가 되어 버렸습니다."

"재미있는 세계명작 하나 읽어 보려고 따져 보는 어려운 영문법,
모르는 단어 찾느라 이리저리 뒤져 봐야 하는 사전.
몇 장 넘겨 보기도 전에 지칩니다."

영어 독해력을 기르려면 술술 읽어가며 내용을 파악하는 것이 중요합니다. 현재 수능 시험에도 대세인 '직독직해' 스타일을 접목시킨 〈**직독직해로 읽는 세계명작 시리즈**〉는 세계명작을 영어 원작으로 쉽게 읽어갈 수 있도록 안내해 드릴 것입니다.

'직독직해' 스타일로 읽다 보면, 영문법을 들먹이며 따질 필요가 없으니 쉽고, 끊어 읽다 보니 독해 속도도 빨라집니다. 이 습관이 들여지면 어떤 글을 만나도 두렵지 않을 것입니다.

명작의 재미를 즐기며 영어 독해력을 키우는 두 마리의 토끼를 잡으세요!

　　〈직독직해로 읽는 세계명작 시리즈〉의 나의 소중한 파트너이
자 오랜 친구 윤수, 나의 브레인 성진과 심한 감기 중에도 작업 일
정 걱정하던 일러스트레이터 은수 씨, 좋은 멘토 디자인 DX, 그리
고 이 책이 출판될 수 있도록 늘 든든하게 지원해 주시는 랭귀지북
스에 감사의 마음을 전합니다.

　　마지막으로 내 삶의 이유가 되시는 하나님께 영광을 올려 드
립니다.

더 콜링 김정희

목차

C O N T E N T S

읽기 가이드

영어 앞에만 서면 숨이 콱콱 막힌다···
〈직독직해로 읽는 〈세계 명작〉〉 시리즈와 함께하세요!

I

어떻게 하면 어려워 보이는 영어 명작을 술술 읽을 수 있을
까요?
우선 문제점부터 살펴봅시다.

(1) 배웠던 문법 따져가며 읽지 않았나요?

관계대명사절부터 to 부정사 어쩌구 저쩌구··· 저절로 골치가 아파옵니
다. 재미있게 읽어볼까 하고 폈던 책을 덮어버리고 맙니다. 골치 아픈 문
법을 따지다 보면 정작 책에서 놓치지 말아야 할 중요한 '내용'은 무엇
인지 감도 잡히지 않습니다.

(2) 뒤에 수식구 찾고 앞에 주어 찾고 왔다갔다 정신없이 읽었나요?

들인 시간에 비해 진도는 몇 장 안 나가고, 그렇게 명작의 재미를 찾지
못하고, 결국 지치고 맙니다. 앞뒤로 왔다갔다 하면서 읽는 것은 시간 낭
비뿐 아니라 의욕 상실의 주범입니다.

II

그럼 어떻게 하면 재미도 있고, 쭉쭉 읽어갈 수 있을까요?

(1) **그래서 제시하는 방법이 직독직해입니다.**

현재 수능에서도 직독직해가 대세인만큼 독해 실력의 향상을 위해서 꼭
필요한 방법입니다.

아무리 복잡하고 긴 글이라도, 문법을 따지기 보다는 전체적인 내용 이
해에 중점을 두며 읽는 방법, 즉 '나무보다 숲'을 보는 방법입니다.

직독직해가 익숙해지면, 그 동안 어려웠던 영문 소설이 어느 새 쉽게 다
가올 것입니다.

(2) **직독직해를 잘하려면 끊어 읽기를 잘해야 합니다.**

그럴려면 영어 문장의 구조에 대한 지식이 필요합니다. 무작정 끊어 읽
기를 한다면, 어디에서 끊어야 할지도 모르고 대충 끊어 읽어서 의미의
연결이 어렵습니다.

III
그러면 어디에서 끊어야 할까요?

(1) 주어가 길면
→ 전체 주어 묶음 뒤에서 끊습니다.

What is done / cannot be undone.

일어난 일은 / 되돌릴 수 없다.

That I have done / is important thing.

내가 했다는 것은 / 중요한 일이다.

(2) 타동사 뒤에 목적어로 명사 또는 대명사가 나오면
→ 그 뒤에서 끊습니다.

We opened it / immediately.

우리는 그것을 열었다 / 바로.

He put his hand / in his pocket.

그는 손을 넣었다 / 주머니 안에.

(3) 타동사 뒤에 목적어의 묶음이 길게 오면

→ 목적어 앞에서 끊습니다.

But she could not understand / why Sara looked different.

하지만 그녀는 이해할 수 없었다 / 왜 새라가 달라졌는지.

People refuse to believe / that a strange new thing can be done.

사람들은 믿기 거부했다 / 낯설고 새로운 것들이 이루어질 수 있다는 것을.

(4) 수식어구를 만난다면

→ 전치사+명사의 묶음 앞에서 끊습니다.

Men / in shirt sleeves / were going in and out.

남자들이 / 셔츠 차림의 / 들락날락 하고 있었다.

The small drudge / before the grate / swept the hearth once.

어린 하녀는 / 난로 앞에 있던 / 난로 바닥을 한 번 쓸었다.

→ 명사+ 현재분사/과거분사/형용사의 묶음 앞에서 끊습니다.

A huntsman /returning with his dogs / from the field, / fell in by
chance / with a Fisherman.

한 사냥꾼이 / 개들을 끌고 돌아오던 / 들판에서 / 우연히 마주쳤다 / 낚
시꾼과.

The sharpest needle / warranted not to cut in the eye / was not
sharper the Scrooge.

가장 날카로운 바늘도 / 바늘귀가 부러지지 않는다고 보장된 / 스크루지
보다 날카롭지 못했다.

→ 명사+관계사의 묶음 앞에서 끊습니다.

Martha / who was a poor apprentice at a milliner's / told them.
마사는 / 숙녀용 모자가게에서 일하는 가난한 견습공인 / 그들에게 말했다.

Two men / who watched the light / had made a fire.
두 남자가 / 빛을 지키는 / 불을 지폈다.

(5) 부사절과 주절이 있다면
→ 그 경계에서 끊습니다.

부사절의 위치는 주절의 앞에 놓일 수도 있고, 뒤에 놓일 수도 있습니다. 부사절의 위치와 상관없이 경계에서 끊고, 부사절과 주절은 서로 독립된 문장 구조를 갖기 때문에 완전히 별도로 해석해야 합니다.

As he was crossing through the water / he lost his footing.

물을 건너고 있을 때 / 그는 발을 헛디뎠다.

A carter was driving a wagon / along a country lane, / when the wheels sank down deep / into a rut.

마부가 마차를 몰고 있었다 / 시골길을 따라, / 그때 바퀴가 깊게 빠져버렸다 / 바퀴 자국에.

(6) to부정사가 '~하기 위해서'라고 해석된다면
→ to 부정사 앞에서 끊습니다.

It took two hands / to do it.
두 손이 필요했다 / 그것을 하기 위해.

She looked behind her / up the long walk / to see if anyone was coming.
그녀는 뒤를 돌아다 보았다 / 긴 산책로 끝을 / 누가 오고 있는지 보기 위해.

이 외에도 여러 가지 방법이 있습니다.
하지만 언어는 수학처럼 공식에 맞춰 공부할 수 없습니다.
탄력성 있게 그 언어가 가지고 있는 매력을 느끼는 것이
가장 중요합니다. 이 모든 방법은 의미가 잘 통하기
위함이라는 것을 명심하세요!
그럼 〈직독직해로 읽는 세계 명작〉 시리즈와 함께
즐거운 영어 공부를 시작해 보세요!

THE BEGINNING OF THINGS
만물의 시작

Away back / in the beginning of things / God made the
아주 오래 전   만물의 시작되던 때   하나님이 하늘과 땅을

sky and the earth / we live upon. At first / it was all dark,
만드셨다   우리가 살고있는.   처음에는   어둠 뿐이었고,

/ and the earth had no form, / but God was building a
땅은 형태가 없었다.   그러나 하나님이 인간을 위한 세상을

home for us, / and his work went on through six long
만드셨고,   작업은 엿새 간 계속되어,

days, / until it was finished as we see it now.
마침내 현재 우리가 보는 모습이 되었다.

On the first day God said, / "Let there be light," / and the
첫째 날에 하나님은 말씀하셨고,   "빛이 있으라,"

black night turned to gray, / and light came. God called
그러자 어두운 밤이 회색 빛으로 변했고,   빛이 나타났다.   하나님은 빛을

the light Day, / and the darkness Night, / and the evening
낮이라 부르셨고.   어두움을 밤이라 부르셨으며,

and the morning made the first day.
저녁과 아침이 지나 첫째 날이 되었다.

Then God divided the waters, / so that there were clouds
그리고 하나님은 물을 나누자,   구름이 위에

above / and seas below, / and He called the clouds
바다가 아래에 놓였고,   구름이 있는 공간을 하늘이라고 부르셨다.

heaven. It was the second day.
이것이 둘째 날이었다.

rise 드러나다 | He 하나님 | bear 지니다 | cattle 소, 가축

Then the seas were gathered together / by themselves, /
그 후에 바다가 한 곳으로 모이자   스스로,

and the dry land rose above them, / and God saw that it
마른 땅이 그 위에 드러났으며,   이것은 하나님이 보시기에 좋았다.

was good. Then He called to / the grass, / and the plants,
그리곤 하나님이 불러내시자   풀과,   식물과,

/ and the trees / to come out of the ground, / and they
나무들을   지면 위로 나오라고,

came bearing their seeds, / and He called the third day
그 모든 것들이 씨를 가진 채로 나왔고,   하나님이 셋째 날을 좋다고 말씀하셨다.

good.

Then God called to the two great lights, / the sun and the
하나님이 두 개의 거대한 빛을 불러내어,   해와 달이라 칭하고,

moon, / to shine clear in the sky, / which had been first
하늘에서 맑게 비추라 하시자,   처음에 어두웠던 하늘이,

dark, / and then gray, / and they rose and set to make /
회색으로 변하더니,   해와 달이 떠올라서 만들어 냈고

day and night, / and seasons and years, / and the stars
낮과 밤을,   계절과 해를,   또한 별들도 나왔다.

came also, / and it was the fourth day.
이것이 넷째 날이었다.

Then God called for / all kinds of fishes / that swim in
그리고 하나님이 불러내시자   온갖 종류의 물고기와

the seas, and rivers, / and for all kinds of birds / that fly
바다와 강에서 헤엄치는,   온갖 종류의 새를   공중에서

in the air, / and they came, / and it was the fifth day.
날아다니는,   물고기와 새가 나왔고,   이것이 다섯째 날이다.

And then God called for the animals / to live on the
하나님이 동물들을 불러내어   땅 위에 살라고 하자,

green earth, / and the cattle and the great beasts, / and
가축과 거대한 짐승들과,

the creeping things came, / and God called them all
땅을 기어다니는 동물이 나왔고,   하나님이 그들을 보시고 모두 좋았다고 하셨다.

good.

After this / he made the first of the great family of Man.
그 이후에 하나님은 최초의 인간 가족을 만드셨다.

He made them / after His own likeness. He made their
하나님은 그들을 만드셨다 그분 자신과 비슷한 모습으로. 그들의 몸을 만들었다

bodies / from the earth, / but their souls He breathed
흙으로, 하지만 하나님이 영혼을 불어 넣으시자,

into them, / so that Man is a spirit, / living in an earthly
인간의 영혼이, 흙으로 만든 몸에 깃들어,

body, / and can understand about God / and love Him.
하나님에 대해 알고 그분을 사랑할 수 있었다.

He blessed them / and told them / to become many, / and
하나님은 인간을 축복하며 말씀하셨다 많은 자녀를 낳고 번성하여,

to rule over all the earth, / with its beasts and birds, and
그리고 땅 전체를 다스리며, 그곳에 사는 짐승들과 새들과, 물고기들을 지배하

fishes, / and it was the sixth day.
라고, 이 날은 여섯째 날이었다.

The Man's name was Adam, / and the woman, / who
그 사람의 이름은 아담이었고, 여자는,

was made from / a piece of Adam's body / nearest to his
만들어진 아담의 몸의 일부로 그의 심장에 가장

heart, / was named Eve.
가까운, 이브라고 불렸다.

Then God's world was finished, / and on the seventh
그러자 하나님의 세상은 완성이 되었고, 일곱째 날에

day / there was rest. God was pleased / with all that was
하나님은 쉬셨다. 하나님은 기뻐하시며 창조한 모든 것을 보시고,

made, / and He made the seventh day holy, / by setting it
일곱째 날을 거룩하게 만드셨다.

apart from all the others. We keep the Sabbath, / or the
다른 날들로부터 떨어뜨려 놓음으로써. 우리는 안식일을 지킨다,

Lord's day / still, / in which his children may rest and
또는 주일을 지금까지, 그분의 자녀들이 쉬며 예배를 드리는.

worship.

Adam and Eve were very happy, / for they had never
아담과 이브는 매우 행복했다, 아무 잘못도 한 적이 없었기

done anything wrong. God gave them / a beautiful wide
때문이다. 하나님은 그들에게 주시며 아름답고 넓은 동산을,

garden, / called Eden, / full of flowers and all kinds of
에덴이라 불리는, 꽃과 온갖 종류의 과일이 가득하고,

fruit, / and with a river flowing through it, / and told
그 사이로 강이 흐르고 있는,

Adam to take care of the garden, / and He sent all the
아담에게 동산을 가꾸라고 말씀하셨고, 온갖 동물과 새를 보내어

animals and birds / to Adam / to be named. God told him
아담에게 이름짓게 하셨다. 또한 하나님이 말씀하

also / that he might eat the fruit / of all the trees of the
시기를 과실을 먹을 수 있으나 정원의 모든 나무들의

garden / except one / — the tree of knowledge of good
하나만 제외하고 — 선과 악을 알게 하는 나무를 —

and evil — / but if he ate of the fruit of that tree / he
만약 그 나무의 과실을 먹으면

should surely die, / and Adam and Eve loved God, / and
반드시 죽을 것이라 하셨다, 아담과 이브는 하나님을 사랑했으므로,

had no wish to disobey Him, / for He was their Father.
그를 거역할 어떤 마음도 없었다. 하나님은 그들의 아버지였기 때문에.

holy 거룩한 | Sabbath 안식일 | worship 예배드리다 | disobey 거역하다

But there was a creeping serpent / in the garden, / and
하지만 그곳에는 기어다니는 뱀이 있었고   동산에,

the evil spirit / that puts wrong thoughts in our hearts /
악한 영이   우리 마음속에 잘못된 생각을 심어 주는

spoke to Eve / through the serpent.
이브에게 말을 했다   뱀을 통해서.

"You shall not die," / he said, / "but you shall be wise
"너희는 결코 죽지 않을 거야,"   뱀이 말했다.   "하지만 하나님처럼 지혜롭게 될 수 있어

like God / if you will eat of this fruit," / and Eve ate of
like God   이 과실을 먹으면,"   그래서 이브가 그 과일을

the fruit, / and gave it to her husband. Then they knew /
먹고,   남편에게 주었다.   그러자 그들은 알게 되었다

that they had sinned, / and when they heard the voice of
자신들이 죄를 지었다는 사실을,   그리고 하나님의 목소리가 들리자

God / in the garden / calling them, / they hid among the
동산에서   자신들을 부르는,   그들은 나무들 사이로 숨었다,

trees, / for they were unhappy and afraid. When the Lord
trees,   불행하고 두려웠기 때문에.

had asked Adam / if he had eaten of the fruit / that was
주님이 아담에게 묻자   과실을 먹었는지

forbidden, / Adam laid the sin upon Eve, / who gave it to
금지된,   아담은 이브에게 죄를 전가했고,   그에게 과실을 전해 준,

him, / and Eve said / that the serpent had tempted her /
him,   이브는 말했다   뱀이 자신을 유혹하여

to eat of the fruit. God knew / that they must suffer for
그 과실을 먹었다고.   하나님은 아셨기에   그들이 직접 저지른 죄로 고통 받아야

their sin, / so He sent them out of the garden / to make a
함을,   동산에서 그들을 내쫓고

garden for themselves, / and to work, / and suffer pain,
그들 스스로 동산을 만들고,   일하며,   고통 받도록 했다,

/ as all who came after them / have done to this day; /
그들의 후손들이   지금까지 그런 것처럼;

but He gave them a great promise, / that among their
하지만 하나님은 그들에게 큰 약속을 주셨다,　　　　　후손의 후손들 중에

children's children / One should be born / who would be
한 아이가 태어날 것이라고

stronger than sin, / and a Savior from it.
인간의 죄보다 강하며,　　　　구세주가 될.

After this / two little children were sent / to comfort
그 일이 있은 후　어린 아이 두 명이 태어났다　　　　　　아담과 이브를 위로하기

Adam and Eve / — first Cain, and then Abel. When they
위해　　　　　　— 첫째는 가인이고, 둘째는 아벨이었다.　　　형제는 자라서

grew up / Cain was a farmer, / but Abel was a shepherd.
가인은 농부가 되었고,　　　　아벨은 양치기가 되었다.

They had been taught to worship God / by bringing the
두 사람은 하나님을 섬기라고 배웠다　　　　　　가장 좋은 것을 가져옴으로써

best of all / they had to Him, / and so Cain brought fruit
하나님께 드릴 수 있는,　　　그래서 가인은 과일과 곡물을 가져와서

and grain / to lay upon his altar, / but Abel brought a
제단에 올려 놓았고,　　　아벨은 새끼 양을 가져왔다.

lamb.

God looked into their hearts and saw / that Abel wished
하나님은 그들의 마음을 들여다 보고 아셨다   아벨은 옳은 일을 하기 원하

to do right, / but Cain's heart was full of sin. Cain was
지만,   가인의 마음은 죄로 가득한 것을.   가인은 화가 나서

angry / because the Lord was pleased / with the worship
주님이 기뻐하신 것 때문에   아벨의 예배를,

of Abel, / and while they talked in the field / Cain killed
들판에서 대화를 하는 동안   가인은 동생을

his brother. When the Lord said to Cain, / "Where is
죽이고 말았다.   주님께서 가인에게 말씀하시자,   "네 동생이 어디

thy brother?" / he answered, / "I know not. Am I my
있느냐?"   가인이 대답했다,   "모릅니다. 내가 동생을 지키는 자입니까?"

brother's keeper?" And the Lord sent him away from
주님께서 가인을 멀리 떨어진 곳으로 보내어,

home, / to wander from place to place / over the earth, /
이 땅에서 저 땅으로 헤메며   세상에서,

and find no rest, / but He promised / that no one should
안식을 찾지 못하도록 하셨다, 하지만 약속하셨다   누구도 가인을 헤치거나,

hurt Cain, / or kill him / as he had killed his brother, / so
죽이지 못하도록   그가 자신의 동생을 죽였던 것처럼,

he went away / into another land / to live.
그렇게 그는 떠나서   다른 곳으로   살게 되었다.

Adam lived many years / after this / and had other
아담은 오랫동안 살면서   이후에   다른 자녀들을 낳았지만,

children, / but at last he died, / when his children's
끝내 아담은 죽었고,   그러자 그의 후손의 자손들이

children / were beginning to spread / over the land.
퍼져 나가기 시작했다   온 세상으로.

wander 헤매다

THE GREAT FLOOD
대 홍수

As the people of the earth / grew to be many more / and
세상의 사람들이 　　　　　　　수가 더욱 많아지고

spread over the plains and hills, / they also grew very
들과 언덕으로 퍼져 나가자, 　　　　　　　그들은 동시에 사악해졌다.

wicked. They forgot God, / and all the thoughts of their
　　　　사람들은 하나님을 잊었으며, 　마음속에 깃든 생각은 죄악 뿐이었다.

hearts were evil. Only Noah / still worshipped God / and
　　　　　　　　　　　오직 노아만 　　　여전히 하나님을 섬기며

tried to do right.
옳은 일을 하고자 했다.

The people had destroyed themselves, / and so God said
사람들은 스스로를 파괴하자, 　　　　　　　하나님이 노아에게 말씀하

to Noah:
셨다:

"The end of all flesh is come; / make thee an ark of
"모든 인류의 종말이 다가왔다; 　　　너는 소나무로 방주를 만들어라."

gopher wood."

He told Noah to make it of three stories, / with a window
하나님은 노아에게 방주를 3층으로 만들어 　　　　　　　꼭대기에 창문을 내고,

in the top, / and a door in the side. It was to be a great
　　　옆에 문을 내라고 하셨다. 　　　　이 방주는 떠다니는 거대한 집이

floating house, / more than four hundred feet long / and
될 것이며, 　　　　　길이는 400피트 이상이고

full of rooms, / and it was to be covered with tar / within
방으로 가득 채워서, 　　　타르로 덮을 예정이었다

and without, / so that the water should not creep in.
안팎을, 　　　물이 스며들지 못하도록.

---

wicked 사악하다 | flesh 육체 | ark 방주 | gopher wood 노아가 방주를 만든 나무, 소나무 전나무 등으로 추정 |
story (건물의) 층 | tar 타르

"I bring a flood of waters / upon the earth," / said the
"나는 홍수를 일으킬 것이며   이 땅 위에,"   하나님이 말씀

Lord, / "and everything that is in the earth shall die."
하셨다,   "이 땅의 모든 생물은 죽을 것이다."

This was to be the house of Noah, / with his wife, / and
이 방주는 노아의 집이 될 것이었다,   그의 부인과,

his three sons and their wives, / during the great flood.
세 아들과 며느리들의,   대 홍수 동안에.

Does the house seem large / for eight people? God had
이 집이 너무 커 보이는가   여덟 명에게는?

told Noah to make room / for a little family of every kind
하나님은 노아에게 방을 만들라고 하셨고   모든 종류의 새와 동물의 가족을 위한

of bird and beast / that lived, / and to gather food of all
살아있는,   모든 종류의 음식을 모으라고 하셨다

kinds / for himself and for them.
자신과 동물 가족을 위한.

So Noah did / all that the Lord had told him to do, / and
그렇게 노아는 행했고   하나님이 명령하신 모든 일을,

seven days before the great storm / he heard the Lord
대폭우가 시작하기 칠일 전에   주님이 부르시는 것을 들었다:

calling:

"Come thou and all thy house into the ark," / and that
"너는 네 가족과 함께 방주로 들어가라."
그래서 바로

very day, / Noah with his wife and his sons, / Shem,
그날에,
노아는 부인과 아들들을 데리고,

Ham, and Japtheth, / and their wives, / went into their
셈, 함, 야벳,
그리고 며느리들을,
거대한 검은 집에 들어갔다,

great black house, / and through the window in the top /
그리고 꼭대기에 난 창문을 통해서

came flying the little families of birds and insects, / from
새와 곤충 가족이 날아 들어왔다,

the tiny bees and humming birds, / to the great eagles,
작은 벌과 벌새부터,
거대한 독수리까지,

/ and through the door / on the side / came the families
문을 통해서는
측면에 있는
동물 가족이 들어왔다,

of animals, / two by two, / from the little mice to the tall
둘씩 짝을 지어서,
작은 쥐부터 키가 큰 기린과,

giraffes, / and the elephants, / and when all had come /
코끼리까지,
그리고 모두 들어오자

the Lord shut them in.
주님께서 문을 닫으셨다.

It rained / forty days and forty nights, / and the waters
비가 왔고
40일 밤낮 동안,

rose higher and higher, / covering the hills, / and creeping
물은 점점 더 불어나서,
언덕을 뒤덮고,

up the mountains, / so that every living thing died /
산 위로 기어올라가,
살아있는 모든 생물이 죽었다

except Noah, / and all that were with him in the ark.
노아를 제외하고,
노아와 방주에 함께한 모든 생물들과.

But after ten months / the tops of the mountains were
열 달이 지난 후에
산봉우리가 모습을 드러냈고,

seen, / and Noah sent out a raven and a dove. The raven
노아는 갈가마귀와 비둘기를 내보냈다.
갈가마귀는 이리저리

flew to and fro, / but the dove came back into the ark, /
날아다녔지만,
비둘기는 방주로 다시 들어왔다,

because she found no place / to rest her foot.
아무 장소도 찾지 못했기 때문에
앉아서 쉴 수 있는.

humming bird 벌새 | raven 갈가마귀 | to and fro 앞뒤로, 이리저리

After seven days / Noah sent her out again, / and she
칠일 후에 　　　　　　 노아가 다시 비둘기를 내보내자, 　　　　 비둘기는 돌아왔다

returned / with an olive leaf in her bill, / and then Noah
올리브 잎사귀를 부리에 물고, 　　　　　　 그제서야 노아는 알았다

knew / that the waters were going away.
물이 줄어들고 있음을.

After seven days again / he sent out his good little dove,
다시 칠일이 지난 후에 　　　　　　 노아는 비둘기를 내보냈고,

/ and she did not come back. So Noah was sure / that the
비둘기는 다시 돌아오지 않았다. 　　　　 그러자 노아는 확신했다

earth was getting dry, / and that God would soon tell him
땅이 완전히 말랐으며, 　　　　　　 하나님이 곧 자신에게 말씀하실 것이라고

/ to go out of the ark.
방주 밖으로 나가라고.

And so he did.
그리고 하나님이 그렇게 말씀하셨다.

Think how glad / the sheep and cows were / to find fresh
얼마나 기뻤을지 생각해 보라 양과 소들이 　　　　 신선한 풀을 발견하고,

grass, / and the birds / to fly to the green trees.
새들이 　　　　 푸른 나무로 날아가게 되었을 때.

Key Expression 🎙

형용사 sure의 쓰임
형용사 sure는 명사를 수식하는 한정적 보어로 쓰이는 용법과 서술적 용법의 쓰임을 구별해서 알아두어야 합니다.

▶ 한정적 용법 - (명사 앞) 확실한, 안정된
▶ 서술적 용법 - sure of[about] sth : ~을 확신하는
　　　　　　　　- sure that 주어+동사 : ~을 확신하는
　　　　　　　　- sure to 동사 : 틀림없이 ~할

ex) So Noah was sure that the earth was getting dry.
　　그래서 노아는 땅이 완전히 말랐다고 확신했다.

bill 부리 | proud 오만한, 자랑스러운 | idol 우상

What a silent world it must have been, / for there were
얼마나 조용한 세상이었을까,　　　　　　　아무도 없었으니

none / but Noah and his family / in all the earth. Noah
노아와 그의 가족 외에는　　　　　온 세상에.

did not forget / how God had saved them, / and he made
노아는 잊지 않았다　　하나님이 그들을 어떻게 구하셨는지,

an altar of stone, / and offered beasts and birds / as a
그래서 돌제단을 만들었고,　짐승들과 새들을 바쳤다

sacrifice. When he looked up to the sky / there was a
희생 제물로.　　노아가 하늘을 바라보았을 때

beautiful rainbow. It was God's promise / that there
아름다운 무지개가 떠 있었다.　하나님의 약속이었다

should be no more floods / upon the earth. He still sends
더 이상 홍수가 없을 것이라는　　세상에.　　하나님은 지금도 무지개

the rainbow / to show us / that He is taking care of this
를 보내신다　　우리에게 보여 주려고　이 세상을 돌보고 있으며,

world, / and will always do so.
　　항상 그럴 것이라는 것을.

Perhaps / the people / who lived after this / — for Noah's
어쩌면　　사람들은　　이 일이 있은 후에 살고 있는

children's children increased very fast — / did not believe
— 노아의 자손의 자손들이 매우 빠르게 늘어났으므로 —　　하나님의 약속을 믿지

God's promise, / for they began to build / a great tower, /
않았을지도 모른다.　　짓기 시작했으니　　거대한 탑이나,

or temple, / on the plain of Shinar; / or perhaps they had
사원을,　　시날 평원에;　　혹은 그들이 오만하고 사악해져서,

grown proud and wicked, / and wanted a temple / for the
　　　　　　　　　　사원을 원했을지도 모른다

worship of idols; / but the Lord changed their speech, / so
우상들을 섬기기 위해;　　그러나 하나님이 인간의 언어를 바꾸자,

that they could not understand each other, / and they were
서로를 이해하지 못하게 되어,

scattered over other countries; / and so each country /
다른 여러 나라로 흩어졌다;　　그래서 그렇게 각 나라가

began to have a language of its own.
각자의 언어를 갖게 되었다.

ABRAHAM—THE FATHER OF THE FAITHFUL
아브라함 ― 믿음의 조상

The people / who lived four thousand years ago / were
사람들은　　　4천 년 전에 살았던

very much like children / who easily forget. They told
어린 아이들과 매우 비슷했다　　　쉽게 잊어버리는.　　그들은 자신의

their children / about the great flood, / but nearly all /
자녀들에게 전했지만　　대홍수에 대해서,　　거의 대부분이

forgot to tell them of the good God / who is the Father of
좋으신 하나님에 대해 전하는 것을 잊었다　　　우리 모두의 아버지이시며,

us all, / whom we should always love and obey. Yet there
우리가 항상 사랑하고 순종해야 하는.

is always one, / if not more, / who remembers God, / and
그래도 꼭 한 명은 있다,　더 있을 수도 있지만,　하나님을 기억하며,

keeps his name alive in the world.
그분의 이름이 이 세상에 계속 살아있도록 지키는 사람이.

Abram had tried to do right, / though there was no Bible
아브람은 옳은 일을 하려고 노력했다,　　성경이 없었지만

/ in the world then, / and no one better than himself / to
그 시대에는,　　자신밖에 없었다

help him / but God, / and one day / He called Abram, /
도와줄 사람이　하나님을 제외하면,　하루는　　하나님이 아브람을 부르셔서,

and told him to go away / from his father's house / into
떠나라고 말씀하셨다　　그의 아버지의 집에서

another country.
다른 나라로.

"A land that I will show thee," / said the Lord, / "and I
"너에게 땅을 보여 주리니,"　　주님이 말씀하셨다,

will make of thee a great nation."
"너로 큰 민족을 이루게 할 것이다."

---

if not more 더 있을 수도 있지만 | nephew 조카 | camel 낙타 | ass 나귀 | skin 가죽, 피부

He also made Abram / a wonderful promise, —
또한 하나님은 아브람과 맺었다　　아주 멋진 약속을, —

"In thee / shall all the families of the earth / be blessed."
"너를 통하여　　땅의 모든 족속이　　　　　　　　복을 얻을 것이다.'

He meant / that sometime / the Savior should be born /
하나님은 의미한 것이다 언젠가　　구세주가 태어날 것을

among Abram's children's children, / and that He should
아브람 후손의 자손들 중에,　　　　　　　그리고 그분이 구세주가 될 것이

be the Savior / of all the nations of the earth.
라고　　　　　　땅의 모든 족속들의.

Abram did / just what God told him to do. He took Sarai,
아브람은 행했다　　하나님이 지시하신 대로.　　　　　그는 사래를 데리고,

/ his wife, / and Lot, his nephew, / and some servants, /
　아내인,　　　또한 조카인, 롯과,　　　　하인 몇 명과,

and cows, and sheep, and camels, and asses, / and went
소, 양, 낙타, 나귀를 데리고,

into the land of Canaan. When they rested at night /
가나안 땅으로 들어 갔다.　　　　밤에 휴식을 취할 때면

Abram and Lot set some sticks / in the ground, / and
아브람과 롯은 나무 막대기를 세워서　　　　땅 위에,

covered them with skins for a tent, / and near by / they
가죽으로 그 위를 덮어 천막을 만들고,　　　　　그 근방에

made an altar, / where Abram offered a sacrifice, / for
제단을 만들어,　　　그곳에서 제물을 바쳤다,

that was the only way / they could worship God / when
그것이 유일한 방법이었기 때문에　　하나님을 섬기는

the earth was young.
예전에는.

Abram went down into Egypt / when there was a lack of
아브람은 이집트로 내려갔지만　　　　음식이 부족해지자

food / in Canaan, / but he came back to Bethel, / where
　음식이　가나안에서,　　　다시 벧엘로 돌아와서,

he made the altar before, / and worshipped God there.
이전에 제단을 쌓았던 곳인,　　　　그곳에서 하나님께 예배를 드렸다.

He was very rich, / for his cattle and sheep had grown
아브람은 매우 부자였다,   그의 가축들이 매우 번성했기에,

into great herds and flocks, / though he had sold many
이집트에서 많은 가축을 팔았음에도 불구하고

in Egypt / for silver, and gold, and food. Abram and Lot
은과 금과 음식을 얻으려고.   아브람과 롯은 자주 이동

moved often, / for their flocks and herds soon ate up the
했다,   가축 무리가 금새 풀을 먹어치웠기 때문에.

grass. Then they rolled up the tents, / and loaded the
그러면 그들은 텐트를 말아서,

camels and asses, / and went where the grass was thick
낙타와 나귀에 싣고,   풀이 무성하고 싱싱한 곳으로 갔다.

and fresh.

They could easily live in tents, / for the country was
그들은 텐트에서 편히 살 수 있었다,   그 땅이 따뜻했기 때문에.

warm. But Abram's herdsmen and Lot's herdsmen /
하지만 아브람과 롯의 목동들은

sometimes quarreled. And so Abram spoke kindly to
때때로 다투었다.   그러자 아브람이 롯에게 다정하게 말을 걸었고,

Lot, / and told him / to take his servants, and flocks, and
롯에게 말했다   하인과 가축 무리를 데리고,

herds, / and go where the pastures were good, / and he
비옥한 초원으로 가라고,   그러면 자신은

would go the other way. So they parted, / and Lot went
그 반대편으로 가겠다고 했다.   그렇게 그들은 헤어졌고,

to the low plains of the Jordan, / but Abram went to the
롯은 요단강 유역의 낮은 평원으로,   아브람은 높은 땅으로 갔다

high plains / of Mamre, in Hebron, / and there he built
헤브론에 있는 마므레의,   그리고 그곳에서 아브람은 또 다른

another altar / to the Lord, / who had given him all that
제단을 쌓았다   주님께 드릴,   그 모든 땅을 자신에게 주신

country / — to him and to his children / forever.
— 그 자신과 자녀들에게   영원토록.

There were warlike people in Canaan, / and once when
가나안 사람들은 전쟁을 좋아하여,

they had carried off Lot / from Sodom, / Abram took his
롯을 데려가자   소돔에서,   아브람은 하인과 목동을

servants and herdsmen / and went out to fight. He had
데리고   싸우러 갔다.

more than three hundred men, / and they took Lot away
아브람에게는 300명 이상의 사람들이 있었고,   적들로부터 롯을 구해 내어,

from the enemy, / and brought him back to Sodom. It
                다시 소돔으로 데려왔다.

was here / that Abram met a wonderful man, / who was
그 장소였다   아브람이 아주 멋진 사람을 만난,

both a king and a priest. His name was Melchisedek, /
왕이자 제사장이기도 했던.   그의 이름은 멜기세덱이었다,

and he brought Abram bread and wine, / and blessed him
그는 아브람에게 빵과 포도주를 가져와서,   그곳에서 아브람을 축복

there.
했다.

After this, / God spoke to Abram / one evening, / and
그 일이 있은 후,   하나님이 아브람에게 말씀하시며   어느 날 저녁,

promised / that he should have a son, / and then while
약속하셨다   그가 아들을 갖게 될 것이라고,

Abram stood outside his tent, / with the great sky / thick
그리고 아브람이 천막에서 나와 서 있자,   웅장한 하늘 아래

with stars above him, / God promised him / that his
무수히 많은 별들이 가득한,   하나님이 그에게 약속하셨다

children's children should grow / to be as countless as
그의 자손의 자손이 자라날 것이라고   별처럼 셀 수 없이 많아질 것이라고.

the stars. That was hard to believe, / but Abram believed
믿기 힘든 말이었지만,   아브람은 하나님을 믿었다

God / always and everywhere.
언제나 어디서나.

---

herdsman 목동 | quarrel 말다툼, 다툼 | pasture 초원 | warlike 호전적인 | carry off 데려가다 | priest
성직자, 제사장

Still no child came to Abram and Sarai, / and Abram was
아브람과 사래에게는 아직 아이가 없었고,

almost a hundred years old, / but God spoke to him again,
아브람의 나이가 거의 백 세가 되었다.   하지만 하나님이 그에게 다시 한 번 말씀하셨고,

/ and told him / that he should be the father / of many
    말씀하시길   그가 조상이 되리라고 하셨다

nations.
많은 민족의.

He told Abram / that a little boy would be born to them, /
하나님이 아브람에게 말씀하셨다   어린 남자 아이가 태어날 것이며,

and his name would be Isaac, / and God changed Abram's
이름은 이삭이라고,   하나님은 아브람의 이름을 아브라함이라고

name to Abraham, / which means "Father of many
바꾸셨고,   "여러 민족의 아버지"라는 의미를 지닌

people," / and Sarai's to Sarah, / which means "Princess."
              사래는 사라라 바꾸셨다,   "공주"라는 의미인.

Abraham was sitting in his tent / one hot day, / when three
아브라함은 천막 안에 앉아 있었고   어느 더운 날,   그때 세 명의 사내

men stood by him. They were strangers, / and Abraham
가 그의 곁에 섰다.   그들은 이방인이었고,   아브라함이 그들에게

asked them / to rest beneath the tree, / and bathe their
청했다   나무 아래에서 쉬라고,   그들의 발을 씻겼다,

feet, / while he brought them food. So Sarah made cakes,
음식을 가져오는 동안.   사라는 떡을 만들고,

/ and a tender calf was cooked, / and these with butter,
    송아지 고기를 요리하여,   버터, 우유와 함께,

and milk, / were set before them. But they were not
우유와,   그들에게 대접했다.   하지만 그들은 이 땅의 사람들이

men of this world; / they were angels, / and they had come
아니었다;   그들은 천사들로,·

to tell Abraham and Sarah / once more / that their little
아브라함과 사라에게 전하러 왔다   한 번 더

child was sure to come. Then the angels went away, / but
그들에게 자녀가 반드시 생길 것이라고. 천사들은 떠났지만,

one of them, / who must have been the Lord Himself /
그들 중에 한 명은,   주님 자신이 분명한

in an angel's form, / stopped to tell Abraham / that He
천사의 모습을 한, 멈춰서 아브라함에게 말씀하셨다

was going to destroy Sodom and Gomorrah, / because
소돔과 고모라를 멸망시킬 것이라고,

the people who lived there / were so very wicked, / and
그곳에 사는 사람들이 아주 많이 사악했기에,

Abraham prayed Him / to spare them / if even ten good
그러자 아브라함은 하나님께 기도했다 그들을 용서해 달라고 혹시 선한 사람 열 명만이라도

men / could be found in them, / for he remembered /
그들 가운데서 찾을 수 있다면, 기억했기에

that Lot lived in Sodom. But the Lord never forgets.
롯이 소돔에서 살고 있는 것을. 하나님은 잊으시는 법이 없다.

The two angels went to Sodom / and stayed with Lot /
두 천사가 소돔으로 가서 롯과 함께 지낸 후

until morning, / when they took him and all his family
아침까지, 롯과 그의 가족을 데리고 나오자

/ outside the city, / and then the Lord said to him, /
도시 밖으로, 주님이 롯에게 말씀하셨다,

"Escape for thy life / — look not behind thee, / neither
"살고 싶다면 도망치거라 — 뒤를 돌아보지 말고,

stay thou in all the plain."
들판에 서 있지도 말고."

And the Lord hid them / in the little town of Zoar, /
그리고 주님은 그들을 숨기셨다 소알이란 작은 마을에,

while a great rain of fire fell / upon the wicked cities of
거대한 불의 비를 내리는 동안 들판의 사악한 도시들 위로,

the plain, / until they became a heap of ashes. Only Lot's
잿더미가 될 때까지. 오직 롯의 부인만

wife looked back / to see the burning cities, / and she
뒤를 돌아보았고 불타는 도시들을 보려고,

became a pillar of salt.
소금 기둥이 되었다.

---

beneath 아래에 | bathe 씻다 | tender 부드러운 | calf 송아지 | spare 용서하다, 구하다 | escape 달아나다,
탈출하다 | heap 더미 | ash 재 | pillar 기둥

The next morning / when Abraham looked from Hebron
이튿날 아침 아브라함이 헤브론에서 바라보자

/ down toward the cities of the plain, / a great smoke was
들판의 도시들 아래쪽으로. 거대한 연기가 그곳에서 솟아

rising from them / like the smoke of a furnace.
오르고 있었다 마치 용광로에서 나는 연기처럼.

At last / the Lord's promise / to Abraham and Sarah
마침내 주님이 맺은 약속이 아브라함과 사라에게

/ came true. A little son was born to them, / and they
현실이 되었다. 그들에게 아들이 태어났고,

called him Isaac. They were very happy, / for though
이삭이라 이름지었다. 그들은 매우 행복했다.

Abraham was a hundred years old, / no child had ever
비록 아브라함이 백 세였고,

been sent them.
그 전까지 자녀가 없었지만.

When he was about a year old / they made a great feast
이삭이 한 살이 되었을 때 그를 위해 성대한 잔치를 열었다,

for him, / and all brought gifts / and good wishes, /
모두 선물을 가져왔고 행복을 빌었다,

yet the little lad Ishmael, / the son of Hagar, / Sarah's
그런데 이스마엘이라는 어린 청년은, 하갈의 아들인, 사라의 하녀였던,

servant, / mocked at Isaac. Sarah was angry, / and told
이삭을 조롱했다. 사라는 화를 내며, 남편에게 말했다

her husband / that Hagar and her boy must be sent
하갈과 그녀의 아들을 내보내야 한다고.

away. So he sent them out / with only a bottle of water
아브라함은 그들을 내보냈다 물 한 병과 빵 한 덩어리를 주고;

and a loaf of bread; / for God had told Abraham / to do
하나님이 아브라함에게 말씀하셨기에

as Sarah wished him to do, / and He would take care
사라가 원하는 대로 하라고, 하나님이 이스마엘을 돌보고,

of little Ishmael, / and make him the father of another
다른 민족의 조상으로 삼겠다고.

nation.

When the water was gone, / and the sun grew very hot, /
물이 다 떨어지고, 태양이 더욱 뜨거워지자,

poor Hagar laid her child / under a bush / to die, / for she
불쌍한 하갈은 아이를 눕히고 덤불 아래 죽도록 두었다,

was very lonely and sorrowful. While she hid her eyes
매우 외롭고 슬펐기 때문에. 하갈이 눈을 가리고 눈물을 흘리며,

and wept, / saying, /
말했다,

"Let me not see / the death of the child," / she heard a
"보지 않게 하라 이 아이의 죽음을," 그녀에게 음성이

voice / out of heaven / telling her not to be afraid.
들려왔다 천국으로부터 두려워하지 말라고 하는.

"Arise, / lift up the lad," / said the voice, / "for I will
"일어나라, 아이를 일으키라," 음성이 말했다,

make him a great nation."
"그를 통하여 큰 민족을 이룰 것이다."

And God opened her eyes / to see a well of water near.
하나님이 하갈의 눈을 열어 근처의 우물을 보게 하셨다.

Then she filled the empty bottle, / and gave the boy a
하갈은 빈 병에 물을 담아, 아이에게 먹였고,

drink, / and God took good care of them / ever after, /
하나님이 그들을 돌봐 주셨다. 그 후로 계속,

though they lived in a wilderness.
비록 황무지에 살았지만.

Ishmael grew up to be an archer, / and became the father
이스마엘은 장정하여 궁수가 되었고, 아랍인들의 조상이 되었다,

of the Arabs, / who still live in tents / as Ishmael did.
여전히 천막 생활을 하고 있는 이스마엘이 그랬던 것처럼.

furnace : 용광로 | lad 청년 | mock 놀리다, 조롱하다 | lay 누이다 | bush 덤불 | sorrowful 슬픈 | weep
눈물을 흘리다 | well 우물 | wilderness 황무지 | archer 궁수

But the Lord let a strange trial come / to the little lad
주님께서는 이상한 시험을 내리셨다   이삭에게도.

Isaac, also. His father loved and obeyed God, / but there
이삭의 아버지는 하나님을 사랑했고 순종했지만,

were heathen people around them, / who worshipped
그들 주위에는 이방인들이 살고 있었다,   우상을 섬기며,

idols, / and sometimes killed their own children / as a
때때로 자녀를 죽여서

sacrifice to these idols. Abraham brought the best of his
우상을 위해 제물로 바치는.   아브라함은 가장 좋은 어린 양과 소를 가져와

lambs and cattle / to offer to the Lord; / but one day /
하나님께 바쳤는데;   하루는

the Lord told Abraham / to take his only son Isaac and
하나님이 아브라함에게 말씀하셨다   외동아들 이삭을 데리고 가서 그분께 바치라고

offer him / upon a mountain / called Moriah / as a burnt
산 위에서   모리아라 불리는

sacrifice to God. Abraham had always obeyed God, /
하나님께 드리는 번제로.   아브라함은 언제나 하나님께 순종했고,

and believed his word, / and now, / though he could not
그분의 말씀을 믿었다.   이때에도,   이해할 수는 없었지만,

understand, / he rose up early in the morning / and took
아침 일찍 일어나서

his young son, / with two servants, / and an ass loaded
어린 아들을 데리고,   두 명의 하인과 함께,   나귀에 땔감을 싣고,

with wood, / to the place of which God had told him.
하나님이 말씀하신 땅으로 향했다.

They were three days on the journey, / but at last / they
그들은 사흘 동안 여행하여,   마침내

came to the high place, / where the city of Jerusalem was
높은 땅에 도달했다,   나중에 예루살렘이 지어진 곳이었다,

afterward built, / and to the very rock / upon which the
그리고 바로 그 바위에   교회가 지어졌다

temple was built / long afterward, / with its great altar
오랜 시간 이후에,

and Holy of Holies.
거대한 제단과 지성소와 함께.

trial 시험 | obey 순종하다 | heathen 야만인, 이방인 | burnt sacrifice 번제, 태워서 드리는 제사 | Holy of Holies 지성소

On Mount Moriah / Abraham had left the young men / at
모리아 산에서   아브라함은 사람들을 남겨둔 채

the foot of the mount, / and went with Isaac / to the great
산 아래,   이삭과 함께 갔다   그 거대한 바위로

rock / on the top of the mount.
산 꼭대기에 있는.

"My father," / said Isaac, / "where is the lamb / for a
"아버지,"   이삭이 말했다,   "양은 어디 있나요

burnt offering?"
번제를 위한?"

"My son, / God will provide himself a lamb / for a burnt
"아들아,   하나님이 직접 양을 준비해 주실 거란다

offering," / said his father, / still obeying God, / and
번제를 위한,"   아버지가 말했다,   여전히 하나님께 순종하고,

believing His word, / that Isaac should be the father of
그분의 말씀을 믿고 있던,   이삭이 많은 민족들의 아비가 될 것이라는.

many nations.

Abraham made an altar of stones, / and bound Isaac /
아브라함은 돌로 제단을 만들고,   이삭을 묶어

and laid him upon it, / but when his hand was lifted / to
그 위에 뉘었다,   아브라함이 손을 들었을 때

offer up the boy, / the Lord called to him from heaven.
아이를 바치기 위해,   하늘에서 주님이 그를 불렀다.

"Lay not thine hand upon the lad," / said the voice, / "for
"그 아이에게 손대지 말라."   음성이 말했다,

now I know / that thou fearest God, / seeing thou hast
"이제야 알고   네가 하나님을 경외하는 것을.   주저하지 않는 것을 보았으니

not withheld / thine only son from me."
                하나뿐인 아들을 바치는 것에

---

burnt offering 번제 | withhold 주저하다 | mourn 애도하다 | bury 장사하다 | burial 장례식

Then Abraham turned / and saw a ram / with its twisted
아브라함이 돌아서자   숫양이 보였다   뒤틀린 뿔이

horns / caught in the bushes, / and he offered it to the
덤불에 걸려 갇혀 있던.   아브라함은 그 양을 주님께 바쳤다

Lord / instead of his son. How glad and grateful Abraham
아들 대신.   아브라함이 얼마나 기쁘고 감사했을까

must have been / that morning, / when he came down the
그 아침에,   그 산에서 내려와,

mountain, / with Isaac walking beside him, / to think / that
이삭과 함께 걸으며,   생각했을 때

he had still obeyed God / when it was hard to do so.
하나님께 순종했다는 것을   그렇게 하기 힘든 상황이었지음에도.

Abraham was an old man / when Sarah died. They had
아브라함은 나이가 많았고   사라가 죽었을 때.

lived together / a long lifetime, / and he mourned for her
그들은 같이 오래 살았다 긴 인생을,   아내의 죽음을 슬퍼했다

/ many days. He bought a field / close by the oak-shaded
오랫동안.   그는 밭을 구입하여   상수리나무로 둘러싸인

plain / of Mamre in Hebron, / and there in a rocky cave
헤브론 땅 마므레의,   암굴 속에 그녀를 묻었다.

he buried her. He was called a Prince of God / by the
아브라함은 하나님의 아들이라 불렸다

Canaanites / because he lived a true, faithful life.
가나안 사람들에게 진실되고 믿음 있는 삶을 살았기 때문이다.

A few years after / he also went to God, / and his body was
몇 해 지나서   그 역시 하나님께 갔고,   그의 육체는 묻혔다

laid / beside Sarah's in the cave-tomb. Ishmael came up
사라의 무덤 곁에.

from the south country to mourn / with Isaac at the burial
이스마엘은 남쪽 나라에서 조문을 위해 찾아왔다   장례식에서 이삭과 함께

/ of their father, / the Friend of God, / and Father of the
그의 아버지의,   하나님의 친구이며,   믿음 있는 자들의 조상인.

faithful.

📖 mini test 1

A. 다음 문장을 해석해 보세요.

(1) It was to be covered with tar / within and without, / so that the water should not creep in.
→

(2) God promised him / that his children's children should grow / to be as countless as the stars.
→

(3) Abraham prayed Him / to spare them / if even ten good men / could be found in them.
→

(4) He rose up early in the morning / and took his young son, / with two servants, / and an ass loaded with wood, / to the place of which God had told him.
→

B. 다음 주어진 문장이 되도록 빈칸에 써 넣으세요.

(1) 하나님은 그분 자신과 비슷한 모습으로 그들을 만드셨다.

He _____.

(2) 하나님은 창조한 모든 것을 보시고 기뻐하셨다.

God _____.

(3) 그들은 하나님을 섬기라고 가르침 받았다.

→

(4) 양과 소들이 신선한 풀을 발견하고, 얼마나 기뻤을지 생각해 보라.

Think _____.

C. 다음 주어진 문구가 알맞은 문장이 되도록 순서를 맞춰 보세요.

(1) 하나님은 그들의 몸을 흙으로 만들었다.
(He / made / their / bodies / from / the earth)
→

(2) 그렇게 노아는 하나님이 하라고 명령하신 모든 일을 행했다.
(all / that / the Lord / had / told / him / to / do)
So Noah _____.

(3) 얼마나 조용한 세상이었을까.
(What / a / silent / world / it / must / have / been)
→

(4) 이스마엘은 장성하여 궁수가 되었다.
(Ishmael / grew / up / to / be / an archer)
→

D. 다음 단어에 대한 맞는 설명과 연결해 보세요.

(1) worship   ▶   ◀ ① a holy table in a church or temple

(2) altar   ▶   ◀ ② to treat with contempt or ridicule

(3) mock   ▶   ◀ ③ to honor or reverence

(4) mourn   ▶   ◀ ④ to feel or express grief or sorrow

ISAAC THE SHEPHERD PRINCE
양치기 왕자 이삭

Before Abraham died, / he thought much about his dear
아브라함은 죽기 전에, 아들 이삭에 대해 많이 생각했다,

son Isaac, / to whom he was going to / leave all that he
아들에게 물려 주겠다고 자신이 가진 모든 것을.

had. The young man / had no mother, no sister, / and
이삭에게는 어머니도 여자 형제도 없었고,

soon he would have no father. So the old man called /
이제 곧 아버지도 돌아가실 터였다. 그래서 아브라함은 불러서

his old and faithful servant, / and told him / to go on a
그의 나이든 믿음직한 하인을, 말했다 여행을 떠나라고

journey / into the land of his fathers, / and bring back
그의 고향으로,

with him a wife for his son Isaac.
아들 이삭의 신부감을 데려오라고 했다.

The children of Nahor, / Abraham's brother, / lived there
나홀의 자손이, 아브라함의 형제인, 아직 그곳에 살고

still, / and Abraham wished / for his son Isaac / a wife of
있어서, 아브라함은 소망했다 아들 이삭을 위해 고향 사람 중에

his own people, / who should be both good and beautiful,
신부감을 얻기를, 선하고 아름다우며,

/ and not like the heathen women of Canaan.
가나안의 이방인 여성과 다른.

So the old servant listened to Abraham / and promised to
그러자 그 하인은 아브라함의 말을 듣고 그렇게 하겠다고 약속했다

do / all that he commanded.
주인이 명령한 대로.

He loaded ten camels with presents / for his master's
그는 낙타 열 마리에 선물을 실었다 주인의 가족에게 줄

family / away in Syria, / and Abraham said: /
멀리 시리아에 살고 있는, 아브라함이 말했다:

command 명령하다 | caravan (사막을 건너는) 대상 | set out 출발하다 | desert 사막 | jar 항아리, 단지, 병

"The Lord shall send His angel / before thee," / and from
"주님이 천사를 보내실 것이다   네 앞에."

his tent door / he saw the little caravan of camels and
그리고 천막 앞에서   낙타를 끌고 가는 하인 무리를 보았다,

servants, / as they set out across the plain, / toward the
그들이 들판을 건너,   toward the

land beyond the river Jordan.
요르단 강 너머로 향하는 것을.

There was a desert to cross / and many dangers to meet,
사막을 건너야 했고   여러 가지 위험을 겪었지만,

/ but the old servant believed in the God / his master
그 하인은 하나님을 믿었기에   주인이 예배한,

worshipped, / and was not afraid.
두려워하지 않았다.

When he came to Haran, / he stopped outside the town /
그가 하란에 도착하자,   마을 밖에 멈추어 섰다

by a well of water. It was early evening, / and the women
우물 옆에.   이른 저녁이었고,   여인들이 다가오고 있었다

were coming / each with a water-jar on her shoulder, / to
각자 어깨에 물 항아리를 이고,

draw water.
물을 긷기 위해.

Key Expression

명사를 수식하는 to 부정사

'to + 동사원형'으로 이루어진 to부정사는 명사를 뒤에서 수식할 경우 형용사적 용법으로 쓰이며 '~하는, ~할'이라고 해석합니다.
이때 수식을 받는 명사는 to부정사의 주어나 목적어의 의미를 가지고 있습니다.
또한 to부정사, 현재분사, 과거분사와 같은 준동사는 모두 명사를 뒤에서 수식하는 역할을 하는데 현재분사는 '진행, 능동', 과거분사는 '수동', to부정사는 '미래'의 의미를 포함하고 있습니다.

ex) There was a desert to cross and many dangers to meet.
건너야 할 사막과 만나게 될 많은 사막이 있었다.
There would be nothing to reap in time of harvest.
추수의 시기에 수확할 곡식이 하나도 없을 것이었다.

47

The old man prayed / that the Lord would show him /
노인은 기도했다   주님이 그에게 보여 주시길

which among these daughters of the men of the city, /
그 마을 남자의 딸 중에서 어떤 이가,

was the one who was to be his young master's wife.
어린 주인의 부인이 될 사람인지.

Before his prayer was ended, / Rebekah, / of the family
그의 기도가 끝나기 전에,   리브가라는 여자가,

of Abraham's brother Nahor, / came bearing her pitcher
아브라함의 형제 나홀의 집안 사람인,   물항아리를 어깨에 메고 이고 다가왔다.

on her shoulder. She looked very kind and beautiful, /
그녀는 매우 친절하고 아름다워 보였고,

and when she had filled her pitcher, / the old man asked
물항아리에 물을 다 채우자,   노인은 물 한 잔을 달라고 했다.

her for a drink of water. Then she let down the pitcher
그러자 그녀는 물항아리를 내려 놓으며

upon her hand / saying: /
말했다:

"Drink, my lord," / and asked / if she should also give
"드세요,"   그리고 물어봤다   물을 줘야 하는지를

water / to his camels. While she was giving him a drink,
그의 낙타에게도.   그녀가 물을 주는 동안,

/ the man showed her some golden jewels / that he had
그 남자는 금으로 된 장신구를 보여 주며

brought, / and when he had asked her name, / and knew
자신이 가져온,   그녀의 이름을 물었고,

that God had sent her to him / for his young master, / he
하나님이 보내주신 것을 알았다   어린 주인을 위해,

gave them to her, / and worshipped the Lord / who had
그는 장신구를 주고,   주님을 찬양했다   자신을 이끄신

led him / to the house of his master's brother.
주인의 형제의 집으로

Then Rebekah ran in / and told Laban, / her brother, /
리브가는 달려 들어가서   라반에게 일렀고,   그녀의 오빠인,

---

pitcher 물항아리, 물주전자 | jewel 보석, 장신구 | feast 축제, 만찬 | costly 값비싼 | haste 서두름, 급함

and the old servant of Abraham had a warm welcome / at
아브라함의 늙은 종을 따뜻하게 맞이했다

the door of Nahor's house.
나홀의 집 앞에서.

"Come in, / thou blessed of the Lord," / they said.
"들어오세요,   하나님의 은총을 입은 이여,"   그들이 말했다.

And after they had cared for the camels and the men, /
그들은 낙타와 사람들을 돌본 후,

there was a hurrying of servants to prepare a feast, / but
하인들에게 서둘러 만찬을 준비하도록 했다.

the old man would not taste food / until he had given the
노인은 음식을 먹었다

message of his master. Then the father and brother of
주인의 전갈을 전한 후에야.   리브가의 아버지와 오빠는

Rebekah, / saw that the Lord had sent for her, / and they
주님께서 리브가를 위해 보내셨음을 알고,

said: /
이렇게 말했다:

"Let her be thy master's son's wife, / as the Lord hath
"리브가를 당신 주인님의 며느리로 데려가세요,   주님이 말씀하신 것처럼."

spoken."

And the old servant bowed / his face to the ground /
늙은 하인은 절했다   그의 얼굴이 땅에 닿도록

worshipping the Lord / who had led him.
주님을 찬양하며   자신을 이끄신.

Then there was feasting / and giving of costly gifts, / and
그리고는 만찬이 시작되었고   값비싼 선물을 주며,

preparing to take a long journey, / for the old servant was
긴 여행을 떠날 준비를 했다.   늙은 하인이 서둘렀기 때문에

in haste / to get back to his master, / and Rebekah, / who
주인에게 돌아가기 위해,   그리고 리브가는,

was willing to go, / took her maid-servants / and rode
기꺼이 떠나기로 한,   여종들을 데리고

away into a far country / to be the wife of Isaac.
먼 나라를 향해 길을 떠났다   이삭의 부인이 되기 위해.

When Isaac was walking / in his field / at sunset, /
이삭이 걷고 있을 때   밭을   해질녘에,

thinking and praying to God, / he looked up / and saw
마음속으로 하나님께 기도를 드리며,   고개를 들자

that the camels were coming, / and he hastened to meet
낙타가 다가오는 것이 보였고,   서둘러 맞이하러 나섰다.

them. When the old servant told Rebekah / that it was
늙은 종이 리브가에게 말하자

his young master, / she alighted from her camel, / and
그가 주인님 아들이라고,   리브가는 낙타에서 내려,

covered herself with a long veil / as was the custom of
긴 면사포로 자신을 가렸다   시리아 여인들의 관습이었기 때문에.

the Syrian women. When the old servant had told the
늙은 하인이 여행 이야기를 전하고,

story of his journey, / he gave Rebekah to Isaac, / and he
리브가를 이삭에게 건네자,

took her to the tent / that had been his mother's, / and she
이삭은 리브가를 데려갔고   어머니가 쓰시던,   리브가는

became his wife, / so that he was no longer lonely and
이삭의 부인이 되었다,   그리하여 이삭은 더 이상 외롭거나 슬프지 않았다.

sad.

Isaac lived to a very great age, / and had two sons, /
이삭은 매우 오래 살았고,   두 아들이 있었다,

Jacob and Esau. He was a gentle, / quiet man, / fond of
야곱과 에서라는.   그는 온화했고,   조용한 사람이었으며,

his family, his flocks, and herds, / and at the place where
그의 가족과 양 떼와 소 떼를 좋아하여,

his father and mother were buried, / he lived among the
아버지와 어머니가 묻힌 곳에서,

fields and oak groves of Hebron / until he died.
헤브론의 밭과 상수리 나무 숲 속에 살았다   그가 죽을 때까지.

---

hasten 서둘러 가다 | alight (말, 배 등에서) 내리다, 하차하다 | veil 면사포 | custom 관습, 풍습 | fond of
좋아하는, 애정을 느끼는 | grove 숲 | twin 쌍둥이 | bow 활 | delicious 맛있는 | red lentils 팥죽 | beg
부탁하다

5

JACOB, A PRINCE OF GOD
하나님의 왕자, 야곱

Jacob and Esau / were the twin sons / of Isaac and
야곱과 에서는   쌍둥이였다

Rebekah.
이삭과 리브가에게서 난.

They did not look alike / as twins often do, / and they
그들은 서로 닮지 않았고   쌍둥이가 대부분 그렇듯이,

were very unlike / in all their ways. As they grew up, /
매우 달랐다   모든 일에 있어서.   아이들이 성장하자,

Esau loved the forests and wild places. He made bows
에서는 숲과 들을 좋아했다.   그는 활과 화살을 만들고,

and arrows, / and was a hunter, / and brought home /
               사냥을 나가서,   집에 가져왔다

wild birds and deer, / for his father was very fond of
새들과 사슴을,   아버지가 고기를 좋아했기에.

such food. Jacob helped his father / with the flocks, / and
           야곱은 아버지를 도와   가축을 돌보고,

learned how to cook food / from his mother, / who loved
요리를 배웠다   어머니로부터,

him more than she loved Esau.
에서보다 야곱을 더 사랑한.

One day / Esau came home / from hunting / tired and
하루는   에서가 집에 돌아와   사냥을 마치고   지치고 배고프던

hungry, / and smelled the delicious soup of red lentils
참에,   맛있는 팥죽 냄새를 맡았다

/ that Jacob was making. He begged Jacob to give him
  야곱이 만들고 있던.   에서가 야곱에게 팥죽을 좀 달라고 하자,

some, / and Jacob, / who wanted to be eldest, / and have
        야곱은,   장자가 되기를 원했고,

the right to the blessing / that fathers gave to the first-
축복의 권리를 원했던   아버지가 장자에게 주는

born / in those days, / said: /
그 당시에,   말했다:

"Sell me this day / thy birthright," / and Esau gave him /
"오늘 내게 팔아라   형의 장자권을."   그러자 에서는 야곱에게 주었다

all his rights as the first born, / for a little food / which he
장자로서의 모든 권리를,   약간의 음식을 위해서

might have had as a free gift.
공짜로 받을 수도 있었던.

Jacob wanted to be counted / in the great promise / that
야곱은 포함되고 싶었다   그 엄청난 약속에

God had given to Abraham, / but Esau despised it.
하나님이 아브라함에게 주신,   하지만 에서는 그것을 무시했다.

Afterward, / when Isaac was old / and his eyes were
그 이후에,   이삭이 나이 들어   눈이 어두워지자,

dim, / he called Esau, / and asked him / to go out into the
에서를 불러,   요청했다   들로 나가

fields / and shoot a deer, / and cook the venison that he
사슴을 잡아와서,   자신이 좋아하는 사슴고기 요리를 만들자고,

loved, / so that he might eat it / and bless his first born /
그래서 그것을 먹고   큰 아들을 축복하겠다고

before he died.
죽기 전에.

Rebekah heard it, / and told Jacob to bring kids from the
리브가가 이 말을 듣고,   야곱에게 무리에서 어린 염소 두 마리를 가져오라 하여,

flock, / which she cooked / and served as venison. Then
자신이 요리해서   사슴고기 요리를 대접했다.

she dressed Jacob in the clothes of Esau, / and told him
그리곤 야곱에게 에서의 옷을 입히고,   말하라고 했다

to say / that it was Esau / who had brought the venison.
자신이 에서라고   사슴고기를 가져온.

Isaac said: /
이삭이 말했다:

"The voice is the voice of Jacob," / but he put his hands
"목소리는 야곱의 목소리이구나."   하지만 야곱의 손을 만져보고,

on him, / and believed it was Esau, / and blessed him.
에서라고 믿었으며,   그를 축복했다.

birthright 생득권, 장자권 | despise 무시하다, 경멸하다 | venison 사슴고기

When Esau came home / and brought venison to his
에서가 집에 돌아와 　　　　　아버지에게 사슴고기를 가져오자,

father, / Isaac said:
이삭이 말했다:

"Who art thou?" / and when Esau said, / "I am thy son,
"넌 누구냐?" 　　그래서 에서가 대답하자, 　　"전 당신의 아들입니다.

/ thy first-born, Esau," / the old man trembled, / and told
첫째 아들, 에서요." 　　이삭은 몸을 떨며, 　　에서에게

Esau / the blessing had been given to another.
말했다 　다른 이에게 축복을 빌었다고.

Poor Esau cried out with grief, / "Hast thou but one
불쌍한 에서는 비통한 마음으로 울었다, 　　"아버지에게는 빌어줄 복이

blessing?" / "Bless me, / even me also, / O my father."
하나뿐입니까?" 　"축복하소서, 　저도, 　　아버지."

And so Isaac blessed him, / but he could not call back /
이삭이 그를 축복했지만, 　　　되돌릴 수는 없었다

the blessing of the first-born. The Lord knew / that Jacob
장자의 축복을. 　　　주님은 아셨다

would grow to be a good man, / and love the things of
야곱이 자라서 좋은 사람이 되어, 　　하나님의 것을 최고로 여길 것이며,

God best, / and that Esau would always / love the things
에서는 언제나 　　　세상의 것들을 최고로

of this world best, / yet it was wrong / of Jacob and
여길 것이라는 사실을. 　그렇지만 옳지 못한 일이었다 　야곱과 리브가가 속이는 것은,

Rebekah to deceive, / for we may not do evil / that good
악을 행하면 안 되기 때문에

may come.
좋은 일을 위해서라도.

After this / Esau hated his brother, / and said he would
이 일이 있은 후 　에서는 동생을 미워했고, 　　그를 죽여버리겠다고 말했다.

kill him.

tremble 떨다 | grief 비탄, 비통 | call back 되부르다 | hate 몹시 싫어하다, 미워하다 | pillow 베게 | hillside
산비탈 | ladder 사다리

So Isaac called Jacob, / and, blessing him again, / sent
그러자 이삭이 야곱을 불러,   다시 한 번 축복하고,

him away into Syria / to the house of Laban, / where
시리아로 보냈다   라반의 집으로,

Rebekah had lived, / and where Abraham's servant went
리브가가 살았던 곳이며,   아브라함의 종이 리브가를 찾으러 갔던 곳으로

to find her / for his master's son.
주인의 아들을 위해.

One night, / when he was not far on his way, / he lay
어느 날 밤,   길을 떠난 지 얼마 되지 않았을 때,   야곱이 잠을

down to sleep, / with a stone for his pillow, / on a hillside
자려고 누웠을 때,   돌을 베게 삼아,   산비탈에서

/ that looked toward his home, / and he dreamed a
자신의 집이 바라 보이는,   아름다운 꿈을 꿨다.

wonderful dream. He saw / a ladder reaching from earth
그는 보았다   하늘에 닿은 사다리와,

to heaven, / and a vision of angels / who were going up
천사들의 환상을   그 사다리를 오르내리고 있는.

and down upon it.

Key Expression

고어 표현의 인칭대명사와 조동사

영문 성경을 읽다 보면 옛말투의 인칭대명사와 조동사가 자주 등장합니다. 한 번 정리해 볼까요.

▶ thou = you(2인칭 단수형 주격)
▶ thy = your(2인칭 단수형 소유격)
▶ thee = you(2인칭 단수형 목적격)
▶ thine = yours(2인칭 단수형 소유대명사)
= your(thy를 모음이나 h로 시작하는 낱말 앞에 쓸 때)
▶ thyself = yourself(재귀대명사)

thou가 주어일 때는 다음과 같은 동사와 함께 사용됩니다.

art(=are), wast(=was), hast(=have), hadst(=had), shalt(=shall), wilt(=will),
canst(=can), wouldst(=would)

ex) "Who art thou?" and when Esau said, "I am thy son."
"넌 누구냐?" 그러자 에서가 대답했다, "전 당신의 아들입니다."
Hast thou but one blessing?
당신에게는 빌어줄 복이 하나뿐입니까?
Of all that thou shalt give me, I will surely give a tenth unto thee.
주님이 제게 주시는 모든 것 중에서, 십일조를 드리겠습니다.

Above it / stood the Lord, / who spoke to Jacob, / and
그 위에는   주님이 서 계셨고,   야곱에게 말씀하시며,

gave to him the promise / that He had first given to
약속을 하셨고   아브라함에게 처음 주셨던,

Abraham, / and told him / that He would go with him, /
말씀하셨다   주님이 야곱과 함께하며,

and bring him again into his own land.
이 땅으로 다시 데려 오실 것이라고.

Jacob was afraid / when he woke, / for he had seen the
야곱은 두려웠다   깨어났을 때,   하늘이 열려 있는 것이 보이고,

heavens opened, / and had heard God's voice. He made
하나님의 음성이 들리자.   그는 제단을

an altar / of the pillow of stone, / and called it Bethel / —
만들어   돌 베개로,   그곳을 벧엘이라 불렀고

the House of God — / and then he vowed / that the Lord
— 하나님의 집이라는 의미의 —   맹세하며   주님이 자신의 하나님

should be his God, / and he added, — /
이 될 것이라고,   말했다, —

"Of all that thou shalt give me, / I will surely give a tenth
"주님이 주시는 모든 것의,   십일조를 바치겠습니다."

unto thee."

When Jacob came to Haran, / he saw the well / from
야곱이 하란에 왔을 때.   우물을 보았다

which his mother used to draw water. There were three
어머니가 물을 길었던.   세 마리의 양이 우물가에

flocks of sheep lying by it, / waiting for all the flocks
누워서,   무리가 모이기를 기다리고 있었다

to gather / in the cool of the day / to be watered. Soon
시원한 곳에서   물을 먹기 위해.

Rachel, / the daughter of Laban, / came leading her
곧 라헬이,   라반의 딸인,   아버지의 양 떼를 몰고 나타났고,

father's flocks, / and one of the shepherds told Jacob /
양치기 중에 한 명이 야곱에게 말했다

whose daughter she was.
자신이 누구의 딸인지.

So Jacob rolled the stone from the well, / and watered the
야곱은 우물가의 돌을 옮기고,   라반의 양 떼에게 물을

flocks of Laban, / his mother's brother. Then he kissed
먹였다.   어머니의 오빠인.   그리곤 라헬에게 입을 맞추고,

Rachel, / and told her / that he was Rebekah's son, / and
          말했다   자신이 리브가의 아들이라고,

she ran and told her father.
그러자 라헬은 아버지에게 달려가 전했다.

There was great joy in Laban's house / because Jacob
라반가의 사람들은 크게 기뻐했다   야곱이 왔기 때문에,

had come, / and after he had stayed a month with them
                그리고 야곱이 그들과 함께 한 달을 지낸 후

/ Laban asked him / to stay and take care of his flocks, /
  라반은 야곱에게 청했다   이곳에 머물며 자신의 양 떼를 돌봐 달라고,

and he would pay him for his work.
그러면 품삯을 지불하겠다고.

Key Expression 🍋

pay의 쓰임

'지불하다'라는 뜻으로 알고 있는 동사 pay는 다음과 같이 1, 3, 4형식에서 다양
한 의미로 쓰입니다.

▶ 1형식 – pay : 이익이 되다, 수지가 맞다
　　　　 – pay + for + (sth) : 값을 치르다
　　　　 (자동사면서 간접목적어와 직접목적어의 의미를 포함)
▶ 3형식 – pay + (sb) + for + (sth) : ~에게 …의 대가를 지불하다
　　　　 – pay + (sth) + to + (sb) : ~에게 …을 지불하다
▶ 4형식 – pay + (sb) + (sth) : ~에게 …을 지불하다

ex) Laban asked him to stay and take care of his flocks, and he would pay him
for his work.
라반은 그에게 이곳에 머물며 자신의 양떼를 돌봐 달라고 청했고, 그러면 품삯
을 지불하겠다고 했다.
One of the brothers opened his bag, and found the money that he had paid
for the wheat in the top of his bag.
형제 중 한 명이 가방을 열고, 밀을 사기 위해 지불했던 돈이 가방의 맨 위에 들
어 있는 것을 보았다.

---

vow 맹세 | tenth 십일조, 십분의 일

Since the day / he had seen Rachel leading her father's
그날 이후로   라헬이 아버지의 양 떼를 이끄는 것을 본

flocks / he had chosen her / in his heart / to be his wife.
야곱은 그녀를 선택했다   마음속으로   아내로 삼기로.

So he said / that he would work for Laban / seven years,
그래서 말했다   라반을 위해서 일하겠다고   칠 년 동안,

/ if at the end of that time / he would give him Rachel /
    그 시간이 끝날 때   라헬을 준다면

for his wife. Laban was quite willing to do so, / and the
자신의 아내로.   라반은 기꺼이 그렇게 하기로 했고,

seven years / seemed to Jacob but a few days, / for the
그 칠 년은   야곱에게는 불과 며칠처럼 느껴졌다,

love he had to Rachel. But, / according to the custom of
라헬을 향한 사랑이 있었기에.   하지만,   그 나라의 관습에 따르면

that country, / the younger daughter could not be given
             여동생이 결혼을 할 수 없었기에

in marriage / before the elder, / and so Laban gave his
언니보다 먼저,   라반은 언니인 레아도 야곱에게 주었고,

daughter Leah also, / and both Leah and Rachel became
            그래서 레아와 라헬 모두 야곱의 아내가 되었다,

the wives of Jacob, / for Jacob lived / in that far away
            야곱은 살았기 때문에,   오래 전의 옛날 시대에

time and country of the early world / when men were
                              남자에게 허락되었던

allowed / to take more than one wife, / and when each
한 명 이상의 부인을 두는 것이,   그리고 그 시대에는 모든

man was both king and priest / over his family and tribe,
남자들이 왕이자 제사장이어서   그의 가족과 부족의,

/ and worshipped God / by offering burnt sacrifices /
   하나님을 예배했다   번제로 제물을 올림으로써

upon an altar.
제단 위에.

tribe 부족 | strengthen 강해지다

58   The Story of the Bible

After twenty years of work with Laban, / in which he
라반의 집에서 20년 간 일한 후,

had earned many flocks and herds / for himself, / Jacob
그곳에서 야곱은 많은 양과 소를 가지게 되었고   혼자 힘으로,

took his wives and the little sons / God had sent him, /
두 명의 부인과 아이들을 데리고   하나님이 보내 주신,

and his flocks and herds, / and started on a journey / to
가축을 이끌고,   여행을 떠났다

his old home. Isaac was still alive, / and Jacob longed
고향집으로.   이삭은 아직 살아있었고,   야곱은 아버지가 무척 보고

to see him. He had lived long in Haran / for fear of his
싶었다.   야곱은 오랫동안 하란에 살았지만   형 에서를 두려워하며,

brother Esau, / and now he must travel / through Edom, /
이제 여행해야 했다   에돔을 통과하여,

Esau's country, / on his way to his old home.
에서의 땅인,   고향으로 돌아오는 길에.

As he was on his way / some of God's angels met him,
여행 중에   야곱은 하나님의 천사들을 만나,

/ and he was strengthened. Still he feared Esau, / and
힘을 얻었다.   그래도 에서를 두려워하여,

sent some of his men / to tell his brother / that he was
사람들을 몇 명 보내었다   형에게 알렸다   자신이 가고 있음을.

coming.

The men came back, / saying / that Esau, / with four
사람들이 돌아와서,   말했다   에서가,   400명의 사람들을

hundred men, / was coming to meet them.
데리고,   그들을 만나러 오고 있다고.

Poor Jacob! He remembered / the sin of his youth, /
불쌍한 야곱!   그는 기억했기에   어렸을 때 자신이 지은 죄를,

when he had stolen the blessing from Esau, / and he was
에서로부터 축복을 훔쳤던 때를,   두려워져서,

afraid, / and prayed God to protect him.
자신을 보호해 달라고 하나님께 기도했다.

He sent his servants again to meet Esau / with great
야곱은 다시 한 번 에서에게 사람을 보냈다

presents of flocks, and herds, and camels, / and after placing
양과 소와 낙타 떼를 잔뜩 선물로 보내며,

his wives and little ones / in the safest place, / he sent all
그리고 부인과 아이를 숨겨 놓은 후   가장 안전한 곳에,   자신이 가진 전부를

that he had / over the brook Jabbok, / and he stayed / on the
보내고   얍복강 건너편으로,   자신은 남아서

other side / to pray. It was as if / he wrestled with a man / all
그 반대편에   기도했다.   장면은 마치   한 남자와 씨름하는 듯 했는데,

night, / and when the day began to break / the man wished
날이 밝기 시작하자   남자는 떠나고 싶어 했지만,

to go, / but Jacob said: /
야곱이 말했다:

"I will not let thee go / except thou bless me."
"당신을 보내지 않겠습니다   나를 축복하지 않으면."

So the man blessed him there, / and call his name Israel; /
그러자 그 남자는 그곳에서 야곱을 축복하며,   이스라엘이라는 이름을 붙여 주었다;

"for as a prince," / he said, / "hast thou power with God and
"왜냐하면,"   그가 말하기를,   "하나님과 사람의 힘을 갖고서,

with men, / and hast prevailed."
승리했기 때문이다."

Then Jacob knew / that the Lord Himself, / in the form of
그제야 야곱은 알았다   주님께서 직접,   사람의 모습을 하고,

a man, / had been with him, / and he had seen Him face to
자신과 함께 있었으며,   직접 그분을 만났다는 사실을.

face.

And as the sun rose / he passed over the brook. When he
해가 떠오르자   야곱은 강을 건너 지나갔다.   고개를 들자

looked up / he saw Esau and his men coming, / and when he
에서가 사람들을 이끌고 오는 것이 보였다,

had told his family to follow him, / he went straight before
그러자 그는 가족에게 자신을 따르라 하고,   곧장 그들에게 갔다,

them, / for he was no longer afraid / to meet his brother.
더 이상 두렵지 않았기 때문에   형을 만나는 것이.

brook 개울, 개천 | wrestle 몸싸움을 하다, 맞붙어 싸우다, 씨름하다

Jacob's prayer had been answered, / and Esau ran to meet
야곱의 기도는 이루어졌고,　에서가 달려와 동생을 맞이하며,

his brother, / and throwing his arms around him, / wept on
팔을 던져 감싸 안았고,

his shoulder. Then they talked / in a loving and brotherly
눈물을 흘렸다.　두 사람은 대화를 나눈 후　다정하게 형제애를 느끼며,

way, / and Esau returned to his home / with the presents
에서는 집으로 돌아갔고　선물을 가지고

/ Jacob had given him, / and Jacob went on his way / into
야곱이 준,　야곱은 자신의 길로 갔다

Canaan / full of joy and thankfulness. He stopped a little
가나안 땅으로　기쁨과 감사함을 가득 느끼며.　그는 잠시 멈춰서

while / in a pleasant place / to rest his flocks and cattle,
멋진 곳에서　가축을 쉬게 했다,

/ but he longed to see the place / where he first saw the
하지만 그 장소를 보고 싶어 했다　하나님의 천사들을 처음 보았고,

angels of God, / and heard the voice of the Lord blessing
자신을 축복하는 주님의 목소리를 들었던,

him, / so they journeyed on to Beth-el, / and there built an
그래서 그들은 벧엘로 여행을 떠났고,　그곳에 제단을 쌓은 후

altar / and worshipped God.
하나님을 예배했다.

Again the Lord spoke to Jacob / at Beth-el, / and called
또 다시 주님의 말씀이 들리며　벧엘에서,　야곱을 이스라엘이라

him Israel, / and blessed him.
부르고,　그를 축복하셨다.

After they left Beth-el, / they came near to Bethlehem, /
벧엘을 떠난 후,　야곱 일행은 베들레헴 근처에 도달했다,

where many hundred years afterward / the Lord Jesus was
그곳에서 수 백년 후　예수님이 태어나셨고,

born, / and there another little son was born to Rachel, /
그곳에서 라헬은 또 다른 아들을 낳았고,

and there too God sent for her, / and took her to Himself, /
또한 그곳에 하나님이 사람을 보내어,　그분 곁으로 라헬을 데려가셨다,

and there her grave was made.
그리고 그곳에 그녀의 무덤이 만들어졌다.

Jacob and Rachel The little boy was named Benjamin,
야곱과 라헬은 아기에게 베냐민이라는 이름을 지어 주었고,

/ and was the youngest of Jacob's twelve sons, / who
그 아이는 야곱의 열두 아들 중 막내였다.   그리고 그 아이

became / the fathers of the twelve tribes of Israel, / and
들은 되었다   이스라엘의 열두 지파의 조상이자,

the princes of a great nation.
큰 민족의 왕자들이.

Jacob was almost home. His great family, / with all the
야곱은 거의 집에 도착했다.   그의 대가족과,

flocks and herds, / had been long on the way, / for they
가축 떼는,   오랫동안 그 길 위에 있었다,

often spread their tents / by the brooks / in the green
자주 천막을 펴야 했기에   강가에   푸른 골짜기 속,

valleys, / that the cattle might rest / and find pasture, /
소 떼가 휴식을 취하고   초원을 찾을 수 있도록,

but at last / the long caravan came slowly / over the fields
하지만 마침내   기나긴 행렬의 무리는 밭으로 서서히 다가갔다

of Mamre to Hebron, / and Isaac, / whom the Lord had
헤브론 땅의 마므레 평원에,   그리고 이삭은,   주님이 아직 세상에 살게 하신

kept alive / to see his son once more, / was there in his
아들을 한 번 더 볼 수 있도록,   그곳에서 천막 안에 있었다

tent / waiting for him.
아들을 기다리며.

But soon after this / he died, / an hundred and eighty
그 후에 얼마 되지 않아   이삭은 죽었고,   백 여든 살의 나이에,

years old, / and Esau came, / and the two brothers laid
에서가 오자,   두 형제는 아버지를 눕혔다

their father / in the cave / that Abraham bought / when
동굴 안에   아브라함이 사서

Sarah died, / and where he had buried Rebekah, / and
사라가 죽었을 때,   리브가를 묻었던,

Jacob became patriarch / in place of his father.
그리고 야곱은 족장이 되었다   아버지를 대신하여.

loving 다정한 | brotherly 형제 같은 | pleasant 쾌적한, 기분 좋은 | long 열망하다 | youngest 막내 | valley
계곡, 골짜기 | patriarch 족장

6

JOSEPH, THE CASTAWAY
조난자 요셉

Of all the sons of Jacob, / Joseph and Benjamin were /
야곱의 아들 중에,　　　　　요셉과 베냐민은

the dearest to him, / because they were the sons of his
가장 사랑한 아들이었다,　　　사랑하는 라헬이 낳은 아들들이었기 때문에,

beloved Rachel, / who had died on the journey / from
　　　　　　　　여행 도중에 죽은

Syria into Canaan. They were also the youngest / of all
시리아에서 가나안으로 향하던. 둘은 가장 어렸다

the twelve sons. When Joseph was about seventeen years
열두 명의 아들 중.　　　요셉은 열일곱 살이 되자,

old, / he sometimes went with his elder brothers / to keep
　　　가끔 형들과 나가

his father's flocks / in the fields. He wore a long coat /
아버지의 양 떼를 돌보았다　들판에서.　　요셉은 긴 외투를 입었는데

striped with bright colors, / which his father had given
화려한 줄무늬의,　　　　　아버지가 요셉에게 준 옷이었다,

him, / because he was a kind and obedient son, / and
　　상냥하고 순종적이며,

could always be trusted.
언제나 믿을 수 있는 아들이었기 때문에.

Once he told his father / of some wicked thing his
하루는 요셉이 아버지에게 전했고　　형들의 잘못을,

brothers had done, / and they hated him for it, / and
　　　　　　　　형들은 그 일로 요셉을 싫어하게 되어,

could not speak pleasantly to him.
말도 건네지 않았다.

castaway 조난자, 표류자 | dearest 사랑하는 | obedient 말을 잘 듣는, 순종적인 | starry 별이 빛나는 | sheaf
다발, 묶음, (밀 등의 곡식) 단 | wonder 궁금해 하다, 생각하다, 놀라다 | reproach 책망하다 | indeed 참으로
정말로

Joseph had many strange and beautiful thoughts / when
요셉은 이상하고 아름다운 생각을 하곤 했다

he looked across the fields to the hills, / and up into the
들판과 언덕들 너머를 바라보고,   별이 반짝이는 하늘을

starry sky / at night. He also had some strange dreams /
올려다 볼 때면   밤에.   때때로 낯선 꿈들도 꾸었다

that he told to his brothers. He said that he dreamed / that
형들에게 들려준.   그는 꿈을 꾸었다고 말했다

they were binding sheaves / in the field, / and that his
곡식 단을 묶고 있었는데   밭에서,   자신의 단이 우뚝 서더니,

sheaf stood up, / while the sheaves of his brothers bowed
            형들의 단이 자신의 단에 절을 했다는.

down to it.

Again / he dreamed / that the sun, and the moon, and
또 다시   그는 꿈을 꿨다   해와, 달과, 열한 개의 별들이

eleven stars / bowed down to him.
            그에게 절하는.

His father wondered / that he should have such thoughts,
야곱은 놀라서   요셉이 그런 꿈을 꿨다는 것에,

/ and reproached him / saying, / "Shall I and thy brethren
그를 책망하며   말했다,   "진정 나와 네 형들이 와서

indeed come / and bow down ourselves to thee to the
            땅에 닿도록 네게 절을 해야 하느냐?"

earth?" / and his brothers said, / "Shalt thou indeed rule
            그의 형제들은 말했다,   "네가 정말 우리를 다스릴 것이냐?"

over us?" / and they hated him.
            그리고 그들은 요셉을 미워했다.

When they were many miles from home / with the flocks
형제들이 멀리 갔을 때   양 떼를 데리고

/ their father sent Joseph to see / if all was well with
아버지가 요셉을 보내어 보고 오라 했다   형들이 모두 괜찮은지.

them. It was a long journey, / and when they saw the boy
긴 여행이었다,   형들은 요셉이 오는 것을 보자

coming / they did not go to meet him, / and speak kindly
맞이하러 가지 않고,   다정하게 말을 걸었다,

to him, / but they said, /
그들이 말했다,

"Behold / this dreamer is cometh. Let us slay him, / and
"보라   여기 꿈꾸는 자가 오는 도다.   우리가 그를 죽이고,

cast him into some pit, / and we will say / some evil
구덩이에 던진 후,   이렇게 말하자

beast hath devoured him, / and we shall see / what will
사악한 짐승이 그를 집어 삼켰다고,   그러면 보게 되겠지

become of his dreams."
그의 꿈이 어떻게 될지."

But Reuben, the eldest, said, /
하지만 장자인 르우벤이 말했다,

"Let us not kill him; / but cast him into this pit," / hoping
"그를 죽이지는 말고;   구덩이에 던져 넣자."

to take him out secretly, / and send him to his father.
몰래 그를 구출해서,   아버지에게 보낼 생각으로.

So when Joseph came near, / they robbed him of his coat
그래서 요셉이 근처에 오자,   그의 화려한 옷을 벗기고,

of many colors, / and cruelly cast him into a pit. After
잔혹하게 구덩이에 던졌다.   이 일이

this / they sat down to eat their bread, / and looking
있은 후 그들은 앉아서 빵을 먹다가,   고개를 드니

up / they saw a caravan coming. It was a company of
대상이 다가오는 것이 보였다.   그들은 이스마엘의 후손들로

Ishmaelites / carrying costly spices / down into Egypt /
값비싼 향신료를 갖고   이집트로

to sell them.
팔러 가는 길이었다.

Then Judah said, /
그때 유다가 말하기를,

"Why should we kill our brother? Let us sell him / to
"어째서 우리가 형제를 죽여야 하지?   그를 팔아버리자

these Ishmaelites."
이 이스마엘의 후손들에게."

Then there passed by some Midianite merchants, / and
그리고 나서 미디안 상인들이 지나가다가,

who drew Joseph out of the pit / and sold him to the
구덩이에서 요셉을 끌어내어   이스마엘 후손들에게 팔았고

Ishmaelites / for twenty pieces of silver, / and he was
은화 20냥에,   그는 끌려 갔다

carried down / into Egypt.
이집트로.

Reuben, / when his brothers went back / to their flocks,
르우벤은,   형제들이 돌아가자   양 떼에게로,

/ went to the pit / to try to save Joseph, / but he was not
구덩이로 갔지만   요셉을 구하려고,   요셉은 없었다,

there, / and Reuben cried out, /
그래서 르우벤은 울부짖었다,

"The child is not, / and I, / whither shall I go?"
"아이가 없어졌으니,   나는,   어디로 가야 하는가?"

The brothers / who had been so cruel to Joseph / brought
형제들은   요셉에게 매우 잔인했던   그의 외투를

his coat / to their father, / all stained with blood. They
가져왔다   아버지에게,   피로 얼룩진.

had themselves dipped it / in the blood of a kid / to
그들은 그 옷을 담갔다   어린 양의 피에

deceive him, / and he mourned long, / and would not be
아버지를 속이려고,   아버지는 오랫동안 애도하며,   편안하지 못했다,

comforted, / for the beloved child / that he believed / had
사랑하는 아이가   그가 생각하기에

been torn in pieces / by evil beasts.
갈기갈기 찢겨 죽었기에   사악한 짐승에게.

---

behold 보다 | slay 죽이다 | cast 던지다 | pit 구덩이 | evil 사악한 | devour 집어삼키다 | cruelly 잔인하게 |
spice 향신료 | merchant 상인 | stained 얼룩진

7

JOSEPH, A SERVANT, A PRISONER,

AND A SAINT
종, 죄수, 그리고 성인 요셉

The king of Egypt, / where Joseph was taken by the
이집트의 왕은,　　　　　요셉이 이스마엘 족속에게 잡혀 끌려간,

Ishmaelites, / was called Pharaoh, / and he had a captain
바로라고 불렸다,　　　　그에게는 친위대장이 있었는데,

of the guard / named Potiphar, / who bought Joseph / for a
　　　　　　　보디발이라는,　　그가 요셉을 샀다

house servant. Though he was the son of a Hebrew prince,
하인으로 쓰려고.　　히브리족 왕자의 아들이었지만,

/ Joseph did his work faithfully and wisely / as a servant,
요셉은 믿음직스럽고 지혜롭게 일했고　　　　하인으로서,

/ and was soon made steward of the house, / and was
곧 그의 집사가 되어,

trusted with all that his master had, / and the Lord made
주인의 모든 재산을 맡아 관리하게 되었다,　　　그리고 주님이 만드셨다

/ all that he did to prosper; / but the wife of Potiphar /
그가 하는 모든 일이 번성하도록;　　하지만 보디발의 아내는

was a wicked woman, / who persuaded her husband / that
사악한 여인이라서,　　　남편을 설득하여

Joseph was a bad man, / and he was sent to prison.
요셉이 나쁜 사람이라고,　　요셉을 감옥으로 보냈다.

Even there / Joseph won the hearts of all, / until the
그곳에서도　　요셉은 모든 이의 마음에 들었고,

keeper of the prison set him over the other prisoners, /
그리하여 감옥의 간수는 요셉에게 죄수의 감독을 맡기고,

and trusted him / as Potiphar had done. It was the Lord in
그를 믿었다　　　보디발이 했던 것처럼.　　요셉 안에 있던 주님이었다

Joseph / who helped him / to win the love and trust / of
그를 도왔던 것은　　믿음과 사랑을 얻도록

those around him.
주변 사람들로부터.

Pharaoh sent two of his servants to prison / because they
바로가 하인 두 명을 감옥으로 보냈다

had displeased him.
바로를 불쾌하게 했기 때문에.

One was his chief cook, / and one was the chief butler,
한 명은 요리 책임자였고,   다른 한 명은 집사장이었다,

/ who always handed the wine cup to the king, / and
언제나 왕에게 술잔을 건네던,

Joseph had the care of them.
그리고 요셉이 그들을 관리해야 했다.

They each had a dream / the same night, / and were
두 사람은 각자 꿈을 꾸었고   같은 날 밤에,   불안해 했다

troubled / because they could not understand them.
            꿈의 의미를 이해할 수 없어서.

Joseph asked them to tell him the dreams, / for God
요셉이 그들에게 꿈에 대해 이야기 해 달라고 했다,

knew what they meant.
하나님은 의미를 아시기 때문에.

Key Expression 🍃

It is ~ that 강조구문

It is와 that 사이에 강조하는 말(주어, 목적어, 부사구)를 넣어 강조하는 구문
을 만들 수 있습니다.
'...한 것은 바로 ~이다'라고 해석하며, 강조하는 대상이 사람일 경우 that대
신에 who를 사용하기도 합니다.

ex) It was the Lord in Joseph who helped him to win the love and trust of those
around him.
주변 사람들로부터 믿음과 사랑을 얻도록 그를 도왔던 것은 바로 요셉 안에 계
신 주님이었다.

saint 성인 | captain of the guard 친위대장 | steward 집사 | prosper 번영하다 | persuade 설득하다 |
displease 불쾌하게 만들다 | butler 집사

So the chief butler told Joseph / that he saw a vine
그러자 집사장이 요셉에게 전했다   가지가 세 개 달린 포도나무를 보았는데,

having three branches, / and the branches budded
가지에 싹이 나서 꽃을 피우고,

and blossomed, / and the blossoms changed into ripe
꽃이 익은 포도송이로 변해서,

grapes, / and he took the grapes / and pressed them into
그 포도를 따서   포도주를 만들어 왕의 술잔에 부어,

Pharaoh's cup, / and handed the cup to the king.
왕에게 건넸다고 했다.

Then Joseph said: / "The three branches are three days.
그러자 요셉이 말했다: "세 개의 가지는 사흘을 의미합니다.

Within three days / the king will take you out of prison,
사흘 안에   왕이 당신을 석방할 것이며,

/ and you shall hand the king's cup to him / as you used
당신은 왕에게 잔을 드리게 될 것입니다   예전에 하던 대로."

to do."

Joseph also asked the butler, / to think of him / when he
요셉은 또한 술 담당 집사에게 요청했다,   자신을 기억해 주고

was again in the king's palace, / and speak to the king /
다시 왕의 궁전에 돌아가면,   왕에게 청하여

to bring him out of prison, / because he had been stolen
자신을 감옥에서 꺼내 달라고,   왜냐하면 고향에서 도둑을 맞았고,

from his own land, / and he had done nothing wrong /
아무런 잘못을 하지 않았기 때문에

that he should be put in prison.
감옥에 갇힐 만한.

Then the chief cook told his dream. He said that he
그러자 수석 요리사가 자신의 꿈 이야기를 했다.   꿈을 꾸었는데

dreamed / that he carried three baskets on his head, / one
세 개의 광주리를 머리에 이고 있었다.

above another.
서로 겹쳐 놓은 채.

vine 포도 나무 | budded 꽃봉오리를 맺은 | blossom 꽃이 피다 | ripe 익은 | press 누르다 | palace 궁전 |
poorly 형편없이

70   The Story of the Bible

In the highest one / was all kinds of cooked meats for
맨 위 광주리에는   바로에게 드릴 온갖 고기 요리가 있었는데,

Pharaoh, / and the birds flew down / and ate from the
          새들이 날아와 앉더니   광주리 속 음식을 먹어버렸다.

basket.

"The three baskets / are three days," / said Joseph / as
"세 개의 광주리들은   사흘을 말합니다."   요셉이 말했다

he said to the butler, / but he told the cook / that in three
집사에게 말했던 것처럼,   하지만 요리사에게 말하길   사흘 안에

days / he would be put to death, / and hanged on a tree, /
처형을 당해,   나무에 매달릴 것이며,

where the birds would eat his flesh.
새들이 그의 시체를 파먹을 것이라 했다.

All this came true, / for Pharaoh's birthday came, / and
이 모든 일이 실제로 이루어졌다.   바로의 생일이 다가와서,

he brought out the chief butler / to serve at a birthday
왕은 집사를 불러내어   생일 잔치에서 술 시중을 들게 했지만,

feast, / but he hanged the chief cook. Yet the chief butler
요리사는 교수형에 처했다.   하지만 그 집사는 요셉을 잊고,

forgot Joseph, / and did not speak to the king / about him
왕에게 이야기 하지 않았다   요셉에 대해서

/ as he might have done.
말하기로 했었지만.

At the end of two long years, / Pharaoh dreamed a
2년이라는 시간이 흐른 후,   바로는 꿈을 꾸었다.

dream. He thought / he stood by the river of Egypt, / and
          그의 생각에   이집트 강가에 서 있었는데,

saw seven cows looking well kept and fat, / came up out
제대로 관리되어 포동포동해 보이는 소 일곱 마리가 보였다.

of the river.
강에서 올라오는.

Behind them / came seven other cows, / looking thin and
그 뒤로   소 일곱 마리가 또 올라왔는데,   마르고 제대로 먹지 못한 듯

poorly fed, / and the thin and poorly fed cows / ate up the
보이는,   마르고 잘 먹지 못한 소들이

well-kept and fat ones.
잘 먹고 통통한 소들을 잡아 먹어버렸다.   71

And Pharoah had a second dream. He thought / he saw
그리고 바로는 두 번째 꿈을 꾸었다.   그의 생각에

seven heads of wheat growing on one stalk / — and
한 줄기에 일곱 개의 이삭이 달려 있는 밀이 보였다

they were all full of grain. After them / came seven thin
— 이삭에는 낱알이 가득했다.   그 다음에   마른 밀 이삭이 일곱 개

heads of wheat / with no grain in them; / and the seven
나왔고   낱알이 들어 있지 않는;   나쁜 밀 이삭들이

bad heads of wheat / ate up the seven good ones.
                        좋은 이삭들을 먹어버렸다.

In the morning / Pharoah was troubled / about these
아침이 되자   바로는 걱정이 되어서   이 꿈들에 대해서,

dreams, / and called for his wise men / who worked
              현명한 신하들을 불렀지만   마법을 부리는,

magic for him, / and they could tell him nothing.
                    아무것도 대답할 수 없었다.

Then the chief butler / standing near the king /
그때 집사가   왕의 곁에 서 있던

remembered Joseph, / and told Pharaoh of the young
요셉을 기억해내고,   바로에게 그 히브리인 젊은이에 대해 이야기 했다

Hebrew / who had told / the meaning of his dream, / and
말해줬던   자신의 꿈의 의미와,

that of the chief cook, / and they had come to pass / as he
수석 요리사 꿈의 의미를,   그리고 그대로 이루어졌다는 것을   그가 말

had said, / so Pharaoh sent for Joseph / and said to him: /
했던 대로,   그러자 바로는 요셉을 불러서   말했다:

"I have heard / that thou canst understand a dream to
"들었다   네가 꿈을 이해하고 해석할 수 있다고."

interpret it."

Joseph answered the king / humbly and wisely:
요셉이 왕에게 대답했다   겸손하고 지혜롭게:

"It is not in me," / he said, / "God shall give Pharaoh an
"제가 아니라,"   그가 말했다,   "하나님께서 바로 왕에게 대답을 주실 것입니다."

answer of peace."

wheat 밀 | stalk 줄기 | grain 곡물, 낟알 | humbly 겸손하게

When the king had told his dream / Joseph said: /
왕이 자신의 꿈을 이야기 하자　　　　　요셉이 말했다:

"The dream is one," / and then he showed him / that
"꿈은 한 가지를 의미합니다."　　그리고 왕에게 보여 주었다

the seven fat cows, / and the seven full heads of wheat
일곱 마리의 살찐 소와,　　일곱 개의 가득 찬 밀 이삭들은

/ meant seven good years / in the land of Egypt, / when
7년 간 풍년이 들 것을 의미하며　　이집트 땅에,

the harvests would be great; / and the seven lean cows, /
그때는 수확이 좋을 것이다;　　그리고 일곱 마리의 여윈 소들과,

and the seven empty heads of wheat, / meant seven years
일곱 개의 빈 밀 이삭들은,　　　　7년 간 기근이 들 것을 뜻하며,

of famine, / when the east winds should spoil the wheat,
　　그때는 동풍이 불어와 밀을 망쳐놓을 것이다,

/ so there would be nothing to reap / in time of harvest /
그래서 수확할 곡식이 하나도 없어서　　추수의 시기에

and the people would want bread. He told the king / that
사람들은 빵을 원하게 될 것이다.　　그는 왕에게 말했다

he had better set a wise man over the land, / who would
지혜로운 자에게 땅의 관리를 맡겨,　　　　곡식의 저장을 관리

attend to saving the grain / during the seven good years,
하도록 하라고　　　　7년의 풍년 동안,

/ so that the people would have bread to eat / in the seven
　　그래서 사람들이 먹을 빵을 가질 수 있도록

years of famine.
7년의 기근 동안.

The king was greatly pleased with Joseph, / and told him
왕은 요셉의 말에 크게 기뻐하며,　　　　그에게 말했다

/ that God had taught him / to interpret dreams, / and
하나님이 그를 가르치셨고　　꿈을 해석할 수 있도록,

had showed him things to come, / and there could be no
앞으로 일들을 보여 주셨으니,　　이보다 더 현명한 사람을 찾을 수

wiser man found / to be set over the land.
없을 것이라고　　이 땅을 다스리는 것에.

harvest 수학 | lean 여윈 | famine 기근 | spoil 망치다 | reap 거두다 | attend to 처리하다 | robe 예복, 가운 |
storehouse 창고 | dearth 부족, 결핍

74　　The Story of the Bible

So he made Joseph a ruler over the whole land, / and
그래서 바로는 요셉을 전 영토를 다스리는 총리로 삼았고,

next to the king / in all things.
왕 다음의 자리에 앉혔다   모든 것에 있어.

He put his own ring on his hand, / and dressed him in
바로는 요셉의 손에 자신의 반지를 끼우고,   그에게 왕자의 예복을 입혔으며,

the robes of a prince, / and gave him an Egyptian name
                       그에게 이집트 인의 이름과

/ and an Egyptian wife, / so that there was no one / in all
이집트 여자를 부인으로 주었다,   그래서 아무도 없게 되었다

the land of Egypt / so great as Joseph, / except the king.
이집트 전체에서   요셉만큼 높은 자가,   왕을 제외하고.

He built storehouses / in every city, / and stored the
요셉은 창고를 짓고   모든 도시에,   곡물을 저장했다,

grain, / until it was like the sand of the sea, / and could
        그리하여 바다의 모래처럼 곡식이,

not be measured.
그 양을 측정할 수 없었다.

In the years of plenty / two sons were born to Joseph,
풍년의 해에   요셉은 두 아들을 얻었다,

/ Manasseh and Ephraim, / and then the seven years of
므낫세와 에브라임이라는   그리고 7년 간의 기근이 찾아왔다.

dearth began to come. When the people began to cry / to
                        사람들이 울부짖기 시작하면

the king / for bread, / he always said, —
왕에게   빵을 달라고,   왕은 항상 이렇게 말했다, —

"Go to Joseph; / what he says to you do."
"요셉에게 가라;   그가 말한 것이 쓸모가 있구나."

And Joseph and his helpers / began to open the
요셉과 그의 협력자들은   곡식 창고를 열어,

storehouses, / and sell wheat / to the Egyptians, / and
              밀을 팔기 시작했다   이집트인과,

to the people of all countries, / for the famine was in all
모든 나라의 사람들에게,   모든 땅에 기근이 들었기 때문에.

lands.

mini test 2

A. 다음 문장을 해석해 보세요.

(1) So the old man called / his old and faithful servant, / and told him to go on a journey / into the land of his fathers, / and bring back with him a wife for his son Isaac.
→

(2) Esau gave him / all his rights as the first born, / for a little food / which he might have had as a free gift.
→

(3) Laban asked him / to stay and take care of his flocks, / and he would pay him for his work.
→

(4) It was the Lord in Joseph / who helped him / to win the love and trust / of those around him.
→

B. 다음 주어진 문구가 알맞은 문장이 되도록 순서를 맞춰 보세요.

(1) 그들은 쌍둥이가 대부분 그렇듯이 서로 닮지는 않았다.
(twins / look alike / as / They / often do / did not)
→

(2) 주님이 제게 주시는 모든 것 중에서, 십일조를 바치겠습니다.
(I will surely give / unto thee / thou shalt give me / Of all that / a tenth)
→

Answer

A. (1) 그래서 아브라함은 나이든 믿음직한 하인을 불러서, 고향에 가서 아들 이삭의 신부감을 데려오라고 했다. (2) 그러자 에서는 공짜로 받을 수도 있었던 장자로서의 모든 권리를 약간의 음식을 위해서 야곱에게 주었다. (3) 라반은 그에게 이곳에 머물며 자신의 양떼를 돌봐 달라고 청했고, 그러면 품삯을 지불하

76 The Story of the Bible

(3) 아버지가 요셉을 보내 그들이 모두 괜찮은지 보고 오라 했다.
(if / was well / to see / sent Joseph / Their father / with them / all)
→

(4) 이 땅을 다스리는 데 더 현명한 사람을 찾을 수 없을 것이다.
(found / no wiser man / There could be / over the land / to be set)
→

C. 다음 주어진 문장이 본문의 내용과 맞으면 T, 틀리면 F에 동그라미 하세요.

(1) The old servant who had been sent to Abraham's home did not find a proper woman.
[T / F]

(2) The Lord knew that Jacob would grow to be a evil man.
[T / F]

(3) Jacob had lived long in Haran for fear of his father.
[T / F]

(4) Pharaoh made Joseph a ruler over the whole land.
[T / F]

D. 의미가 비슷한 것끼리 서로 연결해 보세요.

(1) alight ▶   ◀ ① kill
(2) despise ▶   ◀ ② descend
(3) devour ▶   ◀ ③ scorn
(4) slay ▶   ◀ ④ gulp

Answer

겠다고 했다. (4) 주변 사람들로부터 믿음과 사랑을 얻도록 그를 도왔던 것은 바로 요셉 안에 계신 주님이었다. | B. (1) They did not look alike as twins often do. (2) Of all that thou shalt give me, I will surely give a tenth unto thee. (3) Their father sent Joseph to see if all was well with them. (4) There could be no wiser man found to be set over the land. | C. (1) F (2) F (3) F (4) T | D. (1) ② (2) ③ (3) ④ (4) ①

77

8

JOSEPH — THE SAVIOR OF HIS PEOPLE
요셉 — 민족의 구원자

The famine reached / even to the fruitful land of Canaan,
기근이 다가왔고 　　　　　　풍요로운 가나안 땅까지,

/ and Jacob, / though rich in flocks and herds, / began to
야곱은, 　　　가축이 많이 있었음에도, 　　　　　　빵이 필요해졌다

need bread / for his great family. So he sent his ten sons
대가족을 먹이기 위해. 　　　그래서 열 명의 아들을 이집트로 보내어

down into Egypt / to buy wheat, / keeping Benjamin, the
밀을 사오라 했다, 　　막내인 베냐민만 집에 두고.

youngest at home.

When they came before the governor / they bowed
총리 앞에 도착하자 　　　　　　　　　형제들은 총리에게

down to him / with their faces to the ground. Joseph
허리 굽혀 절했다 　　얼굴이 땅에 닿도록. 　　　　　요셉은 그들을

knew them, / though he acted as if he did not, / and
알아보았고, 　　모르는 척 행동했지만,

remembered his dream / of his brother's sheaves bowing
자신이 꿈이 기억났다 　　　　형들의 곡식단이 자신의 곡식단에게 절하던.

down to his sheaf. At first, / he spoke roughly to them, /
처음에는, 　　그들에게 거칠게 대했다,

and called them "spies." But they said / that they were all
"첩자"라고 부르며. 　　　하지만 그들은 말했다 　자신들은 형제이며,

one man's sons, / and had come to buy food.
음식을 사러 왔다고.

Joseph still spoke roughly to them, / not because he was
요셉은 여전히 거칠게 대했는데, 　　　　화가 났기 때문이 아니라,

angry, / but because he did not wish / them to know him
바라지 않았기 때문이었다 　　　　그들이 자신을 바라보는 것을

/ yet.
아직.

fruitful 소출이 많이 나는 | governor 총리 | spy 첩자 | roughly 거칠게

His heart was full of love for them, / and he was soon
요셉의 마음은 그들에 대한 사랑으로 가득했고,

going to show them great kindness; / but when they told
머지 않아 다정한 모습을 보여 주려 했다;   하지만 그들이 말하자

him / that they had left an old father and a young brother
집에 늙은 아비와 어린 동생을 두고 왔으며,

at home, / and one was dead, / he still acted / as if they
한 명은 죽었다고,   요셉은 계속 행동했다

did not tell the truth.
그들이 거짓을 말하고 있다는 듯이.

He said / that to prove themselves true men / one of them
요셉이 말했다 그들이 진실된 사람임을 증명하려면

should go home / and bring the youngest brother, / and
한 명이 집에 가서   막내 동생을 데려오고

the others should be kept in prison / until they returned; /
나머지는 감옥에 갇혀야 한다고   두 사람이 돌아올 때까지;

and he put them all in prison.
그리고 모두를 감옥에 가뒀다.

After three days, / he said / one might stay / while the
사흘 후,   요셉은 말했다 한 명은 남으라고

others took the wheat home / to their families, / but that
나머지가 밀을 가지고 집으로 간 사이   가족들에게,

they must surely come back / and bring the boy with
하지만 반드시 돌아와 와야 한다고   동생을 데리고.

them.

Then Reuben, / who had tried to save Joseph / from the
그때 르우벤이,   요셉을 구하려 했었던

pit long before, / told his brothers / that all this trouble
오래 전에 구덩이에서,   형제들에게 말했다   이 모든 문제가 그들에게 일어난

had come upon them / for their wickedness / to their
것이라고   악행 때문에

brother Joseph, / and they said to each other / in their
요셉에게 저질렀던,   그리고 그들은 서로에게 말했다

own language:
자신들의 언어로:

"We are verily guilty / concerning our brother; / when
우리가 진정 죄를 지었구나   우리 형제에게;

he besought us, / we would not hear, / therefore is this
그가 간청했을 때,   우리가 듣지 않았으니,

distress come upon us."
이러한 고통이 다가왔구나."

Joseph understood everything they said / though they did
요셉은 그들의 말을 모두 알아 들었다   그들은 그 사실을 몰랐고,

not know it, / for he had been talking to them / through
말하고 있었기에

an interpreter, / and they thought he was an Egyptian.
통역관을 통하여,   그가 이집트인이라고 생각했지만.

Now his heart was so full / that he had to go out of the
그때 요셉은 가슴이 벅차 올라서   방에서 나가 울 수밖에 없었다.

room to weep. But he came back / and chose Simeon to
하지만 다시 돌아와   시므온에게 남으라고 하고

stay / while the others went to Canaan / to bring back
나머지는 가나안으로 가서   베냐민을 데려오라 했다.

Benjamin.

They took the wheat / that they had bought / in bags, /
형제들은 밀을 가지고   자신들이 구입한   가방 속에 넣어,

and went away; / but when they stopped at an inn / to
떠났다;   한 여관에서 멈췄을 때

rest and feed their asses, / one of the brothers opened
휴식을 취하고 나귀를 먹이기 위해,   형제 중 한 명이 가방을 열고,

his bag, / and found the money / that he had paid for the
돈이 들어 있는 것을 보았다   밀을 사기 위해 지불했던

wheat / in the top of his bag. Here was more trouble, /
가방의 맨 위에.   그러자 더욱 혼란에 빠져,

and they were afraid.
그들은 두려워했다.

---

verily 참으로 | guilty 죄책감이 드는 | beseech 간청하다 | distress 고통, 괴로움 | interpreter 통역관 | inn
여관 | bear (책임)지다 | blame 책임

When they came home / to their father / they told him /
형제들이 집에 도착하여　　　아버지에게 이야기 한 후

all that had happened, / and as they opened the bags, /
일어난 모든 일을,　　　　　가방을 열어 보니,

each one found his money. Jacob was deeply troubled; /
각자 가방에 돈이 들어있는 것을 발견했다.　야곱은 깊은 혼란에 빠졌다:

for Joseph was gone, / and Simeon was gone, / and now
요셉은 떠났고,　　　　　시므온도 없는데,

they wanted to take Benjamin.
이제는 베냐민까지 데려오라 했기에

Reuben who had two sons said: / "Slay my two sons / if I
아들이 둘 있는 르우벤이 말했다:　　　"제 아들을 죽이세요

bring him not to thee."
만약 제가 시므온을 데려오지 못한다면."

But Jacob said / Benjamin should not go down to Egypt.
하지만 야곱은 말했다　베냐민이 이집트로 가서는 안 된다고.

But the wheat was gone / in a short time, / and they were
그러나 밀이 떨어져 버렸고　　　짧은 기간에,

likely to starve / so great was the famine, / and at last
굶주리게 될 것 같아서　기근이 매우 심했기 때문에,　　마침내 야곱이 말했다

Jacob said / they must go to Egypt again for food.
　　　　　다시 이집트에 가서 음식을 구해 오라고.

Judah said they would go / if Benjamin would go with
유다가 가겠다고 말했지만　　　　베냐민이 함께 간다면,

them, / but Jacob would not listen to this. He asked them
　　　야곱은 그 말을 들으려 하지 않았다.　　　　야곱이 아들에게 묻자

/ why they told the man / that they had a brother, / and
　그 남자에게 왜 말했는지　　　동생이 있다고,

they replied, / that the Governor had asked them / if their
그들은 대답했다,　　총리가 자신들에게 물었다고

father was yet living / and if they had another brother.
아버지가 아직 살아계신지　　그리고 형제가 있는지.

"Send the lad with me," / said Judah, / "if I bring him not
"아이를 데려가게 해 주세요,"　　유다가 말했다,　　"그 아이를 다시 아버지께 데려

unto thee, / let me bear the blame forever."
오지 않는다면,　　제가 평생 책임지겠습니다."

81

balm 향유 | fine 훌륭한

Then Jacob told them / to take him and go, / and also to
그러자 야곱이 말했다   베냐민을 데리고 가라고,   또 선물도 가져가라고

take presents / of honey, and spices, and balm, and nuts, /
꿀과 향신료와 향유, 견과류를,

and double the money, / so as to return / that which was put
그리고 돈을 두 배로 가져가서,   돌려주라고   가방에 들어 있던 돈을,

in their bags, / and he blessed them, / and sent them away.
그리고 아들들을 축복하며,   떠나 보냈다.

They went down into Egypt, / and stood before Joseph
형제들은 이집트에 가서,   다시 요셉 앞에 섰다.

again. When he saw Benjamin with them / he told the
요셉은 베냐민을 데려온 것을 보자

steward of his house / to make ready a fine dinner for them,
집사에게 말했다   멋진 만찬을 준비하고,

/ and bring them to him at noon, / and he did so.
그들을 정오에 데려오라고,   그러자 집사는 명령대로 했다.

Then the brothers were afraid / that they were all to be
형제들은 두려워하며   감옥에 들어갈까봐,

put in prison, / and at the door of Joseph's house / began
요셉의 집 앞에서

to tell the steward / how they found the money / when
집사에게 말하기 시작했다   자신들이 어떻게 돈을 발견했는지

they opened their bags, / and that they had brought it back
가방을 열었을 때,   그래서 두 배의 돈을 가져왔다고;

doubled; / but the steward spoke kindly to them, / and said
하지만 집사는 친절하게 말했다,

that he had placed their money, / and that they need not
자신이 돈을 가방에 넣었으니,   두려워할 필요 없다고,

fear, / for God had given it back to them.
하나님이 돌려준 돈이기에.

Then he brought Simeon out, / and they made ready / to
그리고 나서 집사는 시므온을 데리고 나왔고,   그들은 준비했다

dine with the Governor at noon, / and to give him their
총리와 점심 식사를 하고,   그에게 선물을 주려고.

presents.

When he came / they bowed down to him / and
요셉이 나타나자   형제들은 그에게 절을 한 후

presented their gifts, / and he asked them / if they were
선물을 전했고,   그러자 요셉이 물었다   그들이 건강한지,

well, / and if the old man of whom they spoke, / was
그리고 그들이 말한 노인이,

still alive, / and they replied that he was. When he saw
아직 살아계신지,   그러자 형제들은 그렇다고 대답했다.   요셉은 베냐민을 보고,

Benjamin, / and knew that he was truly his own brother,
자신의 형제가 맞다는 사실을 알았다.

/ the son of Rachel, / he said: /
라헬의 아들인,   그리고 말했다:

"God be gracious unto thee my son," / and he went
"하나님의 은총이 내리시기를,"

quickly to his own chamber, / lest he should weep before
그리고는 재빨리 침실로 갔다,   그들 앞에서 눈물이 날까봐.

them.

Key Expression

배수 비교 표현

'~보다 몇 배, ~의 몇 배'라는 의미를 나타내는 배수 비교는 배수사와 원급 및 비교급 표현을 사용하여 나타낼 수 있으며 '배수사 + 명사'의 형태도 가능합니다.

▶ 배수사 + 명사
▶ 배수사 + as + 형용사/부사 + as + 비교할 대상
▶ 배수사 + 형용사/부사의 비교급 + than + 비교할 대상

배수사에는 half(절반), twice(2배), three times(3배), ~ times(~배) 등이 있습니다. 이 때 3배 미만인 half와 twice의 경우에는 비교급 배수비교는 사용하지 않습니다.

ex) The portion of Benjamin was five times greater than that of the others.
= five times as great as that of others.
= five times that of others.
베냐민의 몫은 다른 형제들보다 다섯 배나 많았다.

When he came out to them again, / and they sat down
요셉이 다시 나타나자,   형제들은 식사를 하기 위해 자리에

to dine, / he placed the sons of Jacob / by themselves,
앉았다.   요셉은 야곱의 형제들을 앉히고   그들끼리,

/ and the Egyptians of his house / by themselves, /
집 안의 이집트인들을 앉혔다   역시 그들끼리,

and the brothers were placed / according to their ages
형제들은 앉았다   나이에 따라

/ — Reuben at the head / and Benjamin last, / and they
— 르우벤이 가장 상석에 앉고   베냐민이 가장 끝 자리에 앉았다.

wondered among themselves / at this. Joseph also sent
그리고 형제들은 이상하게 여겼다   이를 보고. 요셉은 또한 음식을 덜어줬는데

portions / from his own table / to his brothers, / but the
          자신의 식탁에서   형제들에게,

portion of Benjamin was five times greater / than that of
베냐민의 몫은 다섯 배나 많았다

the others.
다른 형제들보다.

The next morning / their wheat was measured to them,
이튿날 아침   밀의 양을 측정하여 그들에게 주자,

/ and the asses were loaded with it, / and they went
나귀 등에 밀을 실었고,   형제들은 길을 떠났다,

on their way, / but Joseph had told the steward / to put
          하지만 요셉은 집사에게 시켜서

the money of each man / in the top of his bag, / and in
각자의 돈을 넣고   가방 맨 위에,

Benjamin's / to put his silver cup.
베냐민의 가방에는   자신의 은잔을 넣으라고 했다.

When they were a little away from the city, / the steward
형제들이 얼마 못 갔을 때,

overtook them, / and charged them / with stealing his
집사가 그들을 습격하여,   체포했다

lord's silver cup.
주인의 은잔을 훔쳤다면서.

---

gracious 자애로운 | chamber 회의실, 방, 침실 | portion 일 인분의 몫 | overtake 엄습하다, 추월하다 | charge
책임, 고발

The men were so sure / that no one of them had stolen
형제들은 확신하고 있었기에 아무도 은잔을 훔치지 않았다고,

the silver cup, / that they said, /
말했다,

"Let him die / with whom the cup is found, / and the rest
"죽이십시오 은잔을 가진 사람이 있다면, 그리고 나머지 형제

of us / will be your slaves."
들은 당신의 종이 되겠나이다."

So everybody's bag was opened / from the oldest to the
모든 가방이 열렸고 장자의 가방부터 막내의 가방까지

youngest, / and the cup was found in Benjamin's bag.
차례로, 베냐민의 가방에서 은잔이 나왔다.

Key Expression

사역동사 let

let은 5형식의 사역동사로 목적보어로 동사원형을 취합니다.
그러나 다른 사역동사인 make, have과 달리 let에는 '시키다'라는 강제의 의
미라기 보다 '허락하다'라는 의미가 강합니다. 특히 목적어 자리에 본인을 넣어
명령문으로 표현할 때에는 '~하겠다, ~하도록 허락해 달라'의 뜻이 됩니다.
그래서 목적어와 목적보어가 수동의 관계일 때 make나 have의 경우에는 '목적
어 + 과거분사'의 형태가 뒤따르지만, let의 경우 '목적어 + be(동사원형) + 과거
분사'의 형태가 뒤따릅니다.

▶ let + 목적어 + 동사원형(능동)
▶ let + 목적어 + be + 과거분사(수동)
▶ make/have + 목적어 + 동사원형(능동)
▶ make/have + 목적어 + 과거분사(수동)

ex) Let him die with whom the cup is found.
   은잔을 가진 사람이 있다면 죽이십시오.
   O, my lord, let thy servant speak a word in my lord's ears!
   주인님, 당신의 종이 주인님께 한 말씀 드리겠습니다!

Then they rent their clothes for grief, / and loaded the
그러자 그들은 비통해하며 자신들의 옷을 찢고,　　　　　짐을 나귀에 실은 후

asses / and went back to the city, / and when they came
도시로 돌아갔다.　　　　　　그리고 요셉의 집에 이르자,

to Joseph's house, / they fell on their faces / before him, /
머리가 땅에 닿도록 엎드렸다　　　　요셉 앞에,

Joseph tried to speak sternly / and said: /
요셉은 근엄하게 말하려 노력하며　　　　이야기 했다:

"What deed is this you have done?"
"도대체 무슨 짓을 한 것인가?"

Judah said: /
그러자 유다가 말했다:

"What shall we say unto my lord, / or how shall we clear
"주인님께 무슨 말을 할 수 있겠습니까,　　　　어떻게 결백을 증명할 수 있겠습니까?

ourselves? We are my lord's servants."
저희는 이제 주인님의 종입니다."

Then said Joseph: /
그러자 요셉이 말했다:

"The man in whose hand the cup is found / he shall be
"잔이 발견된 사람은

my servant, / and as for you, / get you up in peace / unto
내 종이 될 것이다,　　그리고 나머지는,　　조용히 물러가거라

your father."
아버지가 있는 곳으로."

Then Judah came nearer to Joseph, / and all his soul
그때 유다가 요셉의 곁으로 다가가,　　　　　모든 혼을 목소리에 담아

came forth into his voice / as he said: /
말했다:

"O, my lord, / let thy servant speak a word / in my lord's
"주인님,　　　　당신의 종이 한 말씀 드리겠습니다　　　주인님의 귀에!"

ears!"

rend 찢다 | grief 비탄 | sternly 엄격하게 | deed 행동, 행위

Then he told the story / of their coming down into Egypt,
그리고 나서 그는 이야기를 전했다   자신들이 이집트에 온 경위와,

/ and of the old father and young brother / whom he had
늙은 아버지와 어린 동생에 대해

asked them about; / of the love of this father / for the
요셉이 물어 보았던;   그리고 아버지의 사랑에 대해

little one, / for his mother, / and his brother now dead. He
막내 아들과,   어머니와,   지금은 죽은 동생에 대한.

reminded Joseph / that he had told them to bring the boy
그는 요셉에게 상기시켰다   요셉이 막내를 데려오라고 말한 것과,

to him, / and that they had said, / that if the boy should
그리고 자신들이 했던 말을,   막내가 아버지 곁을 떠나면,

leave his father, / his father would die; / but the governor
아버지는 죽고 말 것이라고;   하지만 총리가 말했기에

had said / "Except your youngest brother come down
"막내를 데려오지 않는다면,

with you, / ye shall see my face no more."
내 얼굴을 다시 보지 못할 것이다."라고

Then Judah told the story / of the father's grief / when he
그리고 또 유다는 이야기를 전했다   아버지가 느낄 비통함에 대해   알게 되면

found / that he must let Benjamin go down into Egypt,
베냐민을 이집트로 보내야 한다는 것을,

/ that they might buy a little food; / how he spoke of his
약간의 음식을 사기 위해서;   그리고 두 아들에 대해서 어떻게

two sons, / that were the sons of Rachel — that one had
말했는지   라헬의 아들들이었던   — 하나는 갈가리 찢겨

been torn in pieces, / and now if mischief should befall
죽었는데,   이제 남은 아이에게도 불행이 일어난다면,

the other, / it would bring his gray hairs / in sorrow / to
아버지의 머리가 희어지고 결국   그 슬픔으로

the grave. He asked Joseph / what he should do / when
죽고 말 거라고.   유다는 요셉에게 물었다   자신이 어떡해야 할지

he returned to his father / without the lad, / seeing that
아버지에게 돌아갔을 때   막내를 데려가지 못한 채,

remind 상기시키다, 다시 한번 말하다 | mischief 나쁜 짓, 해, 피해 | gray hair 흰머리 | sorrow 슬픔, 비애
| bound up 밀접한, 열중하여 | surety 보증인, 보증금 | grieved 슬퍼하는 | terrified 무서워하는, 겁이 난 |
deliverance 구조

his life was bound up in the lad's life, / and Judah begged
아버지의 삶이 막내의 삶과 연결되어 있는 것을 보았으니,　　　그래서 유다는 요셉에게

him, / as he had made himself surety for the lad, / to take
애원했다, 자신이 막내를 데려가겠다고 보장했으니,

him to be his slave, / but to let Benjamin return to his
자신을 종으로 삼고,　　　베냐민은 아버지에게로 돌려보내 달라고

father / with his brothers.
　　　다른 형제들과.

"For how shall I go up to my father," / said Judah, / "and
"제가 어떻게 아버지께 돌아가겠습니까,"　　　유다가 말했다,

the lad be not with me?"
"막내를 데려가지 못하면서?"

Then Joseph could bear it no longer. He told all the
그러자 요셉은 더 이상 참을 수 없었다.　　　그는 모든 이집트인에게 말한 후

Egyptians / to go out of the room, / and then weeping /
　　　방에서 나가라고,　　　눈물을 흘렸다

so that the Egyptians and the people / in the king's house
그러자 모든 이집트인과 사람들이　　　왕궁에 있던

/ heard, / he made himself known to his brothers.
　들었고,　　요셉은 자신의 정체를 형제들에게 알렸다.

"I am Joseph, / your brother," / he said, / "whom you sold
"내가 요셉입니다,　　　당신들의 형제입니다."　　그가 말했다,　　"형들이 이집트인에게

into Egypt," / and he begged them / to come near to him.
팔았던."　　　그리고 그들에게 애원했다　　가까이 오라고.

"Be not grieved / nor angry with yourselves," / he said,
"슬퍼하지 말고　　　스스로에게 화내지도 마세요,"　　　그가 말했다,

/ for he saw that they were terrified, / "for God sent me
　그들이 두려워하는 것을 보았기 때문에,　　　"하나님이 저를 형들 앞에

before you / to save your lives / by a great deliverance. It
보내셨으니　　　형들의 목숨을 구하도록　　크나큰 구원으로

was not you / that sent me hither, / but God, / and he hath
형들이 아닙니다　　　저를 이곳으로 보낸 이는,　　　하나님이십니다,　　그리고 그분이

made me a ruler / throughout all the land of Egypt."
저를 통치자로 만드셨습니다　　이집트 전체를 다스리는."

Then he told them / to hasten and go to his father / and
그리고 나서 그들에게 말했다   서둘러 아버지에게 가서

tell him this, / and ask him to come down / at once, /
이 일을 알린 후,   이곳으로 오시도록 하라고   즉시,

with all his flocks and herds, / and dwell in Goshen, /
가축 떼를 이끌고,   그리고 고센 땅에 살라고.

the best part of Egypt, / for years of famine were yet to
이집트에서 가장 좋은 땅인,   아직 수 년 동안 기근이 계속 될 것이기에.

come.

Then Joseph took little Benjamin in his arms / and wept
요셉은 베냐민을 품에 안고

over him, / and kissed him, / and kissed all his brothers,
눈물을 흘리며,   그에게 입맞추고,   형제들에게도 입을 맞췄다,

/ and after that / his brothers talked with him. The king
그 후에   형제들과 이야기를 나눴다.

heard the story of Joseph's brothers / and was pleased.
왕은 요셉의 형제들 이야기를 듣고   기뻐했다.

Key Expression

see that : ~하도록 조치하다

See that은 원래 See to it that으로 '(that 이하를) 하도록 조치하다, 배려하다, 명심하다, 반드시 ~하게 하다'라는 의미를 가진 관용구문입니다. 이때 it은 전치사 to의 형식적인 목적어, that절은 진목적어로 봅니다.
See to it that은 중간에 'to it'을 생략하고 See that으로 사용하는 경우가 많으니 함께 외워두세요.

ex) See that ye fall not out by the way.
= See to it that ye fall not out by the way.
가는 길에 서로 떨어지지 않도록 하세요.
He told Moses to see that every Israelite should take a lamb from the flock and keep it four days.
주님이 모세에게 말씀하시기를 모든 이스라엘인은 양 한 마리씩을 데리고 가서 나흘 동안 가지고 있도록 조치하라고 하셨다.

He told Joseph / to send wagons / for the wives and little
왕은 요셉에게 명령했다   마차를 보내고

ones of his brothers, / and to tell them / to bring their
요셉 형제의 가족들을 위해,   그들에게 말하라고   아버지를 모셔와서,

father, / and all their cattle and sheep, / and come to live
가축 떼와 함께,   고센에 살라고

in Goshen / where they should have the best of the land /
요셉의 가족들은 가장 좋은 곳을 가져야 하기에

for their flocks and herds.
가축 떼를 위해.

Joseph did as the king commanded, / and also gave them
요셉은 왕의 명령대로 했다.   형제들에게 음식을 주었고

food / for the journey, / and a suit of clothing to each
여행을 위해,   옷 한 벌씩 주었다,

brother, / but to little Benjamin / he gave five suits, / and
하지만 베냐민에게는   옷을 다섯 벌 주었고,

three hundred pieces of silver. He also loaded twenty
은화 300닢도 주었다.   요셉은 또한 나귀 20마리에 실었다,

asses / with the good things of Egypt / as presents to his
이집트의 좋은 물건들을   아버지께 드릴 선물로,

father, / so he sent them all on their journey / saying: /
그리고 모두를 떠나 보냈다   말하며:

"See that ye fall not out by the way."
"가는 길에 서로 떨어지지 않도록 하세요."

When they came to Jacob in Hebron, / they told him the
헤브론에 있는 야곱에게 도착하자,   형제들은 아버지에게 멋진

wonderful story / of the finding of Joseph, / and his heart
이야기를 전했다   요셉을 찾았다는,   하지만 야곱의 마음은

was faint, / for he did not believe them; / but when he
어지러웠다,   그들을 믿을 수 없어서;

had heard all Joseph's messages, / and had seen the gifts,
요셉의 전갈을 듣고,   선물과 마차를 보자,

and the wagons, / he said: /
그가 말했다:

---

hasten 서둘러 하다 | suit 한 벌 | faint 어지러운, 실신할 것 같은

"It is enough: / Joseph my son is yet alive: / I will go and
"그걸로 족하다: 내 아들 요셉이 살아 있다니: 그를 보러 가겠다

see him / before I die."
죽기 전에."

So they began the long journey to Egypt, / for it took
그래서 그들은 이집트로의 긴 여정을 시작했다,   오랜 시간이 걸렸기

a long time / to travel / with a great family, / and with
때문에   여행하는 것은   대가족을 이끌고

thousands of cattle and sheep. At Beersheba / Jacob
수천 마리의 가축을 이끌면서.   브엘세바에서

stopped and worshiped God, / where his father had built
야곱은 멈춰서 하나님을 찬양했다,   그곳은 그의 아버지가 제단을 쌓았던

an altar / years before; / and God told him in the night
곳이었고   수년 전에;   그날 밤에 하나님이 말씀하셨다

/ that he need not fear / to go down into Egypt, / for
두려워하지 말라고   이집트로 가는 것을,

He would there make him a great nation, / and that He
그곳에서 하나님이 그에게 큰 나라를 세우게 하실 것이며,

would bring him back again / to his own land.
다시 불러들일 것이라고   그분의 나라로.

So Jacob with all his children and their little ones, / and
그래서 야곱은 모든 자녀와 손자 손녀들과 함께,

all his flocks and herds / came into Egypt. There were
모든 가축을 데리고   이집트로 왔다.   67명이 있었고,

sixty-seven souls, / and when they had counted Joseph
요셉과 두 아들을 합하면,

and his two sons, / there were seventy.
일흔 명이었다.

Jacob sent Judah on before / to see Joseph / and ask the
야곱은 먼저 유다를 보내   요셉을 만나   고센 땅으로 가는

way to Goshen, / so that they might go directly there /
길을 물어보게 했다.   가족들이 그 곳에 바로 갈 수 있도록

with the cattle and sheep. And when Joseph knew that
가축을 이끌고.   요셉은 아버지가 오고 있다는 소식을 듣고,

his father was coming, / he went to meet him in Goshen,
아버지를 만나려고 고센으로 갔고,

/ and there he wept on his father's neck / a long time, /
그곳에서 아버지의 목을 끌어안고 눈물을 흘렸다   오랫동안,

and Jacob said: /
그러자 야곱이 말했다:

"Now let me die, / since I have seen thy face, / because
"이제 죽어도 여한이 없다.   네 얼굴을 보았으니,

thou art yet alive."
또 네가 지금까지 살아있으니."

After this / Joseph presented five of his brothers to
이후에   요셉은 형제들 중 다섯 명을 왕에게 소개했고,

Pharaoh, / and the king spoke very kindly to them, / and
왕은 매우 다정하게 이야기하며,

gave them the best of the land / for their flocks, / and
가장 좋은 땅을 주었고   가축을 기를,

hired some of them / to oversee his own shepherds.
그 중 몇 명을 채용하여   목동의 관리를 맡겼다.

Joseph brought his father in also / and Jacob blessed
요셉은 아버지도 모셔왔고   야곱은 왕에게 축복을 전했다.

Pharaoh.

So the family of Jacob lived in peace, / and were cared
그렇게 야곱의 가족들은 평화롭게 살았고,   요셉의 보살핌을 받았다,

for by Joseph, / just as the Lord had promised Jacob, /
주님이 야곱에게 약속하셨던 대로,

when in a dream / he saw the angels of God / at Bethel,
꿈 속에서   하나님의 천사들을 보았고   벧엘에서,

/ and heard above them the voice of the Lord / blessing
주님의 목소리가 울려 퍼졌던   그를 축복하며

him, / and saying: /
이렇게 말하던;

"Thou shalt spread abroad / to the West, and to the East,
"너는 널리 퍼질 것이다   서쪽으로, 동쪽으로,

/ and to the North, and to the South, / and in thee / shall
그리고 북쪽과, 남쪽으로,   그리고 네 안에서

all the families of the earth be blessed."
세상의 모든 가족들이 축복을 받으리라."

Joseph carried all Egypt / through the years of famine, /
요셉은 이집트 전체를 다스렸고   기근이 계속되는 동안,

and saved seed / for the people to sow their fields / in the
씨앗들을 보관하여   사람들이 밭에 심을 수 있도록 했다

seventh year / so that they said: /
7년 동안   그러자 사람들이 말했다:

"Thou hast saved our lives."
"당신이 우리의 생명을 살렸습니다."

He afterwards visited his father, / and Jacob made him
이후에 요셉은 아버지를 방문했고,   야곱은 그에게 약속하도록 시켰다

promise / that he would bury him / when he died / in the
자신을 묻어 달라고   자신이 죽으면

tomb of Abraham and Isaac, his father, / in his own land.
아브라함과 아버지 이삭의 무덤 안에,   아버지의 땅에서.

abroad 널리 퍼져, 해외로 | sow 뿌리다, 심다 | redeem 구원하다

When Jacob was near his end, / Joseph brought his two
야곱이 죽을 때가 되자,　　　　　　요셉은 어린 두 아들을 데려왔다,

little sons, / Ephraim and Manasseh, / to his bedside, /
에브라임과 므낫세를,　　　　　　아버지의 침대 곁으로 데려가자,

and the old man gave them his blessing, / laying his right
야곱은 아이들을 축복했다,　　　　　　오른손을 에브라임의

hand upon the head of Ephraim, / the youngest, / and his
머리 위에 올리고,　　　　　　동생인,

left hand on that of Manasseh / the first born, / even as
왼손은 므낫세의 머리에 위에 올린 채,　　　　형인,

Isaac had given the birthright blessing to him / instead of
비록 이삭은 장자의 권리를 자신에게 주었지만,　　　　에서 대신,

to Esau, / and he said: /
그리고 말했다:

"The angel which redeemed me from all evil / bless the
"나를 악으로부터 구원하신 천사가　　　　　　이 아이들을

lads."
축복하소서."

Key Expression

lay와 lie의 구분

lay와 lie는 비슷한 의미를 지닌 자동사-타동사 커플입니다. 뒤따르는 목적어의 유무에 따라 구분하여 사용해야 합니다.
특히 과거형 활용에서 겹치는 부분이 있기 때문에 주의해야 합니다.

▶ lay-laid-laid : [타동사] 놓다, 눕히다, (알을) 낳다
▶ lie-lay-lain : [자동사] 눕다, 놓여 있다, ~한 상태이다

ex) The old man gave them his blessing, laying his right hand upon the head of
Ephraim, the youngest, and his left hand on that of Manasseh the first born.
(→ lay 놓다)
노인은 오른손을 동생인 에브라임의 머리 위에 올리고, 형인 왼손은 므낫세의 머
리에 위에 올린 채, 그들을 축복했다.
Poor Hagar laid her child under a bush to die. (→ lay 눕히다)
불쌍한 하갈은 덤불 아래 아이를 눕혀 죽도록 두었다.
He lay down to sleep, with a stone for his pillow. (→ lie 눕다)
야곱은 돌을 베게 삼아 잠을 자려고 누웠다.
Night was falling, and the waters lay dark before them. (→ lie 놓여 있다)
밤이 깊어지자, 바닷물이 그들 앞에 검게 펼쳐 졌다.

Then he called all his sons together / and told them / what
그리고는 아들을 모두 불러   이야기 했다

should befall them / in the last days. To each one / he
그들이 겪을 일들을   마지막 순간에.   아들 각자에게   야곱은

spoke / as a prophet speaks / who has a vision of things
말하며   예언자처럼   앞으로의 일들을 볼 수 있는,

to come, / and he blessed them there. When he spoke to
그리고 그들을 축복했다.   유다에게 이야기 할 때는

Judah, / he told him / that kings and lawgivers should /
말했다   왕과 법을 만드는 사람들이 나올 것이라고

arise from among his children / until the Saviour of the
그의 자손들 중에서   그리고 마침내 구원자가 오실 것이라고.

world should come.

Jacob was an hundred and forty-seven years old / when he
야곱은 140세였다   죽었을 때,

died, / and there was great mourning for him.
그리고 훌륭한 장례식이 벌어졌다.

Joseph had the body of his father embalmed, / as the
요셉은 아버지의 시신을 미라로 만들었고,

Egyptians had the custom of doing, / and after a long
이집트인들이 관습으로 행하던 대로,

mourning in Egypt, / Joseph and his brothers / and many
이집트에서의 긴 애도의 시간 후,   요셉과 형제들은

Egyptians who were Joseph's friends, / carried the body of
요셉의 친구였던 많은 이집트인들과,   야곱의 시신을 가나안까지

Jacob to Canaan, / in a great procession, / and buried him
옮겼다,   대 행렬을 이루며,

in the cave of Machpelah, / where his fathers were buried.
그리고 막벨라 굴에 시신을 묻었다,   조상들이 묻혀 있는.

After they had returned to Egypt, / the brothers of Joseph
그들이 이집트로 돌아온 후,   형제들은 요셉에게 말했다:

said: /

---

lawgiver 입법자 | embalm 방부 처리하다, 미라를 만들다 | procession 행렬 | nourish 영양분을 공급하다,
키우다

"Perhaps now / he will hate us, / and bring upon us / all
"이제 어쩌면   요셉이 미워할지 몰라,   그리고 끄집어낼지도 몰라

the evil we did to him."
우리가 그에게 행한 악행을."

So they sent to him to ask his forgiveness / for all that
그래서 형제들은 요셉을 찾아가 용서를 구했다   지나간 일들에 대해.

was past. Then Joseph wept, / for he had nothing but love
요셉은 눈물을 흘렸다,   그의 마음속에는 사랑밖에 없었고

in his heart / toward his brothers, / and he wished them to
형제들을 향한,   그들이 자신을 믿어 주기를 바랐기

trust him. He comforted them / and spoke kindly to them,
때문에.   요셉은 형제들을 위로하며   다정하게 말을 걸고,

/ saying: /
이렇게 말했다:

"Fear not: / ye meant evil unto me, / but God meant it
"두려워하지 마세요. 형들은 내게 나쁜 짓 했지만,   하나님께서 그 일을 좋은 일로

unto good. I will nourish you / and your little ones."
바꾸셨어요.   제가 형들을 보살피고   형들의 아이들을 돌보겠어요."

And so through all Joseph's life, / and he lived one
그렇게 요셉은 평생 동안,   110세까지 살 동안,

hundred and ten years, / he was a tender father to all his
모든 가족에게 자상한 아버지였고,

family, / and a wise ruler of the people, / and he died /
백성을 다스리는 현명한 통치자였으며,   죽었다

after making his family promise / to carry his body back
가족과 약속한 후   자신의 시신을 가나안으로 옮겨

into Canaan / to be buried with his fathers / when they
선조들과 함께 묻어 달라고

themselves should go.
그들 자신이 떠나야 할 때.

"For God will surely visit you," / he said, / "and bring
"하나님이 반드시 당신을 만나시리니."   그가 말했다,

you out of this land / into the land which he promised to
"이 땅에서 불러 내어   아브라함에게 약속하신 땅으로,

Abraham, / to Isaac and to Jacob."
이삭과 야곱에게."

9

THE CRADLE THAT WAS ROCKED

BY A RIVER
강물에 흔들리던 요람

After Joseph and all the sons of Jacob had grown old /
요셉과 야곱의 아들 모두 나이가 들어

and had passed away, / their children's children grew in
죽은 후,　　　　　　　　　그들의 후손이 늘어나

numbers / until they became a great multitude.
엄청난 수를 이루었다.

The Pharaoh whom Joseph had served also died, / and
요셉이 섬겼던 바로가 또한 죽고 나서,

the king who followed him / did not like the Hebrews.
그의 뒤를 이은 새 왕은　　　　　　히브리족을 좋아하지 않았다.

He feared them / because they had grown to be strong, /
왕은 히브리족을 두려워하여 그들이 강성해졌기 때문에,

so he set overseers to watch them, / and make them work
감독관을 두어 그들을 감시하고,　　　　　　노예처럼 일을 시켰다.

like slaves.

He treated them cruelly, / and made them lift the great
왕은 그들에게 잔혹하게 대하며,　　　거대한 돌을 옮겨

stones / with which they built the tombs of the kings /
왕의 무덤을 만들게 하고

and temples of the gods. He also tried to kill all the little
신전과.　　　　　　　　　　왕은 또한 아이들을 모두 죽이려 했지만

boys / as soon as they were born, / but the Lord took
태어나자마자,　　　　　　주님이 돌보셨다.

care of them. Also, / the king told his servants, / that
또한,　　　　　왕은 신하에게 시켜,

wherever they found a baby boy / among the Hebrews,
어디서든 남자 아이가 발견되면　　　　히브리족 중에,

---

sout 억센 | rush 골풀 | weave 엮다 | pitch 역청, 송진

/ to throw him into the river Nile, / but the little girls, /
나일 강에 던져 죽이라고 했다.   단 여자 아이는,

they should save alive.
살려두게 했다.

There was a man named Amrom, / who, with his wife
아므람이라는 이름의 사람이,   요게벳을 아내로 맞아,

Jochebed, / had a beautiful little boy / whom they
예쁜 아들을 낳았고   부부는 아들을 무척

tenderly loved. They hid him / as long as they could, /
사랑했다.   부부는 아이를 숨겼으나   가능한 한 오랫동안

and then when he was three months old / and she could
3개월이 지나자

hide him no longer, / she made up her mind / to give him
더 이상 숨길 수 없어서.   요게벳은 결단을 내렸다

into the care of God. She made a little boat, / or ark of
하나님에게 아이를 맡기겠다고.   요게벳은 작은 배를 만들었다,

stout rushes, / that grew by the river. She wove it closer
골풀로 만든 방주를,   강가에서 자라는.   요게벳은 골풀을 촘촘하게 엮어,

than a basket, / and then covered it with pitch / that the
                        송진을 발랐다

water might not enter, / just as Noah covered the great
물이 스며들지 못하도록,   노아가 방주에 칠했던 것처럼

ark / before the flood.
대홍수가 나기 전에.

Then she wrapped her baby carefully / and laid him in
그리고 나서 아기를 조심스럽게 감싸서 　　　　　　　　　작은 배에 눕힌 후,

the little boat, / and set it among the reeds / at the edge of
그 배를 갈대밭 사이에 놓았다

the river Nile. God and His angels watched / the cradle
나일강가에 있는. 　　　하나님과 그의 천사들이 지켜보았고

of the child, / and the river gently rocked it. Jochebed
아기를 태운 요람을, 　강이 요람을 부드럽게 흔들었다.

told the baby's sister / to wait near by / and see what
요게벳은 아이의 누이에게 　　근처에서 기다리면서 　　아기에게 무슨 일이

might happen to him, / and this is what happened, / or
일어나는지 지켜보라고 했다. 　　　이 일이 일어났다,

rather what God prepared for the baby / in the boat of
하나님이 아기를 위해 예비하신 일이었다 　　　　골풀 숲 속의 배 안에 있던.

rushes.

The king's daughter came down to bathe / in the river,
왕의 딸이 목욕을 하러 나왔고 　　　　　　　　　강가로,

/ and as her maidens walked up and down / by the
시녀들이 돌아다니고 있을 때

riverside, / she called one of them / to bring to her the
강변을, 　　　공주가 시녀 한 명을 불러 　　　작은 배를 가져오라고 했다

little ark / that she saw rocking on the river / among the
강물에 흔들리는 것을 보고 　　　　　　갈대밭 사이에서.

reeds. When she had opened it / she saw a beautiful little
공주가 상자를 열어보니 　　　　예쁜 아기가 보였고,

child, / and when it cried / her heart was touched, / and
아기가 울기 시작하자 　　　공주는 측은하게 생각하여,

she longed to keep it for her own.
아기를 기르고 싶어졌다.

read 갈대 | maiden 처녀 | riverside 강변 | nurse 아이를 보는 식모, 젖을 먹이다 | maid 처녀

"This is one of the Hebrew's children," / she said, / and
"히브리인의 아이구나." 공주가 말했다,

as the baby's sister came near / she asked the princess / if
그때 아기의 누이가 다가와 공주에게 물었다

she should go and get a nurse / from among the Hebrew
유모를 불러올지 히브리 여인 중에서

women / to bring it up for her, / and the princess said to
그 아기를 기르도록, 그러자 공주가 말했다,

her, / "Go," / and the maid went and called the child's
"다녀오렴." 그러자 그 누이는 가서 어머니를 불러왔다.

mother. The princess said: / "Take this child away / and
공주가 말했다: "이 아이를 데려가서

nurse it for me, / and I will give thee thy wages."
나 대신 젖을 먹이면, 내가 품삯을 주겠다."

And the mother took her baby joyfully / though she hid
어머니는 기쁜 마음으로 아이를 데려갔고 기뻐하는 마음을 감추면서

her joy in her heart, / and carried him home / to nurse
아이를 집으로 데려와

and bring up / for Pharoah's daughter.
젖을 먹이고 길렀다 바로의 딸 대신.

And the child grew, / and when he was old enough / his
이이가 자라, 나이를 먹자

mother took him to the king's palace, / and he became
어머니는 아이를 왕의 궁전에 데려갔고,

the son of the princess. She called his name Moses, /
아이는 공주의 아들이 되었다. 공주는 아이를 모세라 불렀다.

which means "drawn out," / because she drew him out of
"건져내었다"는 의미로, 자신이 강에서 건져낸 아이였기에.

the water.

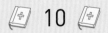

10

MOSES IN MIDIAN
미디안 땅의 모세

Moses had teachers, / and was taught all the learning of
모세에게는 교사가 있어서,   이집트인의 학문을 모두 배웠지만,

the Egyptians, / but his heart was with his own people.
그의 마음은 자신의 백성과 함께였다.

He was grieved / when he saw their burdens, / and heard
그는 슬퍼했고   그들이 고된 노동을 하고 있는 것을 보고,   그들의 울음 소리

their cries / when their taskmasters struck them.
를 들었다   감독관이 그들을 때릴 때.

Once, / when he was a grown man, / he saw an Egyptian
하루는,   성인이 된 모세가,   한 이집트인이 히브리인을 때리는

beating a Hebrew, / and he struck the Egyptian and
것을 보고,   그 이집트인을 쳐서 죽여버렸다,

killed him, / for he thought / he ought to defend his
그의 생각에는   자신의 민족을 지켜야 한다고 여겼기 때문이다:

people: / and when he saw that the man was dead, / he
그리고 그 사람이 죽은 것을 보고,

buried him in the sand. In a day or two / Moses tried to
시체를 모래 속에 묻어 버렸다.   며칠 후   모세가 싸움을 말리려 하자

make peace / between two Hebrews who were fighting, /
싸우고 있던 두 히브리인 사이에서,

and they answered him roughly, / and one of them said: /
그들은 모세에게 거칠게 대들었고,   그 중 한 명이 말했다:

"Who made thee a ruler over us? Wilt thou kill me, / as
"누가 당신을 우리의 지도자로 세웠소?   나도 죽일 셈이오,

thou didst the Egyptian / yesterday?"
당신이 이집트인을 죽였던 것처럼   어제?"

---

burden 무거운 짐, 부담 | taskmaster 작업 감독 | defend 방어하다, 옹호하다 | make peace 화해하다, 중재하다

Then Moses was afraid, / and when the king heard of
그러자 모세는 두려워졌고,   왕이 이 일을 들고,

it, / and tried to take his life, / Moses fled away / out of
모세를 죽이려 하자,   도망쳤다   이집트

Egypt, / through a desert into Midian. There he found
밖으로 나가, 미디안의 사막으로.   그곳에서 우물을 발견하고

a well / and sat down by it to rest. While he sat there /
근처에 앉아 쉬었다.   그가 앉아있을 때

the seven daughters of the priest of Midian / came to
미디안 제사장의 일곱 딸들이   물을 긷기 위해

draw water / for their father's flocks, / and some rough
왔는데   아버지의 가축에게 먹이려고,   거친 목동들이 오더니

shepherds came / and drove them away, / but Moses
제사장의 딸들을 몰아내 버렸다.   하지만 모세가 일어나

stood up / and helped them, / and watered their flocks.
그 여자들을 도왔고,   가축에 물을 먹였다.

When their father knew / that a noble stranger had been
제사장이 그 사실을 알고   고귀한 이방인이 딸에게 친절을 베풀었다는 것을,

kind to his daughters, / he asked him to come into his
모세를 자신의 집으로 초대하여,

house, / and eat bread with him, / and stay as long as
식사를 대접하고,   원하는 만큼 머무르라고 했다.

he would. So Moses stayed / and Zipporah, / one of the
그렇게 모세는 머물렀고   십보라가,   일곱 딸 중 한 명인,

seven sisters, / became his wife.
모세의 부인이 되었다.

---

flee 도망치다 | priest 제사장 | drive someone away 떠나게 만들다 | noble 고귀한 | bondage 구속 | father-in-law 장인 | wilderness 황무지 | oppressed 억압당하는

But Moses did not forget his people. God was preparing
하지만 모세는 자신의 백성을 잊지 않았다.   하나님이 모세를 준비시키셨고

him / to lead them out of bondage, / and he learned many
자신의 백성을 구속에서 풀어주기 위해,   그는 많은 것을 배웠다.

things, / during the years / that he kept the sheep of his
기간 동안   장인의 양 떼를 돌보던

father-in-law / in the wilderness.
황무지에서.

One day / he led his flocks across the desert / to Mount
하루는   모세가 양 떼를 끌고 사막을 건너고 있었다

Horeb or Sinai. There he saw a bush all bright within /
호렙산이나 시내산으로.   그곳에서 그는 환하게 빛나는 덤불을 보았다

as if it burned. He drew nearer to see / why the bush was
마치 불타고 있는 듯이.   그가 가까이 다가가자   왜 덤불이 타지 않는지 알아보

not consumed, / and heard the voice of the Lord calling
려고,   주님이 부르는 목소리가 들렸다.

him. The Lord told him / to come no nearer, / and to put
주님이 말씀하셨다   가까이 다가와

off his shoes, / for he stood on holy ground. Then the
신을 벗으라고,   거룩한 땅에 서 있었기 때문에.

Lord told him / that He was the God of his fathers, / and
그리고 말씀하셨다   자신은 모세의 조상의 하나님이며,

that He had heard the cry / of his oppressed people / in
울음 소리를 들었다고   억압받는 백성들의

Egypt.
이집트에 있는.

"I know their sorrows," / said the voice / from the midst
"나는 그들의 슬픔을 알고 있다,"   목소리가 들렸다   불꽃 가운데서.

of the fire, / "And I am come down / to deliver them out
"그래서 내가 내려왔도다

of the hand of the Egyptians, / and to bring them up out
그들을 이집트인의 손에서 구해내고,   이집트 땅에서 데리고 나와

of that land / into a good land, / and a large / — unto a
좋은 곳으로 인도하기 위하여,   넓은 땅으로

land flowing with milk and honey."
— 젖과 꿀이 흐르는 땅으로.

Then the Lord said / that Moses must go to the new
주님이 말씀하셨다   모세가 새 바로에게 가서,

Pharaoh, / for the old king was dead, / and bring the
전 왕이 죽었기 때문에,   이스라엘의 자손을

children of Israel / out of Egypt. Moses was a very
데려와야 한다고   이집트 밖으로.   모세는 매우 미천한 사람이라,

humble man, / and he could not believe / that Pharaoh
믿을 수 없었다

would listen to him / or that the Hebrews would follow
바로가 자신의 말을 듣고   히브리인들이 자신을 따르리라고,

him, / but the Lord said, /
하지만 주님이 말씀하셨다,

"Certainly / I will be with thee."
"반드시   내가 너와 함께 하리라."

And as a sign / that it should be so, / He said / that after
증표로써   그렇게 되리라는,   주님이 말씀하셨다

Moses had brought his people / out of Egypt, / they
모세가 그의 백성을 데리고 나온 후   이집트 밖으로,   그들이

should serve God / in this mountain.
하나님을 찬양해야 한다고   이 산에서.

But Moses had many fears. He knew / that he had been
하지만 모세는 매우 두려웠다.   그는 알았다   자신이 자라났음을

brought up / as an Egyptian, / and he feared / that his
이집트인으로서,   그래서 두려웠다

people would not listen to his words.
백성들이 자신의 말을 듣지 않을까봐.

Then the Lord showed signs / to Moses to help his faith.
그러자 주님이 기적을 보이셨다   모세에게 믿음을 주기 위해.

He turned the rod in Moses' hand / into a serpent, / and
주님은 모세가 들고 있던 막대를   뱀으로 바꾸었고,

then when he was afraid of it, / the Lord told him / to
그가 뱀을 두려워하자,   말씀하셨다

take it in his hand / and it became a rod again.
그 뱀을 잡으라고   그러자 뱀은 다시 막대로 변했다.

He also turned his hand white / with leprosy, / and then
주님은 또 모세의 손을 희게 바꾸신 후   문둥병에 걸린 듯,

changed it again / to natural flesh, / and told Moses, /
다시 바꾸셨다   정상적인 손으로,   그리고 모세에게 말씀하셨다,

that these, and other signs / he should show in Egypt / —
이와 같은 기적을   모세가 이집트에서 보이게 될 거라고

to prove that he was sent of God.
— 그가 하나님이 보낸 사람임을 증명하기 위해

But Moses felt himself to be so weak and faithless / as a
하지만 모세는 자신이 약하고 미덥지 않은 사람이라 생각해서

leader of his people, / that he still cried out / that he was
백성의 지도자로서,   여전히 외쳤다

"slow of speech, / and of a slow tongue," / and when the
자신은 "말이 느리고,   혀가 둔한 자,"라고   그러자 주님이 말씀

Lord said, / "I will teach thee / what thou shalt say," / he
하셨다,   "내가 너를 가르치리라   무슨 말을 해야 할지,"

did not believe, / but begged the Lord / to send by whom
그는 믿지 못하고,   여전히 주님께 애원했다   다른 사람을 보내시라고

he would, / only not by him.
자신이 아닌,

Then the Lord said / that Aaron, the brother of Moses /
그러자 주님이 말씀하셨다   모세의 형 아론이

could speak well, / and that he should go with him / to
말을 잘하기에,   모세와 함께 가서

Pharoah and to his people, / and should speak for him, /
바로와 모세의 백성들에게,   모세를 대신하여 말할 것이라고,

but that the wisdom and power of God / should be with
하지만 하나님의 능력과 지혜는   모세에게 있을 것이기에,

Moses, / and that he should do wonders / with the rod in
모세는 기적을 행하게 될 거라고   손에 막대를 들고.

his hand.

humble 겸손한, 미천한 | rod 막대 | leprosy 나병, 문둥병 | faithless 믿을 수 없는

📖 mini test 3

A. 다음 문장을 해석해 보세요.

(1) He said / that to prove themselves true men / one of them
should go home / and bring the youngest brother, / and the
others should be kept in prison / until they returned.
→

(2) The old man gave them his blessing, / laying his right hand
upon the head of Ephraim, / the youngest, / and his left hand
on that of Manasseh / the first born.
→

(3) He spoke / as a prophet speaks / who has a vision of things to
come, / and he blessed them there.
→

(4) She could hide him no longer, / she made up her mind / to
give him into the care of God.
→

B. 다음 주어진 문장이 되도록 빈칸에 써 넣으세요.

(1) 그들은 총리에게 얼굴이 땅에 닿도록 허리 굽혀 절했다.

They bowed down to him _____.

(2) 요셉은 그렇지 않은 척 행동했지만 그들을 알아보았다.

Joseph knew them, _____.

(3) 그는 그들 앞에서 눈물이 날까봐 재빨리 자신의 침실로 갔다.

He went quickly to his own chamber, _____

_____.

A. (1) 요셉은 그들이 진실된 사람임을 증명하려면 그들 중 한 명이 집에 가서 막내 동생을 데려오고, 나머지는 두 사람
이 돌아올 때까지 감옥에 갇혀야 한다고 말했다. (2) 노인은 오른손을 동생인 에브라임의 머리 위에 올리고, 왼손은 형
인 므낫세의 머리에 위에 올린 채, 그들을 축복했다. (3) 야곱은 앞으로의 일들을 볼 수 있는 예언자처럼 말하고, 그곳

(4) 베냐민의 몫은 <u>다른 형제들보다 다섯 배나 많았다</u>.

The portion of Benjamin was ▮▮▮▮▮▮▮▮▮
▮▮▮▮▮▮▮▮ .

C. 다음 주어진 문구가 알맞은 문장이 되도록 순서를 맞춰 보세요.

(1) 그들에게 닥친 이 모든 문제는 동생 요셉에게 저지른 자신들의 악행에서 비롯된 것이다.
(to their brother Joseph / had come / all this trouble / for their wickedness / upon them)
→

(2) 은잔이 발견되면 가진 사람을 죽이십시오.
(him / with whom / Let / is found / die / the cup)
→

(3) 가는 길에 서로 떨어지지 않도록 하세요.
(by / that / See / fall / not / ye / the way / out)
→

(4) 대가족을 이끌고 여행하는 것은 오랜 시간이 걸렸다.
(to travel / took / a great family / It / with / a long time)
→

D. 다음 단어에 대한 맞는 설명과 연결해 보세요.

(1) verily   ▶   ◀ ① dto free from the captivity

(2) rend   ▶   ◀ ② in truth

(3) redeem   ▶   ◀ ③ a group of individuals moving along

(4) procession   ▶   ◀ ④ to tear in piece

11

THE ROD THAT TROUBLED EGYPT
이집트를 불안에 떨게 한 지팡이

So Moses took his wife and his sons / and returned
모세는 부인과 아들을 데리고   이집트로 돌아왔고,

to Egypt, / and the rod of God was in his hand; /
하나님의 지팡이가 그의 손에 들려 있었다:

and Aaron, sent of God, / came to meet him in the
하나님이 보내신 아론이,   맞이하러 황무지에 나오자,

wilderness, / and there Moses told him / all that was in
그곳에서 모세가 말했다   마음속에 있던 모든

his heart, / and all that God had sent him to do.
생각과,   하나님이 지시하신 모든 일을.

When they came into Egypt / they gathered the Israelites
그들은 이집트에 도착하자   이스라엘 백성을 불러 모아,

together, / and Aaron spoke to them, / and they believed
아론이 이야기를 했다,   그러자 사람들은 그의 말을

his words, / and the signs / that Moses showed them.
믿었고,   증표들도 믿었다   모세가 그들에게 보인.

Key Expression ♟

부정어에 의한 도치

부정의 의미를 가진 말이 강조를 위해 문장 맨 앞에 위치할 경우 뒤따르는 주어와
동사의 어순이 바뀌는 도치현상이 납니다.
도치 시에는 조동사나 be동사가 있을 경우 이를 앞으로 빼며 일반동사는 do 동사
를 이용합니다.

▶ 부정어 + 조동사/be동사/do동사 + 주어 + 동사원형

ex) I know not the Lord, neither will I let Israel go.
나는 주님을 모르고, 이스라엘 백성을 보내지도 않을 것이다.

---

brick 벽돌 | clay 점토 | straw 지푸라기 | crush 으스러뜨리다

Afterward, / they went to Pharoah / and gave him the
그 이후, 사람들은 바로에게 가서 주님의 말씀을 전했다,

message of the Lord, / and Pharoah said:
그러자 바로가 말했다:

"I know not the Lord, / neither will I let Israel go."
"나는 주님을 모르고, 이스라엘 백성을 보내지도 않을 것이다."

And he began to oppress the Israelites / more than he
그리고 왕은 이스라엘인을 억압하기 시작했다 이전보다 더욱,

had ever done before. They made bricks of clay / mixed
이스라엘인들은 점토로 벽돌을 만들어 지푸라기를

with straw, / that hardened in the sun, / and were as
안에 넣고, 햇빛에 말려서, 돌처럼 단단한 벽돌을

lasting as stone, / but he forced them / to find the straw
만들었는데, 왕은 그들에게 강요했다 직접 지푸라기를 구해

/ wherever they could, / and make as many bricks as
어디에서든지, 이전과 같은 수의 벽돌을 만들어 내라고,

before. This they did / until no more straw could be
그들은 지시에 따랐지만 더 이상 지푸라기를 찾을 수 없게 되었고,

found, / and their Egyptian masters beat them cruelly /
이집트인 감독관들은 그들을 잔인하게 구타했다

because they failed / to make the full number of bricks.
실패했다는 이유로 할당량의 벽돌 수를 채우는데,

Then they turned upon Moses and Aaron and said, / that
그러자 그들은 모세와 아론에게 가서 말했다,

they had put a sword in the king's hand / to slay them.
두 사람이 왕의 손에 칼을 쥐어준 것이라고 자신들을 죽이라고,

Where could Moses turn / except to the Lord who had
모세가 의지할 곳이 어디일까 자신을 보내신 주님 외에?

sent him? The Lord heard him / and made to him again
주님께서 그의 말을 듣고 다시 한 번 약속을 하셨고,

the great promise, / as he did at the burning bush, / and
불타는 덤불에서 했던 것처럼,

Moses told the people, / but they could not believe it, /
모세가 사람들에게 말했지만, 사람들은 믿지 않았다,

for they were crushed under their cruel burdens.
자신들이 지고 있는 커다란 부담에 눌려 있었기에,

And now / the Lord sent Moses and Aaron again to
그러자 이번에는 주님이 모세와 아론을 다시 한 번 바로에게 보내어,

Pharoah, / to show by sign and miracle, / that their
증표와 기적을 통해 보이셨다,

message was from Him. They took the rod / that Moses
주님으로부터 온 메시지를. 그들은 지팡이를 들었고

brought from Mount Horeb, / and Moses told Aaron to
모세가 호렙산에서 가져온, 모세가 아론에게 그 지팡이를 던지라고 하자

cast it down / before the king, / and it became a serpent.
왕 앞에, 지팡이는 뱀으로 변했다.

Pharoah called his wise men and wizards, / and they did
바로는 그의 현명한 신하와 마법사들을 불렀고, 그들도 같은 마술을

the same, / only Aaron's rod swallowed up their rods, /
부렸지만, 아론의 지팡이가 그들의 지팡이를 삼켜버리기만 했다,

and Pharoah would not listen to their words.
그런데도 바로는 그들의 말을 들으려 하지 않았다.

But in the morning / when Pharoah walked by the river
그날 아침 바로가 강가를 걷고 있을 때

/ the two men stood by him / and said again: / The Lord
두 사람이 그의 옆에 서더니 다시 말했다:

God of the Hebrews / hath sent me unto thee / saying:
히브리인의 하나님께서 나를 왕께 보내셨으며 이렇게 말씀하셨습니다:

/ "Let my people go / that they may serve me / in the
"나의 백성을 보내 주거라 그들이 나를 섬길 수 있도록

wilderness,"
황무지에서,"

And then Aaron struck the waters of the river Nile / with
그리고 나서 아론이 나일강을 내리치자

his rod, / and the waters turned to blood.
그의 지팡이로, 강물이 피로 변했다.

In all the land, / in every stream and pond / there was
이집트 전체에서, 모든 연못과 시내에 핏빛 물이 흘렀고,

blood, / so that the fishes died / and no one could drink
물고기들이 죽어서 누구도 그 물을 마실 수 없었다.

the water.

But because the wizards could turn water to blood also,
하지만 마법사들도 역시 강물을 피로 바꿀 수 있기에,

/ Pharoah's heart was hardened / toward Moses and
바로는 결심을 굳혔다 　　　　　　모세와 아론을 향한.

Aaron.

While the people were digging wells for water, / Aaron
사람들이 물을 얻기 위해 우물을 파는 동안,

stretched forth his rod / over the river again, / and frogs
아론이 다시 한 번 지팡이를 뻗자 　　강물 위로,

came up from it, / and spread over all the land / and
개구리들이 물 속에서 나와, 　　모든 땅에 퍼져서

filled the houses of the people. This also the magicians
사람들이 집을 가득 채웠다. 　　　　이 일 또한 마법사들도 따라 했지만,

did, / but so great was the plague / that the king said: /
전염병이 너무 심했기 때문에 　　　왕이 말했다:

"I will let the people go."
"네 백성을 보내 주겠다"

"When shall I entreat / for thee and for thy people / to
"제가 언제 간청하면 될까요 　　　왕과 백성들을 위해

destroy the frogs / from thee and thy houses?" / said
개구리 떼를 없애달라고 　　여러분의 집에서?" 　　　모세가 말하자;

Moses; / and Pharoah told him to do so the next day.
바로는 바로 다음 날 그렇게 해 달라고 했다.

So on the next day / Moses prayed to the Lord / that the
그래서 이튿날에 　　　　모세는 주님께 기도드렸고

frogs might go out of the land, / and the Lord answered
개구리 떼를 이 땅에서 쫓아달라고, 　　　주님께서 그의 기도에 답하셨다;

his prayer; / but when Pharoah saw that the frogs had
하지만 바로는 개구리가 없어지자

been destroyed / his heart grew hard, / and he would not
결심이 확고해져서,

listen to Moses and Aaron.
모세와 아론의 말을 들으려 하지 않았다.

dust 먼지, 티끌 | lice 이 (louse의 복수) | swarm 곤충의 떼 | settle 자리 잡다, 앉다 | sweep out 쓸어 내다 |
sickness 질병 | boil 종기 | yield 양보하다

Then another plague was brought / upon the Egyptians.
그러자 또 다시 전염병이 일어났다   이집트에.

The dust of the land was changed to lice / that covered
땅의 먼지가 이로 변해

man and beast, / and this was followed by swarms of
사람과 짐승을 덮었으며,   이어서 파리 떼가 나타나

flies / that settled upon all the land / except Goshen /
모든 땅을 뒤덮었다   고센을 제외하고

where the Israelites lived.
이스라엘 백성이 살고 있던.

Then Pharoah said: /
그러자 바로가 말했다:

"Go, / sacrifice to your God / in this land," / but they
"가거라,   너희 하나님께 제물을 바치라   이 땅에서,"   하지만 그들은

would not worship / in Egypt, / and Pharoah at last told
예배하려 하지 않았고   이집트에서는,   그러자 마침내 바로가 말했다

them / that they could go into the wilderness, / but they
황무지로 나가도 되지만,

must not go very far away. So Moses prayed, / and the
멀리 나가서는 안 된다고.   그래서 모세가 기도를 올려,

swarms of flies were swept out of Egypt, / but Pharoah
파리 떼를 이집트 땅에서 쓸어내 버렸지만,   바로는 또 자신의

did not keep his word.
약속을 지키지 않았다.

Then a great sickness fell / upon the cattle and sheep
그러자 큰 질병이 일어났다   이집트의 소와 양에.

of the country, / though the flocks and herds of the
이스라엘 백성의 가축은 무사했지만:

Israelites were free from it; / and this was followed by / a
또한 뒤를 이어

breaking out of boils / upon men and beasts everywhere,
종기병이 생겼다   모든 사람과 짐승에게,

/ even upon the magicians, / but Pharoah's heart was still
심지어 마법사에게도,   하지만 사악한 바로는 여전히

too wicked / to yield to God.
하나님께 굴복하지 않았다.

Then came a great storm of hail over Egypt, / such as
그러자 이번에는 우박 폭풍이 이집트를 덮었다,

had never been known / in that sunny land. It killed the
전혀 알려지지 않았던   그 따뜻한 땅에서는.

cattle in the fields, / and destroyed the grain that was
우박은 들판의 소를 죽이고,   다 자란 곡식을 파괴했으며,

grown, / and broke the trees and herbs. The lightnings
나무와 약초를 꺾었다.   또한 번개가 쳐서

fell also / and ran upon the ground, / and when it was
        땅 위에서 번쩍였고.   이 모든 것이 끝난 후에도

over / the heart of Pharaoh was still hard against God.
        바로의 마음은 여전히 돌처럼 굳은 채 하나님께 맞서려 했다.

Then Moses told Pharaoh / that the face of the earth
그러자 모세가 바로에게 말했다   땅이 뒤덮일 것이며

would be covered / with clouds of locusts / that would
                        구름같이 많은 메뚜기 떼로

eat every green thing / left by the storm, / if he did not
모든 풀을 먹어치울 것이라고   폭우가 남겨 놓은,   만약 그가 하나님의

let God's people go. This frightened Pharaoh's servants
백성을 보내지 않는다면.   이 말에 바로의 신하들은 겁을 먹고

/ and they begged him / to send them away, / and though
        바로에게 애원했지만   그들을 보내 달라고,

he would not let their wives and little ones go, / he said:
바로는 아내와 아이들은 보내려 하지 않았고,   이렇게 말하며:

"Go now, / ye that are men, / for that ye did desire," / and
"지금 가거라,   단 남자들만,   너희들이 원하는 곳으로,"

he drove them out of his presence.
사람들을 좇아냈다

Then at the Lord's word, / Moses arose and stretched
그러자 주님의 말씀에 따라,   모세가 일어나 지팡이를 뻗었고

forth his rod / over Egypt, / and the plague of locusts
                이집트 땅 위에,   메뚜기 떼가 몰려와,

came, / driven by the East wind, / and covered the land /
        동풍에 실려,   땅을 뒤엎어

until there was no green thing left / in Egypt.
풀이 모두 없어져 버렸다   이집트 땅에서.

Then Pharaoh sent for Moses and Aaron / in great haste,
그러자 바로는 모세와 아론을 찾아   서둘러,

/ and confessing his sin, / begged to be forgiven / and
자신의 죄를 시인하고,   용서를 구하며

to be saved from, / "this death only," / and, at Moses'
구원해 달라 청했다.   "이 죽음만이라도."   그래서, 모세가 기도하자,

prayer, / a mighty west wind drove the army of locusts /
강한 서풍이 불어와 메뚜기 떼를 몰아냈다

into the Red Sea.
홍해 속으로.

Key Expression ❢

follow의 해석

follow는 '따라가다'라는 의미 외에도 '뒤를 잇다, (결과가) 뒤따르다, 뒤이어 ~를 하다' 등 다양한 의미를 가지고 있습니다.
특히 followed by와 같이 수동태로 쓰일 경우 by 뒤에 오는 대상들이 차례차례로 이어진다는 의미로 해석하면 자연스러워요.

ex) The dust of the land was changed to lice that covered man and beast, and this was followed by swarms of flies that settled upon all the land.
땅의 먼지가 이로 변해 사람과 짐승을 덮었으며, 이어서 파리 떼가 나타나 모든 땅을 뒤덮었다.
(→ 뒤이어 ~하다)

He ordered his chariots and horsemen to follow them.
그는 자신의 마부와 말 탄 신하들에게 그들을 쫓으라고 명령했다.
(→ 뒤를 쫓다)

Whenever it moved the people followed, and when it stood still, they rested.
그것이 움직이면 백성들이 그 뒤를 따랐고, 그것이 멈추면, 백성들도 쉬었다.
(→ 따르다)

The king who followed him did not like the Hebrews.
그의 뒤를 이은 새 왕은 히브리족을 좋아하지 않았다.
(→ 뒤를 잇다)

---

hail 우박 | herb 약초 | lightning 번개 | locust 메뚜기 | frighten 겁먹게 하다

But again / the heart of Pharaoh turned against God, /
하지만 또 다시　　바로의 마음은 하나님께 반대했고,

and the Lord brought thick darkness over the land / for
그러자 주님은 짙은 어둠을 불러 내었다

three days, / only in the homes of the Hebrews / there
사흘 동안,　　　오직 히브리족의 집에서만　　　　　빛을 볼 수

was light. Then Pharaoh was willing to let them / take
있었다.　　그러자 바로는 기꺼이 그들에게 허락했다

their wives and their little ones, / but not their flocks and
아내와 아이들을 데려가라고,　　단 양과 소는 제외한 채,

herds, / and because they would not leave them behind,
그런데 그들이 가축을 두고 가려 하지 않았기 때문에,

/ Pharaoh drove Moses and Aaron from him / in anger, /
바로는 모세와 아론을 몰아내며　　　　　화난 모습으로,

saying:
말했다:

"See my face no more."
"다시는 내 앞에 나타나지 말라."

But the Lord proposed to break / the hard heart of
그러나 주님께서는 꺾겠다고 작정하셨다　　바로의 굳은 마음을.

Pharaoh. He told Moses / to see that every Israelite
주님이 모세에게 말씀하셨다　 모든 이스라엘인은 데려가도록 하라

should take / a lamb from the flock / and keep it four
양 한 마리씩　　　　그리고 나흘 동안 가지고 있도록

days. Then, at evening, / he was to kill it, / and dip a
하라.　　그리고 나흘째 되는 날 저녁에,　그 양을 죽여서,

branch of hyssop in its blood, / and strike it / against the
우슬초 묶음을 양의 피 속에 담근 후,　　　그 피를 칠하라　　문의 양 옆 벽과,

sides of his door, / also over it, / leaving three marks of
문 위에,　　　핏자국 세 개를 남긴 채.

blood there. Then he was to close his door / and no one
그리고 문을 닫은 후　　　　　아무도 밖으로 나오지

was to go out of it / until morning.
않을지어다　　아침이 될 때까지.

propose 제안하다, 작정하다 | dip 담그다 | branch 묶음 | hyssop 히솝(박하과의 작은 풀), 우슬초 | unleavened
이스트를 넣지 않은 | throne 왕좌 | captive 포로

They were to roast the lamb / and eat of it, / and be ready
백성들은 양을 구워서   고기를 먹고,   여행 채비를 할지어다

for the journey / they were to make, / and it should be to
떠나게 될,   그리고 이 풍습은 영원히 지켜

them forever / the feast called the Passover. They were
지리라   유월절이라 부르는.   고기는 누룩을 넣지

to eat it with unleavened bread, / and the feast should
않은 빵과 먹어야 하며,   이 축일은 영원히 지켜지리라

be kept forever / from the first to the seventh day of the
매달 1일부터 7일까지,

month, / a holy feast to the Lord.
하나님께 드리는 거룩한 의식으로써.

And this is why it was called the feast of the Passover.
이것이 바로 유월절이라 불리는 축일이 생겨난 유래이다.

At midnight, / after the lamb was killed / in each house
자정이 되자,   양을 죽인 후   이스라엘인의 각 가정

of the Israelites, / and the doors were shut, / the Lord
에서는,   문을 닫았고,

passed through the land, / and wherever he saw the blood
주님께서 그 땅을 지나시며,   피가 보이는 집은 모두

/ on the side posts and the top of the door, / he passed
문의 양 옆과 위쪽에,   그냥 지나가셨고,

over that house, / and it was safe, / but in every Egyptian
그 집은 안전했다.   하지만 이집트인 가정에서는 모두

house / the first born died, / from the child of Pharaoh
맏아들이 죽었다,   왕인 바로의 자식부터,

who sat on the throne, / to the child of the captive in the
감옥에 갇힌 사람의 자식에 이르기까지,

cell, / and all the first born of cattle.
또한 소의 첫 새끼까지도.

The next morning / a great cry went up from the land of
이튿날 아침   이집트 전역에서 대성통곡이 울렸다,

Egypt, / for there was not a house / where there was not
한 집도 없었기 때문에   가족 중 아무도 죽지 않은 집이.

one dead.

Then Pharaoh was quite ready / to let the Israelites go.
그제서야 바로는 결심이 섰다 / 이스라엘 백성을 보내겠다는.

"Take all you have and be gone," / he said.
"너희가 가진 모든 것을 갖고 떠나라." / 그가 말했다.

They were all ready, / and rose up very gladly / to join
이스라엘인들은 모두 준비를 마쳤기에, 매우 기뻐하며 일어나

the great procession, / led by Moses and Aaron, / that
대규모 행렬에 동참했다, / 모세와 아론에게 이끌려,

gathered in Goshen, / and started on its long journey /
고센에 모여 있던, / 그리고 긴 여행이 시작되었다.

toward the east.
동쪽으로 향하는.

They had heard of the land of their fathers, / and now
그들은 선조의 땅에 대해 들은 적이 있었고,

they were going home / to be slaves no more. They were
이제 고향으로 가는 중이었다 / 더 이상 노예가 아닌 채.

a family of seventy souls / when they came into Egypt,
이스라엘인은 일흔 명이었지만 / 이집트에 처음 왔을 때는,

/ four hundred and thirty years before, / and now they
430년 전에,

went out a great nation, / as the Lord had promised /
이제 큰 민족이 되었다, / 주님이 약속하셨듯이

when he blessed their fathers.
선조를 축복하셨을 때.

The feast of the Passover has been the chief one / held
유월절은 가장 중요한 축일이다

by the Israelites, / from the time of their coming out of
이스라엘 백성이 지키는, / 이집트에서 탈출하던 때부터

Egypt / until now, / and since Jesus held the Passover
이집트에서 / 지금까지, / 그리고 예수님께서 유월절 만찬을 여셨기에

feast / with his disciples / on the night that he went forth
제자들과 함께 / 죽음을 앞둔 그 날 밤에,

to death, / it has become to all Christians / the Sacrament
유월절 저녁은 모든 기독교인들에게

of the Lord's Supper.
성찬식이 되었다.

 12

FOLLOWING THE CLOUD
구름을 따라가다

"God led the people," / says the Word, / as they came
"하나님이 백성을 인도하셨다," 라고 성경에는 씌어 있다.

up out of Egypt. He gave them the two leaders / by
이집트에서 탈출하던 때. 하나님은 지도자 두 명을 보내어

whom He had broken the power of Pharaoh, / and set
바로의 힘을 무너뜨리고,

His people free, / and He also set a great cloud in the
백성을 자유롭게 하시고, 공중에 거대한 구름을 만들어서,

air, / just above and before them, / to lead them in the
그들의 바로 위에, 옳은 길로 이끄셨다.

right way. It was to them / the presence of the Lord. By
그 구름은 그들에게 있어 주님의 존재였다.

day / it rose white and beautiful against the blue sky, /
낮에는 푸른 하늘에 구름이 희고 아름답게 떠올라,

and moved slowly before them. At night / it stood still
그들 앞에서 천천히 움직였다. 밤이면 구름은 그곳에 멈춰 서서

/ while they rested, / and shed light over all the camp, /
그들이 쉬는 동안, 천막 위에 빛을 드리웠고,

for there seemed to be a fire within the cloud / at night.
그 모습은 마치 구름 속에 불이 타는 듯 보였다 밤에는.

gladly 기꺼이 | disciple 제자 | sacrament 성찬식 | the Lord's Supper 주의 만찬, 성찬 | presence 존재,
임재

How safe and happy they must have felt / away from the
그들이 얼마나 안전하고 행복해 했을까.   사악한 이집트 감독관들

cruel taskmasters of Egypt, / and the Lord's presence,
로부터 멀어졌으니,   그리고 주님의 존재가,

/ spreading a wing of cloud over them. They were not
그들 위로 구름의 날개를 드리우고 있었다.

led by a straight way / to Canaan, / for a warlike people
그들은 곧장 향할 수는 없었지만   가나안으로,   호전적인 사람들이 살고 있었기

lived / in the land / which they must pass through, / but
때문에   그 땅에   그들이 반드시 지나야 하는,

they were led / at first / through a country without cities
지나갔다   처음에는   도시나 군대가 없는 나라들을,

or armies, / where they would not trouble many people
그곳에서는 많은 사람들에게 불편을 주거나

/ or be troubled by them. They bore with them / the
문제가 생기지 않았다.   그들은 계속 간직했다

embalmed body of Joseph, / for they had promised to
요셉의 시신을 미라로 만들어,   요셉의 시신을 선조들과 함께 묻기로

bury him with his fathers / in the cave of Machpelah; /
약속했기에   막펠라 동굴 속에;

and they also had much wealth / in herds, and flocks, and
또한 그들은 부를 축적했다   소 떼와, 양 떼와, 금과, 은에 있어서.

gold, and silver. Pharaoh thought of this / after they had
바로는 이런 생각이 들자   그들이 떠난 후,

gone, / and his wicked heart grew harder than before, /
사악한 마음이 전보다 굳어져서,

so he ordered his chariots and horsemen / to follow them,
자신의 마부와 말 탄 신하들에게 명령했다   그들을 쫓으라고,

/ and they found the Israelites / camped by the Red Sea.
그리하여 바로의 신하들은 이스라엘인들을 찾아냈다   홍해 근처에 야영 중이던.

warlike 호전적인 | chariot 마차 | horseman 기수, 마부

Then there was great fear and mourning / in the camp /
그러자 엄청난 공포와 슬픔이 일어났다   야영지에서

when they saw the army of Pharaoh coming, / but Moses
바로의 군대가 다가오는 것을 보고,   하지만 모세가

cried: /
외쳤다:

"Fear ye not, / stand still / and see the salvation of the
"두려워 말고,   가만히 서서   주님의 구원을 지켜보시오.

Lord. The Lord shall fight for you, / and ye shall hold
주님께서 여러분을 위해 싸우시리니,   여러분에게는 평화가 함께할

your peace."
것이오."

Then the Lord told Moses / to speak to the people / that
그러자 주님께서 모세에게 명하셨다   사람들에게 말하도록

they go forward. He also told him / to lift up his rod /
앞으로 나아가라고.   또한 말씀하셨다   지팡이를 들고

and stretch his hand over the sea / and divide it, / and the
바다 위로 뻗어   바다를 가르라고,

children of Israel should go on dry ground / through the
그러면 이스라엘 백성이 육지로 갈 수 있을 거라고

midst of the sea. Night was falling, / and the waters lay
바다 한 가운데를 건너.   밤이 깊어지자,   검은 바닷물이 그들 앞에 펼쳐

dark before them, / but the angel of God, / the pillar of
졌지만,   하나님의 천사가,   구름과 불기둥의 모습

cloud and fire, / moved from its place before them / and
으로 나타나,   그들 앞에서 움직였고

went behind them, / while Moses and Aaron led them on.
뒤를 따랐다,   모세와 아론이 사람들을 이끌고 가는 동안.

dawn (하루가) 밝다, 시작되다 | shore 해안

Then the presence of the Lord was a cloud and darkness
그때 주님의 존재는 구름이며 어둠이었지만

/ to the Egyptians, / but it gave a light by night / to the
이집트인에게는, 밤을 밝혀 주었다 이스라엘

Israelites. A strong east wind drove the waters apart /
백성에게는. 강한 동풍이 불어와 바다를 갈랐고

all night, / so that there was a way through the sea, / and
밤새도록, 그러자 바다 한가운데에 길이 생겨나고,

the waters were a wall / upon their right hand and on
바닷물은 벽이 되었다 그들의 양 옆에.

their left. Pharaoh's army saw the broad path / through
바로의 군대는 넓은 길을 보고 바다 가운데

the sea, / and followed fast / after the Israelites, / but as
생긴, 빠르게 쫓아갔다 이스라엘 인의 뒤를,

morning dawned / the Lord looked from the cloud / and
하지만 동이 트자 주님이 구름 사이에서 보시고

troubled the Egyptians. Their chariot wheels came off, /
이집트인에게 시련을 안기셨다. 그들의 마차 바퀴는 빠져 버렸고,

and all went wrong with them.
모든 일이 엉망이 되어버렸다.

At last / the Lord told Moses / to stretch his hand forth
마지막으로 주님께서 모세에게 말씀하셨고 손을 바다 위로 뻗으라고,

over the sea, / that the waters might come back / upon
바닷물이 다시 돌아와

the Egyptians, / and he did so; / and as the sun rose, / the
이집트인을 덮도록, 모세는 말씀에 따랐다; 그러자 해가 떠오르며,

sea swallowed up the Egyptian host, / and their bodies
바다는 이집트인들을 삼켜버렸고,

were cast upon the shore. There on the other side / stood
그들의 시체가 해안가로 던져졌다. 반대편에서는

the great host of Israel, / and saw the salvation of God, /
이스라엘 백성들이 서서, 하나님의 구원을 목격했고,

and they believed in Him, and in Moses His servant.
그들은 하나님과 그의 종인 모세를 믿게 되었다.

Then a great shout went up / from the host of Israel.
그리고 엄청난 함성이 일어났다   이스라엘 백성으로부터.

Moses led them in a song of praise, / and Miriam, the
모세는 찬양의 노래로 백성들을 이끌었고,

sister of Aaron, / took a tambourine, / and the women
아론의 누이인 미리암이,   탬버린을 들자,   여인들이 그 뒤를 따라

followed her / in dances / as they answered / in a chorus
         춤을 추며   대답했다   찬양의 노래를 합창

of praise: ―
하며.

"Sing ye to the Lord, / for He hath triumphed gloriously;
"주님을 찬양하라,   그분이 영광스럽게도 승리하셨고;

/ the horse and the rider / hath he thrown into the sea."
말과 말을 탄 병사들을   바다에 던지셨으니."

Key Expression ❗

take up : 계속하다

take up은 '계속하다'라는 의미로 특히 '이미 끝난' 데서 시작하여 계속하다'라
는 뜻을 가진 숙어입니다.
take up은 이 외에도 다음과 같이 다양한 의미로 쓰입니다.

▶ take something up : (옷을) 기장을 줄이다
▶ take up something : ~을 집어 들다
▶ take up something : (시간·공간을) 차지하다
▶ take up with somebody : (특히 평판이 좋지 않은) ~와 어울리다
▶ take up for : ~의 편을 들다
▶ take something up : ~을 치우다
▶ take somebody up on something : ~에게 …에 대해 의문을 제기하다
▶ take something up with somebody : ~에게 …에 대해 이야기 하다

ex) Soon they took up their journey, the cloudy pillar going before.
곧 그들은 다시 여행을 시작했고, 구름 기둥이 앞에서 인도했다.
So Moses hewed them from the rock and took them up into Mount Sinai.
모세는 바위를 잘라낸 후 그것들을 가지고 시내산으로 올라갔다.

---

triumph 대성공 | bitter (맛이) 쓰다 | palm tree 야자나무, 종려나무 | complain 불평하다

Soon they took up their journey, / the cloudy pillar going
곧 그들은 다시 여행을 시작했고, 구름 기둥이 앞에서 인도했다.

before. There was but little water / by the way, / and after
물이 거의 없어서 가는 길에,

three days of thirst, / they came to the waters of Marah, /
사흘 동안 갈증을 느끼다가, 마라의 강에 도착했다.

but they were bitter, / and the people cried to Moses, /
하지만 물이 써서, 사람들이 모세에게 외쳤다.

"What shall we drink?"
"우리는 무엇을 마셔야 합니까?"

Then the Lord showed him a tree / which he cast into the
그때 주님께서 모세에게 나무 토막 하나를 보이셨고, 모세가 그것을 물에 던지자,

waters, / and they were made pure and sweet. Soon after
물은 깨끗해지고 달게 되었다. 얼마 후 그들은

they came to Elim, / where there were / twelve wells of
엘림에 도착했는데, 그곳에는 있었고 열두 개의 우물과,

water, / and seventy palm trees, / and there they rested.
70그루의 종려나무가 있어서, 그곳에서 쉬었다.

Again / they took up their journey / and passed through
또 다시 그들은 여행을 떠났고 사막의 땅을 지나게 되었다,

a desert land, / where they could get no food, / and again
그러나 그곳에서 음식을 얻을 수 없게 되자,

they complained to Moses / because he had brought
사람들은 다시 모세에게 불평했다 모세가 자신들을 데리고 왔기에

them / into the wilderness / to die. They did not yet
황무지로 죽게 되었다고, 그들은 아직 믿지 않았다

believe / that God could supply / all their need.
하나님이 주실 것이란 사실을 필요한 모든 것을.

"I will rain bread from heaven / for you," / said the Lord
"내가 빵을 비처럼 내리리라 너희를 위해," 주님께서 모세에게

to Moses. He was ready to provide, / if they would only
말씀하셨다. 주님은 기꺼이 내려주셨다,

believe in Him and obey Him.
사람들이 그분을 믿고 따르기만 한다면.

Moses called them to come near / before the Lord / while
모세는 사람들에게 가까이 오라고 했고　　　　주님 앞에

Aaron should speak his word to them. As they came near
아론이 주님의 말씀을 전했다.　　　　　　사람들이 가까이 다가와서

/ and looked toward the wilderness / where the cloud
황무지 쪽을 바라보자　　　　　　구름이 멈춰 있던,

stood, / the glory of the Lord shone out of it. The Lord
주님의 영광이 구름 밖에서 빛났다.

had heard them speak harshly to Moses / for bringing
주님은 사람들이 모세에게 심하게 말하는 것을 들으셨다

them into a desert / to die, / but he said, /
자신들을 사막으로 데려와　　죽게 된 것에 대해, 하지만 말씀하셨다,

"At even ye shall eat flesh, / and in the morning / ye shall
"저녁에는 고기를 먹게 될 것이고,　　　　아침에는

be filled with bread."
빵으로 배를 채우리라."

Key Expression

2형식 감각동사의 용법

look(~처럼 보이다, ~하게 보이다)과 같이 오감을 나타내는 동사를 감각동사라고 합니다. 감각동사는 뒤에 보어를 동반하는 2형식 동사이므로 부사처럼 해석하지만 형용사가 와야 합니다.

보어 자리에 명사가 올 경우에는 'like +명사'의 형태로 써야 합니다.

2형식 감각동사에는 look 외에도 sound(~처럼 들리다), taste(~한 맛이 나다), smell(~한 냄새가 나다), feel(~한 느낌이다) 등이 있습니다.

ex) It tasted like wafers made with honey.
　　그것은 꿀로 만든 얇은 빵 맛이 났다.
　　She looked very kind and beautiful.
　　그녀는 매우 친철하고 아름다워 보였다.

---

speak harshly 불쾌히 말하다 | quail 메추라기 | dew 이슬 | frost 서리 | fretful 조바심치는, 까다로운, 칭얼대는

And his word came true. Great flocks of quails came up
그리고 그분의 말씀은 현실이 되었다.   엄청난 메추라기 떼가 날아오더니

/ and covered the camp / at sunset, / so that they caught
야영지를 덮었고   해질녘에,   그래서 사람들은 새를 잡아 먹었다;

them for food; / and in the morning / the dew lay around
아침이 되자   이슬이 내려앉았고,

them, / and when it had risen, / there lay on the ground
해가 뜨자,   땅 위에 널려 있었는데

/ a small, round, white thing, / something like frost, or a
작고 둥근 흰 것들이,   서리나 씨앗과 비슷하게 생긴.

little seed, / and it tasted like wafers made with honey.
꿀로 만든 얇은 빵 맛이 났다.

The Lord told Moses / that the people must gather /
주님이 모세에게 말씀하셨다   사람들은 거둬야 하며

just enough to eat through the day, / and no more. The
하루 동안 먹을 만큼만,   더 이상은 안 된다고.

morning before the Sabbath / they must gather enough
또 안식일 전날 아침에는   이틀 분량을 거둬야 한다고,

for two days, / for none would fall / on the Sabbath. This
아무것도 내리지 않을 것이기에   안식일에는.

was the bread / that the heavenly Father provided for his
이것은 빵이었고   하나님 아버지께서 자녀에게 주시는

children / through all the years of their journey / from
여행하는 동안 줄곧

Egypt to Canaan, / and they called it "Manna."
이집트에서 가나안으로,   사람들은 이를 "만나"라고 불렀다.

There were hard things to bear / in the wilderness. Often
견디기 힘든 어려움도 있었다   황무지에서.

when they wanted water / for their little ones and their
종종 물이 필요할 때   아이와 가축에게 줄,

cattle, / and could not find it, / they were like fretful
물을 찾지 못하면,   칭얼대며 울었다

children / when they were tired and thirsty. Once, / at
지치고 목이 말라서.   한번은,

Horeb, / Moses struck a rock / with his wonderful rod, /
호렙에서,   모세가 바위를 치자   경이로운 지팡이로,

and water sprung out in a stream.
물이 흘러나와 샘을 이뤘다.

There were enemies also / in the way. The Amelikites
적들도 있었다   길에는.   아멜렉인이 와서

came out / to fight with the Israelites. The strong men
이스라엘인과 싸웠다.

went to meet the enemy, / but Moses stood on a hill /
강한 사람들은 나가서 적과 맞섰지만,   모세는 언덕에 서 있었고

with the rod of God in his hand, / and Aaron and Hur
손에 지팡이를 든 채,   아론과 훌이 그 옆에 있었다.

were with him. While Moses held up the rod, / Israel
                    모세가 지팡이를 들고 있는 동안에는,   이스라엘이

prevailed; / but when he let down his hand / Amalek
우세했지만;   모세가 팔을 내리면

prevailed.
아멜렉이 우세했다.

But Moses grew tired / and they placed a stone / for
하지만 모세는 지쳐버렸고   아론과 훌이 돌을 놓아

him to sit upon, / and Aaron and Hur held up his hands
모세가 앉을 수 있게 하고,   모세의 팔을 들었다

/ on either side / until the going down of the sun, / when
    양쪽에서   해가 질 때까지,

Amalek was conquered. Moses built an altar there, / and
그래서 아멜렉은 패배했다.   모세는 그곳에 제단을 세우고,

called it / "*The Lord my Banner."
그것을 불렀다   "여호와 닛시"라고.

They were now drawing near the Mount, / where Moses
이스라엘 백성은 이제 그 산 근처에 이르렀다.

saw the burning bush, / and heard the Lord calling him /
모세가 불타는 덤불을 보았고,   주님의 부름을 들었던

to be the leader of his people.
이스라엘 백성의 지도자가 되라는.

---

* The Lord my Banner 여호와 닛시. '여호와는 나의 깃발'이라는 의미로 여호와는 나의 깃발이며 승리라
는 뜻을 나타내는 말이다.

prevail 이기다, 승리하다 | banner 깃발 | granite 화강암 | cliff 절벽

They were far out / of their way to Canaan, / but it was
그들은 멀리 벗어나 버렸는데   가나안으로 향하는 여정에서,

in the Lord's purpose / to bring them into obedience and
그것은 주님이 의도하신 일이었다   사람들에게 순종과 믿음을 주기 위해

faith / before he brought them into the promised land.
약속의 땅으로 데려가기 전에.

They had lived long among the Egyptians, / and were
그들은 오랫동안 이집트인 사이에서 살았기에,

very far from being like Jacob and Joseph, / but there
야곱이나 요셉과는 매우 달랐지만,

were good and true men / like Aaron, and Joshua, and
선하고 진실한 사람도 있었다   아론과 여호수아, 훌과 같은,

Hur, / who helped Moses. It was about three months /
모세를 도왔던.   석 달 가량 흘렀을 때

after the children of Israel left Egypt, / that they came
이집트를 떠나온 지,   시내 광야에 도달했다.

into the wilderness of Sinai. There the "Mount of God" /
그곳에는 "하나님의 산"이라 불리는

still lifts its great granite cliffs / toward the sky. There are
거대한 화강암 절벽이 높이 솟아 있었다   하늘을 향해.

high valleys midway / where it is cooler than below, / and
산 중턱에는 높은 계곡들이 있어   산 아래보다 시원했기에,

there the people encamped / and waited to hear what God
사람들은 그곳에 천막을 치고   하나님의 말씀을 기다렸다,

would say to them, / for God talked with Moses on the
하나님이 그 산에서 모세에게 말씀하셨기에.

Mount.

He said / He had chosen them, / if they would obey his
하나님은 말씀하셨다   이스라엘을 선택하셨다고,   그분의 말씀에 순종한다면,

voice, / to be a holy nation. He told Moses / to tell the
거룩한 나라를 이룩하도록.   하나님은 모세에게 말씀하셨다

people to be ready, / and on the third day / He would come
사람들에게 준비하도록 전하라고, 사흘째 되는 날   내려오실 거라고 하셨다

down / in the sight of all the people / on Mount Sinai.
모든 백성이 보는 가운데   시내산 위에.

And so it was, / as the people looked / there was a thick
그리고 그렇게 되었다.   사람들이 보고 있을 때

cloud upon the Mount, / from which came thunder and
짙은 구름이 산 위에 나타났고,   구름 속에서 천둥 번개가 치며,

lightning, / and the sound of a great trumpet, / while the
웅장한 나팔 소리를 내자,

mountain trembled / as with an earthquake. Only Moses
산이 흔들렸다   지진이 나는 것처럼.

and Aaron could approach the holy Mount, / and from it /
오직 모세와 아론만이 거룩한 산에 다가갈 수 있었고,   그곳에서

God gave to Moses the laws / that the people were to live
하나님이 모세에게 율법을 전하시자   백성들이 지키고 살아야 하는,

by, / and Moses wrote them all down / that he might read
모세가 그 모든 것을 글로 옮겼다

them to the people. A company of the Elders of Israel went
백성들에게 읽어줄 수 있도록.   이스라엘의 제사장들도 산에 올라가

up / and saw the glory of God / afar off, / but God called
하나님의 영광을 보았지만   멀리서,

Moses up into the Mount, / and the cloud closed him round,
하나님은 산 속으로 모세를 부른 후,   구름으로 주변을 감쌌다.

/ while the Lord gave him / the laws for a great nation, /
주님께서 내리시는 동안   위대한 나라를 위한 율법과,

and the pattern of the tabernacle / which He wished him to
교회의 양식을   모세에게 만들라고 하시는

make / for a church in the wilderness.
황야의 교회를 위해.

Forty days and forty nights / Moses was on the Mount
40일 밤낮 동안   모세는 산 속에서 하나님과 함께 있었고,

with God, / and then God gave him / the ten great
그리고 나서 하나님은 모세에게 내리셨다

commandments / written with his own hands / on tablets of
십계명을   직접 새긴   돌판 위에,

stone, / that he might give them to the people. They were to
그러자 모세가 그것을 사람들에게 전했다.   십계명은 지켜야

be kept / as the rules of life / for all people in all times.
했다   삶의 법칙으로   모든 시대의 모든 사람들이.

Forty days and nights seemed a long time / to the people
40일은 매우 긴 시간처럼 느껴졌다

camped around the Mount. Perhaps / they thought / Moses
시내산 주변에 있던 사람들에게는.   어쩌면   그들이 생각하기에

would never come back to lead them, / for they began to
모세가 다시 돌아와 자신들을 이끌지 않을지도 몰랐기 때문에,   사람들은 이집트 신에 대해

think of the gods of Egypt, / and asked Aaron to make one
생각하기 시작했고,   아론에게 하나 만들라고 요청했다.

for them. So to please them / he told them to bring him /
사람들을 만족시키기 위해   아론은 사람들에게 가져오라 한 후

their gold ornaments, / and he melted them / and made a
금 장신구를,   그것을 녹여서   황금 송아지를 만들고

golden calf / such as the Egyptians worshiped, / and before
이집트인이 섬겼던 것처럼,   그 앞에

it / they made an altar, / and they worshiped the calf.
제단을 만들어,   황금 송아지를 찬양했다.

The Lord who sees all things / told Moses to go down / to
주님이 모든 광경을 보시고   모세에게 내려가라고 말씀하셨다

the people / for they were worshiping an idol. So Moses
백성에게로   그들이 우상을 찬양하고 있었기 때문에.

went down a little way / and met Joshua, / and they both
모세가 내려가다가   여호수아를 만났고,   두 사람은 함께 내려가

went down / and saw / the people feasting, / and singing,
보았다   사람들이 잔치를 벌이며,   노래하고 춤추는 모습을,

and dancing, / and Moses cast the tablets of stone / upon
그러자 모세는 돌판을 던졌고

the ground / and they were broken. The heart of Moses, /
땅 위에   돌판은 깨져 버렸다.   모세의 마음도.

too, / was almost broken, / but he destroyed the golden calf,
또한,   거의 깨져 버렸다.   하지만 그는 황금 송아지를 부수고,

/ and punished the people / for their great sin, / and then
사람들에게 벌을 내린 후   그들이 지은 큰 죄에 대해,

went up to the Mount / to plead for the life of his people.
산으로 올라가   사람들을 구해 달라고 애원했다.

---

trumpet 나팔 | tabernacle 회막, (고대 유대인의) 이동 예배소 | ornament 장신구 | calf 송아지 | idol 우상 |
plead 애원하다

"O this people have sinned a great sin," / he cried, / "and
"이 백성들이 큰 죄를 지었습니다."   모세가 외쳤다,

have made them gods of gold, / yet now if thou wilt
"금으로 신상을 만들었습니다.   하지만 이제 주님께서 그들의 죄를

forgive their sin, / and if not, blot me, / I pray thee, / out
용서하옵소서,   아니면 저를 지우시옵소서,   기도 드리오니,

of the book which thou has written," / so great was the
주님께서 쓰신 생명의 책에서."

love of Moses for his people.
그렇게 백성을 향한 모세의 사랑은 컸다.

There was a time of repentance / among the people /
회개의 움직임이 있었고   백성들 사이에

after this, / and Moses and his servant Joshua reared
이 일이 있은 후,   모세와 그의 종인 여호수아는 천막을 치고

a tent / outside the camp / and called it the Tabernacle
              야영지 밖에   그것을 '회막'이라 불렀다.

of the congregation. It was for worship / until the true
이곳은 예배를 위한 곳이었다

Tabernacle should be built / according to the pattern /
진짜 회막이 만들어질 때까지   양식에 따라

given in the Mount. All who sought the Lord went to
산에서 받은.   주님을 찾는 사람들은 모두 예배하러 회막에 갔고,

worship there, / and the pillar of cloud came and stood /
                    그러면 구름 기둥이 다가와 섰다

at the Tabernacle door / while Moses talked with God, /
회막 문 앞에   모세가 하나님과 대화를 나누는 동안,

and all the people saw it and worshiped.
그리고 모든 백성은 그 모습을 보며 경배했다.

Moses prayed again for the people, / and the Lord said: /
모세는 또 다시 백성을 위해 기도 드렸고,   그러자 주님이 말씀하셨다:

"My presences shall go with thee, / and I will give thee
"나의 임재가 너희들과 함께하리라,   그리고 너희들을 쉬게 하리라."

rest."

---

the book 생명의 책 | rear 세우다, 건립하다 | congregation 신도, 회중 | seek 찾다, 구하다 | hew 자르다

134   The Story of the Bible

The Lord called Moses again / into the mount, / and told
하나님은 모세를 다시 불렀고   산 속으로,

him to bring with him / two tablets of stone / and He
가져오라고 하셨다   두 개의 돌판을

would again write / the ten commandments / upon them.
그리고 직접 다시 새기셨다   십계명을   돌판 위에.

So Moses hewed them from the rock / and took them up
모세는 바위를 잘라낸 후   그 돌판을 가지고 시내산으로

into Mount Sinai. Then the Lord came down again / in
올라갔다.   그러자 주님이 다시 내려 오시더니

a thick cloud / and talked with Moses, / and wrote upon
짙은 구름 속에서   모세와 이야기 하셨고,   돌판 위에 기록하셨다.

the tablets of stone.

Key Expression ❗

가정법 미래

가정법 중에서 미래에 대한 강한 의심, 또는 실현 불가능하거나 일어날 가능성이
거의 없는 일을 가정할 때 '가정법 미래'를 사용합니다.
가정법 미래는 if절에 현재형 동사를 사용하는 조건절과 구별해야 하는데 가정
법 미래의 경우 주관적인 확신이 강하게 들어나는 표현이라 할 수 있습니다.
가정법 미래의 형태는 다음과 같습니다.

▶ If + 주어 + would/should/were to + 원형 동사,
  주어 + 조동사 현재 or 과거형 + 원형 동사
  → 이때 주절에 쓰는 조동사는 will(would), shall(should), can(could), may(might)
    를 사용합니다.
  → if절에 would를 사용하면 주어의 소망이나 의지를, should를 사용하면 미래에
    대한 강한 의심을, were to를 사용하면 실현 불가능한 일을 표현합니다.

ex) If you would know all the beautiful and costly and curious things that were
made for this church in the wilderness, you will find them described in the
last chapters of Exodus.
만약 여러분이 황야의 교회를 위해 만들어진 이 모든 아름답고 값진 기이한 물
건들에 대해 알고 싶다면, 출애굽기의 마지막 장에서 찾아볼 수 있다.
He was ready to provide, if they would only believe in Him and obey Him.
사람들이 그 분을 믿고 따르기만 한다면 주님은 기꺼이 주실 터였다.

After forty days / Moses came down to the people /
40일 후　　　　　　　　　모세가 백성들에게 내려왔다

bringing the commandments with him, / but his face
계명들을 가지고,　　　　　　　　　　　하지만 모세의 얼굴이 빛나

shone / with a strange light / that the people never saw
고 있어서　　신비한 기운으로　　　사람들이 전혀 본 적 없었던,

before, / and they were afraid of him. It was something
사람들은 그를 두려워했다.

above the light of the sun, / for Moses had seen the Glory
그 빛은 태양빛보다 강한 빛이었다,　　　모세가 주님의 영광을 보았기 때문이었다.

of the Lord.

While they still camped / around the mount / they began
사람들은 여전히 야영 중이었고　　산 주변에서

to build the Tabernacle. Moses told the people / to bring
그동안 회막을 만들기 시작했다.　　　모세는 사람들에게 말해

gold, and silver, and brass, and wood. They also brought
금과 은, 놋과 나무를 가져오게 했다.　　　사람들은 또한 가져와서

/ precious stones, and oil for the lamp, / and fine linen, /
보석과 등잔 기름,　　　　　　　　　　　가는 베실을,

and they gave so willingly / that at last Moses told them /
이것들을 기꺼이 바쳤고　　　　　　그러자 마침내 모세가 말했다

that there was more than enough.
충분하다고.

These were put / in the hands of two wise men / whom
이 물건들은 건네졌고　　현자 두 명의 손에

the Lord had chosen / and taught to do the work, / and
주님이 선택하셨고　　　　일을 하도록 가르치신,

they had willing helpers / among the people, / for wise
자진해서 돕는 사람들이 있었다　　　백성들 중에,

hearted women did spin with their own hands, / and bring
지혜로운 여인들은 직접 실을 자아서,

what they had spun, / of blue, and purple, and scarlet, and
짠 것을 가지고 왔다,　　　　청색, 자색, 홍색실과 가는 베실로

fine linen / to make the hangings of the Tabernacle.
　　　　　　회막의 벽걸이를 만들기 위해.

If you would know / all the beautiful and costly and
만약 알고 싶다면   이 모든 아름답고 값진 기이한 물건들에 대해

curious things / that were made for this church in the
                         황야의 교회를 위해 만들어진,

wilderness, / you will find them / described in the last
            찾아볼 수 있다

chapters of Exodus.
출애굽기의 마지막 장에서.

The Israelites camped a long time / in the high valleys
이스라엘인은 오랫동안 머물렀고   높은 계곡에

/ around the Mount of God, / and at last set up the
  하나님의 산 주변,   마침내 회막을 완성했다.

Tabernacle. It was so made / that it could be taken down
회막은 만들어졌다   분해하여

/ and carried with them / when they journeyed, / for it
  들고 갈 수 있도록   여행할 때,

was a beautiful tent. Over it / the pillar of cloud stood.
아름다운 천막의 모습이었기에.   천막 위에는 구름 기둥이 서 있었다.

Whenever it moved / the people followed, / and when
구름 기둥이 움직이면   백성들이 그 뒤를 따랐고,

it stood still, / they rested. Within the Tabernacle / they
구름 기둥이 멈추면,   백성들도 쉬었다.   회막 안에는

placed a beautiful chest of wood / overlaid with gold, /
아름다운 나무 궤를 놓아   도금한,

which ever after held their most precious things, / the
가장 값진 물건을 보관했다,

tablets of stone / written upon by the Lord himself.
바로 돌판이었다   주님께서 직접 쓰신.

brass 놋 | precious stone 보석 | oil 기름 | linen 베 | spin 실을 잣다 | purple 자주색 | scarlet 주홍색 |
hanging 벽걸이 | curious 기이한, 궁금한 | chest 궤 | overlaid 도금이 된

This "Ark of Testimony," as it was called, / had rings at
"증거궤"라 불린 이것에,   측면에 고리를 달고

the sides / through which men laid strong rods / by which
그 고리에 튼튼한 막대를 걸어

to carry it, / and so had the golden table for bread, / and
들고 갔다,   또 빵을 올려놓는 금으로 만든 탁자와,

the golden altar of incense. There was a beautiful seven-
향을 피우기 위한 금으로 만든 제단도 있었다. 아름다운 일곱 개의 순금 촛대도 있어서

branched candlestick of pure gold / in which olive oil
그 안에 올리브 기름을 태웠다

was burned / for a sacred sign, / and there was a brazen
신성한 증표로써,   또한 번제단도 있었다

altar / for burnt offerings, / and a great brazen bowl for
재물을 태워 바치기 위한,   또 손을 씻기 위한 놋그릇과,

washing, / and other things / to be used in the worship of
다른 여러 가지 것들이 있었다

the Sanctuary.
성소에서 드리는 예배에 쓰이는.

Key Expression

fall on one's face : 엎드리다

fall on one's face는 '(얼굴을 땅에 대고) 엎드리다, 엎어지다'라는 의미입니다. 또한 '완전히 실패하다'라는 의미로 쓰이기도 합니다.
이와 같이 뒤에 오는 신체 부위에 따라 다음과 같이 다양한 숙어가 만들어집니다.

▶fall on one's face : 엎드리다, 엎어지다, 앞으로 고꾸라지다
▶fall on one's back : 뒤로 자빠지다
▶fall on one's hips/behind/butt/buttocks : 엉덩방아를 찧다

ex) When the people saw the answer of the Lord they fell on their faces before
    him.
    백성들은 주님의 대답을 보자 얼굴을 땅에 대고 엎드렸다.

There were beautiful garments, also, / for the priests,
아름다운 의복도 있었다,   제사장들이 입는,

/ Aaron and his sons, / and for Aaron / there was a
아론과 아들들인,   아론의 옷에는

wonderful breast-plate of gold / set with twelve precious
금으로 만든 멋진 흉패가 달려 있었다   열두 개의 보석을 박아 넣고,

stones, / bearing the names of the twelve tribes of Israel.
이스라엘 열두 지파의 이름을 새겨 넣은.

When all was finished, / and the Tabernacle was set up,
모든 준비가 끝나고,   회막이 완성되자,

/ the cloud that veiled the presence of the Lord came /
하나님의 임재를 가렸던 구름이 다가와

and covered it, / and the glory of the Lord filled it, / so
회막을 덮었고,   하나님의 영광이 그곳을 채웠다,

that Moses could not enter; / but the Lord spoke to him
모세는 들어갈 수 없었지만;   주님의 목소리가 들렸다

/ from the cloud, / and told him / how the priests should
구름 속에서,   주님이 말씀하셨다   제사장이 어떻게 이끌어야 하는지

order / the worship of the Lord / there.
주님께 드리는 예배를   그곳에서.

Afterward, / Aaron and his sons offered burnt offerings
이후에,   아론과 아들들은 번제를 드렸다

/ for their sins, / and the sins of the people, / in the way
그들의 죄와,   백성들의 죄에 대해,

the Lord had commanded, / and fire from the Lord came
주님이 명하신 방식대로,   그리고 주님으로부터 불꽃이 내려와

down / and consumed the offering.
제물을 태웠다.

When the people saw the answer of the Lord / they fell
백성들은 주님의 대답을 보자

on their faces before him.
얼굴을 땅에 대고 엎드렸다.

Ark of Testimony 증거궤 | sacred 신성한 | brazen 놋쇠로 만든 | garment 의복 | breast-plate 흉패 | veil
가리다 | consume 소모하다. 먹다. 마시다

In the second month of the second year / the cloud rose
이듬 해 2월에

from over the Tabernacle, / and then the people knew /
구름이 회막 위에서 일어나자.   백성들은 알게 되었다.

it was time to go on their Journey. So they took down
여행을 떠나야 할 때가 되었다는 것을.   그래서 회막을 분해하여

the tent of the Tabernacle / and put all things in order
                              모든 물건을 정리했다

/ for the journey. Each of the twelve tribes / descended
여행을 위해.   열두 지파는 각자

from the twelve sons of Jacob / marched by themselves,
야곱의 열두 명 아들의 뒤를 이은   무리를 지어 행진했다.

/ carrying banners, / and having captains. In the midst of
깃발을 들고,   대장을 세워서.   그들 가운데에서

them all / marched the Levites / carrying the Ark and the
레위지파 사람들이 걸었다   궤와 휘막의 각 부분을 들고,

different parts of the Tabernacle, / and when the cloud
                                그러다가 구름이 멈추면,

stood still, / they stopped / and set up the Tabernacle, /
            그들도 멈춰 서서   회막을 세웠고,

while the people formed their camp / all around it / in the
그동안 사람들은 천막을 쳤다   그 주위에

order of their tribes.
지파의 순서에 따라.

Key Expression 🔑

put ~ in order : 정리하다
put ~ in order는 '~을 정리하다'의 의미를 가진 숙어입니다. put 대신 set
을 사용할 수도 있습니다.

ex) So they took down the tent of the Tabernacle and put all things in order for
the journey.
그래서 그들은 여행을 위해 회막을 분해하여 모든 물건을 정리했다.

Still the manna fell / with the dew / at night, / and the
여전히 만나가 내렸고   이슬과 함께   밤이면,

people gathered it / in the morning, / and when they tired
사람들이 그것을 거뒀다   아침이 되면,   사람들이 만나에 싫증을 내면,

of it, / the Lord sent them quails again.
주님은 다시 메추라기 떼를 보내셨다.

Over and over / the people complained and rebelled, /
계속해서   사람들은 불평하고 반항했지만,

but the Angel of the Lord's Presence still hovered over
주님의 천사들이 그 위에 머물면서,

them, / and led them / toward the promised land. Forty
사람들을 이끌었다   약속의 땅으로.   40년 동안

years / they were on the journey / that was so easily made
사람들은 여행했다   야곱의 아들들이 쉽게 했었던

by the sons of Jacob / when they went back and forth to
밀을 사기 위해 오갔을 때

buy wheat / in the time of famine; / and forty-two times /
기근의 시절에;   그리고 42번이나

did they encamp on the way, / yet the mercy of the Lord
도중에 야영을 했다   하지만 주님의 자비는 그들을 실망시키지

never failed them, / and they were brought into their own
않았고,   그들의 땅에 도착할 수 있었다

land / at last. Then the cloud was no longer needed to go /
마침내.   이제 구름은 더 이상 움직일 필요가 없었지만

before them, / but long after, / when they built a beautiful
그들 앞에서,   한참 후에,   사람들이 아름다운 성전을 짓고

temple / at Jerusalem / in which to put the sacred Ark of
예루살렘에   그 안에 증거궤를 놓자,

Testimony, / the cloud came again / and filled the temple /
구름이 다시 다가와   성전을 가득 채웠다

with the glory of the Lord.
주님의 영광으로.

over and over 여러 번, 반복하여 | rebel 반란을 일으키다, 반역하다 | hover 맴돌다 | mercy 자비

A. 다음 문장을 해석해 보세요.

(1) The dust of the land was changed to lice / that covered man and beast, / and this was followed by swarms of flies / that settled upon all the land.
→

(2) The feast of the Passover has been the chief one / held by the Israelites, / from the time of their coming out of Egypt / until now.
→

(3) The Lord told Moses / that the people must gather / just enough to eat through the day, / and no more.
→

(4) If you would know / all the beautiful and costly and curious things / that were made for this church in the wilderness, / you will find them / described in the last chapters of Exodus.
→

B. 다음 주어진 문구가 알맞은 문장이 되도록 순서를 맞춰 보세요.

(1) 나는 주님을 모르고, 이스라엘 백성을 보내지도 않을 것이다.
[let / the Lord, / I know / go / neither / I / not / will / Israel]
→

(2) 그리고 왕은 <u>이전보다 더</u> 이스라엘인을 억압하기 시작했다.
[before / ever / had / than / he / more / done]
And he began to oppress the Israelites ⬚⬚⬚⬚⬚⬚

⬚⬚⬚⬚⬚⬚⬚⬚⬚⬚ .

Answer

A. (1) 땅의 먼지가 이로 변해 사람과 짐승을 덮었으며, 이어서 파리 떼가 나타나 모든 땅을 뒤덮었다. (2) 유월절은 이집트에서 탈출하던 때부터 지금까지 이스라엘 백성이 지키는 가장 중요한 축일이다. (3) 주님이 모세에게 말씀하시길 사람들은 하루 동안 먹을 만큼만 거둬야 하며, 더 이상은 안 된다고 하셨다. (4) 만약

(3) 그것은 꿀로 만든 얇은 빵 맛이 났다.
   (like / with / made / honey / tasted / It / wafers)
   →

(4) 백성들은 주님의 대답을 보자 <u>그 앞에 얼굴을 땅에 대고 엎드렸다</u>.
   (their / before / they / on / fell / him / faces)
   When the people saw the answer of the Lord ⬚⬚⬚⬚⬚⬚⬚⬚⬚

   ⬚⬚⬚⬚⬚⬚⬚⬚ .

C. 다음 주어진 문장이 본문의 내용과 맞으면 T, 틀리면 F에 동그라미 하세요.

(1) Pharaoh was willing to let Moses' people go when he saw the
   miracle of God.
   (T / F)

(2) Pharoah's men followed Moses across the Red Sea.
   (T / F)

(3) God sent Moses' people bread and flesh.
   (T / F)

(4) Moses' people were on journey for forty days.
   (T / F)

D. 의미가 비슷한 것끼리 서로 연결해 보세요.

(1) entreat   ▶   ◀ ① triumph
(2) yield   ▶   ◀ ② decoration
(3) prevail   ▶   ◀ ③ plead
(4) ornament   ▶   ◀ ④ surrender

13

IN THE BORDERS OF CANAAN
가나안 국경에서

While the host of Israel was in camp at Paran, / the Lord
이스라엘 백성들이 바란에 진을 치고 있는 동안,　　　　　　　　주님께서 모세

told Moses / to send men before them into Canaan / to
에게 말씀하셨다　　사람들을 미리 가나안으로 보내

spy out the land.
정탐하라고.

So he sent twelve men / who walked through the land /
그래서 모세는 열두 명을 보냈다　　그 땅을 돌아다니며

and saw the people, and the cities and the fields and the
사람들과 도시와 들판과 과일을 살펴 볼.

fruits. They were forty days searching the land / and
그들은 40일 동안 그 땅을 살피고

they brought from the brook Eschol / a cluster of grapes
에스골 골짜기에서 가져왔는데　　　　　　　포도송이를

/ so large / that two of them bore it / on a staff / between
크기가 매우 커서　두 사람이 지고 올 정도였다　　　막대기에 꿰어　　포도송이

them. They also brought / some pomegranates and figs.
사이에.　　또한 가지고 왔다　　　　석류와 무화과도.

When they came into the camp / they said / that the
그들은 야영지로 돌아와서　　　　　　　말했다

country where they had been / was good, / and flowing
자신들이 다녀온 그 나라는　　　　　　비옥하고,

with milk and honey, / but the people were strong, /
젖과 꿀이 흐르는 땅이었다고.　　하지만 사람들이 강성하고,

and the cities had very high walls. They said / they saw
도시는 매우 높은 성벽으로 둘러싸여 있다고.　　또 말했다

giants there.
그곳에서 거인을 보았다고.

---

border 국경 | Eschol 에스골, 헤브론 땅 근처의 개울 | cluster 송이 | pomegranate 석류 | fig 무화과 |
grasshopper 메뚜기

Caleb, / who was one of the twelve, / and a good and true
갈렙은,　　열두 명의 정찰대원 중 한 명인,　　　　착하고 진질한 사람으로,

man, / said: /
　　이렇게 말했다:

"Let us go up at once / and possess it, / for we are well
"당장 올라가서　　　　　　그 땅을 차지합시다,　　우리는 충분히

able to overcome it," / but the men who were with
이길 수 있습니다."　　　하지만 그와 같이 갔던 사람들은

him / were afraid of the giants, / and said / they felt
　거인을 두려워하여,　　　　　　말했다　　자신들은

like grasshoppers / before them. Then there was great
메뚜기 같았다고　　　거인 앞에 서니.　그러자 큰 통곡 소리가 일어났다

weeping / among the people / all that night, / and they
　　사람들 사이에　　　　그날 밤 내내,　　　그리고 나서 사람

said,
들이 말했다.

"Let us make a captain, / and let us return into Egypt."
"지도자를 선출하고,　　　　이집트로 돌아갑시다!"

Moses and Aaron were greatly troubled, / but the
모세와 아론은 매우 곤란해 했지만,

two good men, / Caleb and Joshua, / stood up / and
선한 두 사람이,   갈렙과 여호수아가,   일어나서

encouraged the people, / saying that they need not fear,
사람들의 용기를 북돋았다,   두려워할 필요가 없다며,

/ for the Lord had given them the land, / yet they were
주님께서 그 땅을 주셨으니,   하지만 사람들은 돌로

ready to stone / Caleb and Joshua.
치려고 했다   갈렙과 여호수아를.

Then the Lord spake to Moses / from the Tabernacle, /
그때 주님께서 모세에게 말씀하셨고   장막 안에서,

and the people saw his glory. He said / the people were
사람들은 주님의 영광을 보았다.   주님이 말씀하시길

unbelieving and disobedient, / and for this reason / they
사람들이 믿음이 없고 순종하지 않아서,   그때문에

could not enter the promised land. He said, / that all
약속의 땅에 들어갈 수 없는 것이다.   또 말씀하시길,

who were twenty years old and upward / would die in
스무살이 넘은 사람들은 모두   황무지에서 죽으리라,

the wilderness, / except Caleb and Joshua, / who had
갈렙과 여호수아 외에는,

followed the Lord wholly. He also said / that the people
주님을 온전히 따랐던.   다시 말씀하시길

would be forty years in the wilderness, / and only the
사람들은 황무지에서 40년 간 보낼 것이며,

youth and the children would live to enter Canaan.
청년과 어린이만 살아서 가나안에 들어가리라.

There was mourning and repentance then / because of
그러자 애도와 회개의 움직임이 일어났고

the word of the Lord, / and the people promised again / to
주님의 말씀으로 인해,   사람들은 다시 한 번 약속했다

believe and obey, / but over and over / they lost faith and
주님을 믿고 따르기로,   하지만 계속해서   사람들이 믿음을 잃고 반항하자,

rebelled, / and great storms of trouble fell upon them.
엄청난 재앙이 그들에게 일어났다.

encourage 격려하다, 용기를 북돋우다

Once the earth opened / and many were swallowed up;
땅이 갈라지자 많은 사람들이 그 속으로 빠져 버렸고;

/ a sudden sickness destroyed thousands. Near Mount
갑자기 전염병이 일어나 수천 명이 죽었다. 호르 산 근처에는,

Hor, / where Aaron died, / fiery serpents ran among
아론이 죽은 장소인, 사나운 뱀이 사람들 사이로 지나갔고,

the people, / and all who were bitten by them died; /
뱀에 물린 사람들은 모두 죽었다;

but there was full forgiveness and cure / for those who
하지만 용서받고 치유 받았다

turned to the Lord. When the fiery serpents entered the
주님께 돌아온 사람들은. 사나운 뱀이 야영지에 들어왔을 때

camp / Moses lifted a brazen image of a serpent up / on
모세는 놋으로 만든 뱀을 세웠는데

a pole / so high / that it could be seen / all over the camp,
장대 위에 매우 높이 장대가 보였고 야영지 전체에서,

/ and whoever looked upon it lived. It was a sign / of the
그것을 본 사람들은 모두 살아났다. 그것은 징표였다

coming Saviour.
앞으로 오실 구원자의.

Between the marches and the battles / with heathen
행군과 전쟁 중에 이방인들과의,

tribes, / some of whom were giants, / Moses wrote in a
그 중 일부는 거인이었던, 모세는 책에 기록했다

book / the laws that God gave him / for the government
하나님께서 주신 법률을 백성들을 통치하기 위해.

of the people. They were wise laws, / the keeping of
현명한 법률이었고, 그 법을 지키면

which / would bring health, peace and blessedness / to
건강, 평화, 축복이 따를 터였다

the people. He gave the book to the Levites / who carried
사람들에게. 모세는 그 책을 레위지파에게 주었고 언약궤를 들었던,

the Ark, / and they were to keep it always / beside the
그들은 항상 간직하며 언약궤 옆에 놓고,

Ark, / and often read it aloud to the people.
종종 사람들에게 큰 소리로 읽어 주었다.

Moses said many things to the people, / and as Jacob
모세는 사람들에게 많은 것을 말했고,

blessed his twelve sons, / so Moses blessed each of the
야곱이 열두 아들을 축복했기에,　　모세는 열두 지파를 축복했다

twelve tribes / that descended from them, / for he was
열두 아들의 자손들인,　　　　　왜냐하면 모세는

near the end of his long life. The Lord had told him /
긴 인생의 마지막을 앞두고 있었기 때문이었다.　주님이 말씀하셨다

that He should take him to Himself / before the people
모세를 데려갈 것이며　　　　　사람들이 가나안 땅에 들어가기

entered Canaan, / and that Joshua must lead the people
전에,　　　　여호수아가 사람들을 이끌어야 한다고

/ into the promised land. So when they had reached
약속의 땅으로.　　　　그래서 사람들이 가나안 국경에 도착하여,

the borders of Canaan, / and were encamped near the
요단강 근처에 진을 치자,

Jordan, / the Lord called his tried servant up into Mount
주님께서 충실한 종을 느보산 위로 부르셨고,

Nebo, / that he might see the land beyond the Jordan,
그곳에서 모세는 요단강 너머의 땅을 볼 수 있었다.

/ where the twelve tribes were to find their promised
열두 지파가 약속된 땅을 발견하게 될 곳이었다.

home. Then the Lord gave him a view of the land, / and
주님께서 모세에게 그 땅을 보여 주시고,　　　　　그곳에서

there he died, / as Aaron died on Mount Hor.
모세는 죽었다,　　　아론이 호르산에서 죽었던 것처럼.

No one saw Moses die, / and no one knows where he was
아무도 모세가 죽는 것을 보지 못했고,　　그가 묻힌 곳도 알지 못했다,

buried, / for the Lord buried him. He was one hundred
주님께서 그를 장사지내셨기에.　　　모세의 나이는 120살이었으나,

and twenty years old, / and yet as strong as a young man.
여전히 젊은이처럼 강건했다.

After his death / Joshua became the leader of Israel.
모세가 죽은 후　　　여호수아가 이스라엘 백성의 지도자가 되었다.

fiery 불타는 | pole 장대 | government 통치, 통치 체제 | descend 내려오다

149

14

A NATION THAT WAS BORN IN A DAY
하루 만에 태어난 국가

The time had come / for the people to cross the river
때가 왔다   사람들이 요단강을 건너

Jordan, / and enter their own land, / and the Lord told
자신들의 땅에 들어갈,   그러자 주님께서 여호수아에게

Joshua / to prepare the people for their last journey /
말씀하셨다   사람들에게 마지막 여행을 준비시키라고

before going over Jordan. Joshua first sent two men /
요단강을 건너기 전에.   여호수아는 먼저 두 명을 보내어

over the river / to see the land.
강 건너에   정탐하도록 했다.

They went to the walled city of Jericho, / and to the
두 사람은 여리고 성에 가서,

house of a woman named Rahab. The king heard / that
라합이라는 여인의 집에 갔다.   왕은 듣고   이방인이

they were there / and sent for them, / but the woman hid
그곳에 있다는 소식을   사람을 보냈지만,   라합은 그들을 숨겼다

them / under the flax / that she was drying on the roof
삼대 속에   지붕 위에 널어 놓았던.

of her house. Afterward / she let them down / by a rope
이후에   라합은 그들을 내려보냈고   밧줄로

/ through a window / (for her house was built / on the
창문을 통해   (그녀의 집은 지어졌기에

town wall), / and they escaped. They promised Rahab /
마을 성벽 위에),   그들은 도망쳤다.   그들은 라합에게 약속했다

before they went, / that if she would hang a long line of
떠나기 전에,   그녀가 붉은 줄은 매달아 놓는다면

scarlet thread / from the window on the wall, / that when
창문 밖 벽에,

they came to take the city / she should be saved / and all
도시에 침입할 때   라합을 살려주겠다고

her family / because of her kindness to them.
가족들까지   친절함에 대한 보답으로.

After they had returned to the camp / they told Joshua
두 정찰병은 야영지로 돌아온 후   여호수아에게 말했다

/ that the Lord would surely give them the land, / for
하나님께서 분명히 그 땅을 주실 것이라고.

the people were afraid of them. Then they rose up / and
성 안 사람들이 자신들을 두려워하고 있으니.   그러자 이스라엘인은 자리에서 일어나

marched to the banks of the Jordan / and waited / for
요단강 가로 진군한 후   기다렸다

Joshua to lead them over. Some of them remembered /
여호수아가 이끌어 주기를.   몇몇 사람들은 기억하고 있었고,

how they had passed / through the Red Sea, / and others
자신들이 어떻게 건넜는지   홍해를 가르고,   다른 사람들은

had heard it / from their parents, / and they now waited
그 이야기를 들었다   부모로부터,   그래서 이제 그들은 기다렸다

/ to see the salvation of God. Joshua told them to follow
하나님의 구원을 보려고.   여호수아는 사람들에게 제사장을 따르라고

the priests, / and the Levites who would bear the Ark of
했고,   레위인에게 언약궤를 메고 가도록 했다,

the Covenant, / so when Joshua said: /
그래서 여호수아가 이렇게 말하자:

Key Expression

as ~ as 원급 비교

A = B의 의미를 표현하고자 할 때 'as + 형용사/부사 원급 + as ~'의 형태로 사용하여 '~만큼 …한'이라고 해석합니다.

참고로 첫 번째 as 앞에 not을 붙여 not as[so] + ~ +as…가 되면 '…만큼 ~하지 않은'이라 해석하여 두 번째 as 뒤의 것이 더 우월하다는 비교의 의미를 가지게 됩니다.

ex) He was one hundred and twenty years old, and yet as strong as a young man.
모세의 나이는 120살이었으나, 여전히 젊은이처럼 강건했다.
If it should be cut he would be as weak as other men.
만약 머리를 자른다면 그도 다른 사람들처럼 힘이 약해질 것이다.

---

flax 삼대 | camp 야영지, 진지 | march 행진하다, 진군하다 | bank 둑, 제방 | salvation 구원 | Levites 레위인

"Behold / the Ark of the Covenant of the Lord of all
"보시오   주님의 언약궤가

the earth / passeth over before you / into Jordan," / the
여러분 앞을 지나   요단강으로 향하는 것을,"

people followed.
사람들이 그 뒤를 따랐다.

The Jordan lay spread / before them / like a lake, / for it
요단강은 펼쳐져 있었다   그들 앞에   호수처럼,

was the time of year / when it overflowed all its banks, /
그런 시기였기 때문에   강물이 흘러 넘치는,

but when the feet of the priests / who bore the Ark / were
하지만 제사장의 발이   궤를 들고 있던

dipped in the edge of the water, / the waters from above
강가로 들어가자,   표면에 흐르던 물이 멈추더니

stopped / and rose like a wall, / while the waters below
벽처럼 솟아오르고,   표면 아래의 물은 흘러가 버려

flowed away / into the Dead Sea, / and left a wide path
사해로,   넓은 길이 만들어졌다

/ for the people to walk in, / and the Ark stood still / in
사람들이 걸어갈 수 있도록,   그리고 궤는 가만히 서 있었다

Jordan / until everyone had passed over. Then twelve
요단강에   모든 사람들이 건너갈 때까지.   그리고 나서 열두 명이,

men, / one out of every tribe, / took a stone from the bed
각 지파에서 한 명씩,   강 바닥의 돌을 주워서

of the river / and carried it over / for a memorial altar, /
가지고 갔다   기념비를 만들기 위해,

so that when any should ask / in years to come, / "What
그리하여 누군가가 묻는다면   미래에,

do these stones mean?" / someone might tell them / how
"이 돌들은 무엇입니까?"라고   대답할 수 있을 것이었다   하나님이

the Lord led Israel / through Jordan / into their own land.
어떻게 이스라엘 백성을 이끌고   요단강을 건너   그들의 땅으로 들어갔는지.

overflow 넘치다 | heap 쌓다

After the Ark had come up / from the bed of Jordan, /
언약궤가 올라온 후   요단강 바닥에서,

and there was not one / of all the thousands of Israel / left
한 명도 없게 되자   수천 명의 이스라엘 백성 중   남아

behind, / the waters came down / from the place where
있는 사람이,   물이 밀려 내려왔고   멈추어 있던 곳에서,

they had stayed, / and flowed down into the Dead Sea, /
     그리고 사해로 흘러 내려갔고,

and overflowed the banks of Jordan / as before.
요단강에 흘러 넘쳤다   전처럼.

The stones were heaped / in Gilgal where they camped, /
돌이 수북이 쌓였고   진을 치고 있던 길갈에,

and directly before them / rose the walls of Jericho, / and
바로 앞에는   여리고 성벽이 솟아 있었다,

here they kept the passover. For forty years / they had
이곳에서 이스라엘 백성은 유월절을 지켰다.   40년 동안

been fed with manna / from heaven / as they camped or
그들은 만나를 먹었지만   하늘에서 떨어지는   여행하거나 야영할 때

journeyed / in the wilderness, / but now they began to
     황무지에서,   이제 그들은 먹기 시작했고

eat / the grain and the fruits of the land, / and the manna
     그 땅의 곡식과 열매를,   만나는 떨어지지 않았다

fell / no more.
     더 이상.

Nearly five hundred years before / the family of Jacob
거의 500년 전   야곱의 가족은

/ left this land / to go down into Egypt / where Joseph
     이 땅을 떠나   이집트로 갔다   요셉이 있었던.

was. They grew to be a great people, / but they were
     그들은 거대한 민족이 되었지만,   노예였다.

slaves. Then the Lord sent Moses / to make them free, /
     그러자 주님께서 모세를 보내어   그들을 자유롭게 하셨고,

and they began the long journey, / which at last / brought
그들은 긴 여행을 시작하여,   마침내

them to their own land.
자신들의 땅에 도착했다.

Forty years / they were on the journey, / and all this time
40년 동안　　　그들은 여행을 했고,　　　　　　　　　그 기간 내내

/ they were pilgrims, / but on the day / that the Jordan
그들은 순례자들이었다.　　　하지만 이 날에는　　요단강이 흐름을 멈추고,

ceased to flow, / and parted / while they passed over / into
갈라져　　　그들이 강을 지나　　　　　　　땅으로

the land / promised to their fathers, / they became a nation.
들어가는 동안　조상에게 약속되었던.　　　　　　그들은 나라를 이루었다.

The land was before them, / and they had only to obey /
약속의 땅이 펼쳐져 있었고,　　　　　그들은 순종하여

the Lord and his servant Joshua / to conquer and possess
주님과 그분의 종 여호수아에　　　　그 땅을 정복하고 소유하기만 하면 되었다.

it.

As they filled the valley of the Jordan / before Jericho, / the
이스라엘 백성이 요단강 골짜기를 가득 채우자　　　　여리고 앞에 있는,

hearts of the heathen fainted for fear, / for they knew / that
이방인은 두려움에 떨었다.　　　　　　　　알고 있었기에

only the Lord could divide a river / to let his people pass.
오직 주님만이 강을 갈라　　　　　　백성들이 건너게 될 수 있음을.

Joshua went out of the camp / to look at Jericho, / the
여호수아는 야영지 밖으로 나가　　　　여리고 성을 바라보았다.

walled city. It was shut up / for fear of the Israelites, / and
성벽의 도시였던.　성문은 굳게 닫혀 있었고　이스라엘 백성을 두려워했기 때문에,

there was no one to be seen.
아무도 보이지 않았다.

Suddenly / Joshua saw a warrior standing / with a drawn
갑자기　　　군사 한 명이 서 있는 것이 보였다

sword in his hand.
손에 칼을 든 채.

pilgrim 순례자 | cease 중지다 | conquer 정복하다 | possess 소유하다 | valley 골짜기 | warrior 군사 |
adversary 적, 상대방 | ram 숫양 | horn 뿔

"Art thou for us," / said Joshua, / "or for our adversaries?" /
"너는 아군이냐," 여호수아가 말했다. "아니면 적군이냐?"

and the warrior angel answered,
그러자 군사의 모습을 한 천사가 대답했고,

"Nay! But as Captain of the host of the Lord, / am I now
"아니다! 주님의 군대 총사령관으로,

come," / and Joshua fell on his face before him.
지금 왔다." 여호수아는 그에게 절을 했다.

He knew then / that it was the Lord / who would conquer
그때 여호수아는 알게 되었고 주님이란 것을 여리고 성을 함락시킬 이는,

Jericho, / and he was told / how the people were to help him.
들었다 어떻게 사람들이 그분을 도와야 하는지.

So Joshua called the priests, / and told them to take up the
그러자 여호수아는 제사장들을 불러, 언약궤를 가져오라 한 후,

Ark, / and he told seven priests to go / before it / bearing
일곱 명의 제사장에게 가라고 했다 언약궤 앞에서

trumpets of rams' horns. Then the army of Israel, / ready for
양 뿔 나팔을 들고. 그리고 이스라엘 군대는, 전쟁 준비를 한

war, / followed, / half of them marching before the Ark, /
후, 뒤를 따랐다. 절반은 언약궤 앞에서 진군하고,

and half of them coming after, / and as the trumpets gave a
나머지 절반은 그 뒤를 따르며, 그리고 나팔 소리가 크게 울리자,

great sound, / they marched once around the city, / and then
이스라엘 군대는 도시 주위를 한 바퀴 돈 후,

went to camp.
진지로 돌아갔다.

Key Expression 🍏

have only to : ~하기만 하면 된다
have only to는 '~하기만 하면 된다'라는 의미를 가진 구문입니다. to 뒤에는 동사 원형이 옵니다.

ex) They had only to obey the Lord and his servant Joshua to conquer and
possess it.
그들은 주님과 그분의 종 여호수아에 순종하여 그 땅을 정복하고 소유하기만 하
면 되었다.

This they did / once every day / for seven days, / but on
그들은 이렇게 했고   매일 한 번씩   칠 일 동안,

the seventh day / they marched around the city seven
칠 일째가 되자   도시 주위를 일곱 번 돌았다.

times, / and as the priests blew the trumpets / for the last
그리고 제사장들이 나팔을 불자 마지막으로 돌 때,

time, / Joshua cried with a mighty voice,
여호수아가 큰 목소리로 외쳤다.

"Shout! For the Lord hath given you the city."
"소리치시오! 주님이 여러분에게 이 도시를 주셨소."

Then as a great shout went up / from the people, / the
큰 외침 소리가 울려퍼지자   사람들로부터,

walls of the city fell down flat, / so that the soldiers of
도시의 성벽이 무너져 버렸고,   이스라엘의 군병들이 성벽을 올라가,

Israel went up, / every man straight before him, / and
모든 사람이 성으로 진격하여,

took Jericho.
여리고를 함락시켰다.

And Rahab was not forgotten. The Lord cared for her
그리고 라합을 잊지 않았다.   주님께서 라합의 집을 돌보셔서

little house / on the wall, / and she, with all her family, /
성벽 위에 있던,   라합과 가족들은

were brought into the Camp of Israel.
이스라엘의 진지로 데려왔다.

And so / by the conquest of Jericho / the new nation of
그리고 그렇게 여리고 성이 정복됨으로써   새로운 나라 이스라엘이

Israel / began to possess its land.
그 땅을 소유하게 되었다.

counsel 조언하다, 충고하다 | prophetess 여자 예언자 | mighty 힘이 센

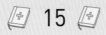

SAMSON THE STRONG
강한 자, 삼손

All the days of Joshua / — and he lived to be an hundred
여호수아가 살아있는 동안 줄곧　　— 그는 110세까지 살았는데—

and ten years old — / the Israelites were conquering / the
이스라엘 민족은 정복했고

people who lived in Canaan, / and dividing it among the
가나안 땅에 사는 사람들을,　　　　　그 땅을 지파들끼리 나누었다.

tribes. Joshua was a father to them, / as Moses had been, /
여호수아는 그들의 아버지였다,　　　　모세가 그랬듯이,

and when at last they were at rest, / each tribe / within its
그리고 마침내 휴식이 찾아오자,　　　　각 지파는

own borders, / and they had begun to build their houses,
자신들의 영역 안에서,　　집을 건축하기 시작했고,

/ and plant their fields, / Joshua spoke words of loving
　밭을 가꾸었다.　　　여호수아가 애정어린 충고를 전하자

counsel / to the people, / and they set up a stone / under an
　　　　백성들에게,　　　사람들은 돌을 세웠고　　상수리 나무

oak tree, / as a sign / that they would always serve the Lord
아래,　　증표로써　　언제나 주님을 섬기고

/ and keep the law, / and then he went to be with God. After
　율법을 지키겠다는,　　　그리고 나서 여호수아는 하나님 곁으로 떠났다.　　여호수아

his death / Israel was ruled by wise men called judges, /
가 죽은 후　　이스라엘은 '사사'라 불리는 현인들이 다스렸고,

who helped them to conquer the land / little by little. Some
그들은 이스라엘인을 도와 땅을 정복했다　　　조금씩.

of them were good men and brave warriors / as Othniel and
사사 중 몇몇은 선하고 용감한 전사였고

Gideon and Jephthah / and one was a prophetess named
옷니엘과 기드온, 입다처럼　　　　드보라라는 여자 예언자도 있었으며,

Deborah, / a noble mother in Israel, / and one was a mighty
이스라엘의 귀족 여성인,　　　　힘센 용사도 있었다.

man of strength, / Samson, the son of Manoah.
바로 마노아의 아들, 삼손이었다.

The people of Israel had turned away from the Lord,
이스라엘 백성이 주님에게서 등을 돌리게 되자,

/ and could no longer conquer their enemies, / but the
그들은 더 이상 적들을 정복하지 못했고,

Philistines had conquered them, / and had been their
블레셋 사람들이 이스라엘인을 정복하여,   그들의 지배자가 되었다

masters / for forty years, / when the Lord sent Samson /
40년 동안,   그때 주님께서 삼손을 보내셨다

to deliver them. He was not a wise man / like Moses or
그들을 구원하기 위해.   삼손은 현명한 사람은 아니었지만   모세나 여호수아처럼,

Joshua, / but he had great strength, / and the Lord used
그에게는 엄청난 힘이 있었고,   주님은 삼손을 이용하여

him / against the Philistines.
블레셋과 맞서 싸우셨다.

Once / a young lion came roaring against him, / and he
한 번은   어린 사자가 삼손에게 으르렁거리며 다가오자,   삼손은 사자를

caught it / and rent it in two, / as if it had been a kid.
잡아   둘로 찢어 죽여버렸다,   마치 사자가 어린 아이인듯.

When he passed the same way / afterward / he saw /
같은 곳을 지나가던 중   나중에   삼손은 보았다

that the bees had built a nest / in the body of the lion, /
벌이 집을 지어서   사자의 몸 안에,

and it was full of honey. At his marriage feast / — for he
사자 몸이 꿀로 가득했다.   자신의 결혼식 피로연 때

married a Philistine woman — / he made a riddle / for
— 그는 블레셋 여인과 결혼했는데 —   삼손은 수수께끼를 냈다

the young men to guess: /
젊은이들에게 추측해 보라고:

"Out of the eater came forth meat, / and out of the
"먹는 자에게서 먹는 것이 나오고,   강한 자에게서,

strong, / came forth sweetness."
단 것이 나왔느니라."

---

roar 으르렁거리다 | nest 둥지, 집 | riddle 수수께끼 | guess 예측하다, 추측하다 | honey comb 벌집

They tried for seven days / to guess the riddle, / but they
칠 일 동안 노력했으나   수수께끼를 풀려고,   사람들은 풀

could not, / and then they told Samson's wife / to find it
수 없었고,   삼손의 부인에게 말했다

out for them, / or they would burn her house. She begged
답을 알아 오라고,   그러지 않으면 집을 불태워 버리겠다고.   부인은 삼손에게

him with tears / to tell her, / and at last / he told her / of
눈물로 애원했고   답을 알려 달라고,   그래서 마침내   삼손이 이야기 하자

the honey comb in the body of the lion, / and she told the
사자의 몸 안에 생긴 벌집에 대해,   부인은 젊은이들에게

young men, / so that at the end of the seventh day / they
전했다.   그리하여 칠 일 째 되던 날

said to Samson,
젊은이들이 삼손에게 말했다,

"What is sweeter than honey?" / and "what is stronger
"꿀보다 단 것은 무엇인가?"   그리고 "사자보다 강한 것은 무엇인가?"

than a lion?"

Key Expression

as if ~ : 마치 ~인 것처럼

as if는 '마치 ~인 것처럼'이라는 의미로 가정법 문장과 함께 사용하는 가정법
의 특수한 형태입니다. 현재의 상황을 가정할 때에는 가정법 과거를, 과거의 상황
을 가정할 때에는 가정법 과거완료를 사용합니다.

▶ 주절 현재시제, as if + 주어 + 과거동사/were ~
  → 마치 ~인 것처럼

▶ 주절 과거/현재완료 시제, as if + 주어 + had + 과거분사 ~
  → 마치 ~였던 것처럼

ex) Once a young lion came roaring against him, and he caught it and rent it in
two, as if it had been a kid.
한 번은 어린 사자가 삼손에게 으르렁거리며 다가오자, 삼손은 마치 사자가 어린
아이인듯 사자를 잡아 둘로 찢어 죽여버렸다.

He saw that he had been betrayed, / so he paid his debt,
삼손은 자신이 배신당했음을 알았고,   그래서 그 빚을 갚은 후,

/ a suit of clothes to each guest, / and went home to his
손님에게 각자 옷 한 벌씩을 주어,   아버지의 집으로 갔다.

father's house. Afterwards / when he found / that his
그 이후에   알게 되자

wife had been given to another / he tied firebrands / to
부인이 다른 이들에게 답을 알려준 사실을   햇불을 묶은 후

the tails of three hundred foxes, / and sent them / among
여우 300마리의 꼬리에,   여우를 풀어 놓아

the wheat fields of the Philistines / so that the fields were
블레셋 사람들의 밀밭에   밭이 불타 버렸다.

set on fire.

Once / the men of Gaza tried to kill him / when he was
한 번은   가사 사람들이 삼손을 죽이려고 했다

within their city, / but he rose at midnight / and took
도시 안에 있었을 때,   하지만 삼손은 한밤 중에 일어나

the city gates, with its posts and bar, / and carried them
성문과 문설주와 빗장을 떼어,   어깨에 매고 갔다

away on his shoulders / to the top of the hill. Again / the
언덕 꼭대기로.   다시 한 번

Philistine lords had promised a great deal of money / to
블레셋 사람들은 엄청난 돈을 주겠다고 약속했고

a woman, / if she would get Samson to tell her / what
삼손의 부인에게,   삼손에게 대답을 얻어낸다면

made him so strong, / so she begged him to tell her.
그를 강하게 만든 이유에 대해,   그러자 그녀는 삼손에게 애원했다.

Three times / she thought she knew the secret, / and told
세 번씩이나   그녀는 자신이 비밀을 알았다고 생각하여,   블레셋 사람들

the Philistines, / but they could not bind him. At last /
에게 말했지만,   그들은 삼손을 잡을 수 없었다.   결국

he was tired of her questions, / and said to her plainly /
삼손은 부인의 질문에 지쳐서,   솔직하게 말했다

— that from a child / no razor had ever touched his hair.
— 어려서부터   머리카락에 칼을 대지 않았기 때문이라고.

betray 배신하다 | debt 빚 | fireband 횃불 | post 문설주 | bar 빗장 | bind 묶다 | razor 삭도, 면도칼

If it should be cut / he would be as weak as other men.
만약 머리를 깎는다면   자신도 다른 사람들처럼 힘이 약해질 것이라고.

Then she watched / and cut his hair / while he slept, / and
그러자 삼손의 아내는 지켜보다가 삼손의 머리를 깎고   자는 동안,

the Philistines bound him / and carried him to Gaza, /
블레셋 사람들이 그를 묶어서   가자로 끌고 갔다,

where they made him blind, / and forced him / to grind /
그곳에서 그를 장님으로 만든 후,   강제로 시켰다   곡식 빻는 일을

in the mills of a prison house. The Philistines were glad /
감옥의 방앗간 안에서.   블레셋 사람들은 기뻐했다

because Samson was their prisoner / at last, / and so they
삼손이 그들의 죄수가 되었기에   마침내,

came together / in a great feast / to sacrifice to their god
그래서 함께 모여서,   축제를 열고   자신들의 다곤 신에게 제물을 바쳤다,

Dagon, / for they said,
             그들이 말하기를,

"Our god has delivered Samson / into our hands." While
"우리의 신이 삼손을 넘겨 주셨다   우리의 손에,"

they were merry / they said:
그들은 기뻐하며   말했다:

"Let us send for Samson / to make sport for us," / and
"삼손을 불러   재주를 부리게 합시다,"

he was brought out of the prison. It was very sad / to see
그리하여 삼손은 감옥 밖으로 끌려 나왔다.   매우 슬픈 일이었다

the strong judge of Israel, / weak and blind, / led by a
이스라엘의 강한 사사를 보는 것은,   약하고 장님이 된 채,   작은 사내에게

little lad, / and making sport for the people / in front of
끌려 나와,   사람들을 위해 재주를 부리는 모습을   그들의 신전 앞에서.

their temple. All the lords of the Philistines were there, /
모든 블레셋인들은 그곳에 있었다,

and upon the broad roof of the temple / were about three
신전의 넓은 지붕 아래

thousand people / watching Samson / while he showed
3,000명 가량의 사람이 모여
삼손을 보았다
삼손이 자신의 힘을 자랑하는

his strength, / for his hair had grown / and his strength
동안,
삼손은 머리가 자라났기 때문에
힘도 다시 돌아오는 중이었다.

was returning. At last / as he was standing between two
마침내
삼손은 두 개의 거대한 기둥 사이에 서서

great pillars / that held up the roof, / he prayed, / lifting
지붕을 받치고 있던,
기도했다,

his sightless eyes to God: /
보이지 않는 눈을 들어 하나님을 바라보며:

"O Lord God, / remember me, / I pray thee, / and
"오 하나님,
저를 기억하시고,
제 기도를 들으소서,

strengthen me only this once."
이번 한 번만 힘을 주시옵소서."

Then he clasped his arms around the pillars / on either
그리고 나서 팔로 기둥을 감싸 안고

side of him, / and bowing himself / with all his might,
좌우에 있던,
몸을 굽히며
모든 힘을 다하여,

/ saying, / "Let me die with the Philistines," / he drew
말했다,
"블레셋 사람들과 같이 죽게 하소서."

the great pillars with him, / and the house fell / with
삼손이 거대한 기둥을 끌어당기자,
건물이 무너졌다

all that were upon it, / on all that were within it. So
건물 위에 모든 것과,
건물 안에 있던 모든 것들도 함께.
그렇게

died Samson / who judged Israel / twenty years, / yet a
삼손은 죽음을 맞았다
이스라엘을 사사했던
20년 동안,

woman, Deborah, / who was also one of the judges in
하지만 드보라라는 여성은,
역시 이스라엘의 사사 중 한 명인,

Israel, / was stronger than he, / for the Lord *looketh on
삼손보다도 강했다,
주님께서는 마음 속을 꿰뚫어 보시기에.

the heart.

*looketh : look의 3인칭 단수 현재형으로 쓰였던 고어 표현

A. 다음 문장을 해석해 보세요.

(1) All who were twenty years old and upward / would die in the wilderness, / except Caleb and Joshua, / who had followed the Lord wholly.
→

(2) When the fiery serpents entered the camp / Moses lifted a brazen image of a serpent up / on a pole / so high / that it could be seen / all over the camp, / and whoever looked upon it lived.
→

(3) Some of them remembered / how they had passed / through the Red Sea, / and others had heard it / from their parents.
→

(4) Once / a young lion came / roaring against him, / and he caught it / and rent it in two, / as if it had been a kid.
→

B. 다음 주어진 문장이 되도록 빈칸에 써 넣으세요.

(1) 그들 중 두 사람이 그것을 막대기에 꿰어 가지고 왔다.

→

(2) 먹는 자에게서 먹는 것이 나오고, 강한 자에게서, 단 것이 나왔느니라.

→

(3) 그는 긴 인생의 마지막을 앞두고 있었다.

→

(4) 주님께서 여호수아에게 말씀하시길 <u>사람들에게 마지막 여행을 준비시키라</u>고 하셨다.

A. (1) 주님을 온전히 따랐던 갈렙과 여호수아 외에는, 스무 살이 넘은 사람들은 모두 황무지에서 죽으리라. (2) 사나운 뱀이 야영지에 들어왔을 때 모세는 놋으로 만든 뱀을 장대 위에 세웠는데 매우 높아서 야영지 전체에서 보였고, 그것을 본 사람들은 모두 살아났다. (3) 몇몇 사람들은 자신들이 어떻게 홍해를 가르고 건넜는지 기억하고 있었고, 다른 사람들은 부모로부터

164 The Story of the Bible

The Lord told Joshua _____

_____ .

C. 다음 주어진 문구가 알맞은 문장이 되도록 순서를 맞춰 보세요.

(1) 만약 머리를 깎는다면 그도 다른 사람들처럼 힘이 약해질 것이다.
(weak / should be / If / as / he / other men / would be / as / it / cut)
→

(2) 그들은 주님과 그분의 종 여호수아에게 순종하기만 하면 되었다.
(They / had / only / to / obey / the Lord / and / his servant / Joshua)
→

(3) 아무도 보이지 않았다.
(one / be / was / There / seen / to / no)
→

(4) 누구도 모세가 죽는 것을 보지 못했고, 그가 묻힌 곳도 알지 못했다.
(knows / saw / was buried / Moses / and / no one / No one / die, / he / where)
→

D. 다음 단어에 대한 맞는 설명과 연결해 보세요.

(1) fiery　　▶　　◀ ① act of saving them from harm, destruction

(2) salvation　　▶　　◀ ② a person that opposes or resists

(3) adversary　　▶　　◀ ③ intensely impetuous, or passionate

(4) clasp　　▶　　◀ ④ to seize with the hand

터 그 이야기를 들었다. (4) 한번은 어린 사자가 삼손에게 으르렁거리며 다가오자, 삼손은 마치 사자가 어린 아이인듯 사자를 잡아 둘로 찢어 죽여버렸다. | B. (1) Two of them bore it on a staff between them. (2) Out of the eater came forth meat, and out of the strong, came forth sweetness. (3) He was near the end of his long life (4) to prepare the people for their last journey | C. (1) If it should be cut he would be as weak as other men. (2) They had only to obey the Lord and his servant. (3) There was no one to be seen. (4) No one saw Moses die, / and no one knows where he was buried. | D. (1) ③ (2) ① (3) ② (4) ④

165

RUTH
룻

In the days when the judges ruled in Israel, / there was
사사들이 이스라엘을 다스리던 시대에,

a famine in the land, / and an Israelite, / who lived in
그 땅에 흉년이 있었다,　　　　　　그래서 한 이스라엘인이,　　　베들레헴에 살던,

Bethlehem, / took his wife and his two sons into Moab /
부인과 두 아들을 이끌고 모압으로 갔다

where there was food. After a while the Israelite died, /
먹을 것이 있었던.　　　　　　그가 죽고 얼마 후,

and the two sons married women of Moab.
두 아들은 모압 여자와 결혼했다.

After two years / the sons died also, / and their mother, /
2년 후　　　　　　두 아들 역시 죽자,　　　어머니인,

Naomi, / longed for her home in Bethlehem, / for there was
나오미는,　　　베들레헴에 있는 집이 그리워졌다,

no longer a famine there. So she took Ruth and Orpah, /
그곳의 흉년이 끝났기에.　　　　　　그래서 룻과 오르바를 데리고,

her sons' wives, / and started on the journey / into the land
며느리인,　　　　　　여행을 시작했다

of Israel.
이스라엘 땅으로.

But before they had gone far / Naomi said; /
하지만 얼마 가지 않아　　　　　　나오미가 말했다;

"Go! Return each to her mother's house; / the Lord deal
"가거라! 너희 친정으로 돌아가거라;

kindly with you, / as ye have dealt / with the dead, and
하나님께서 은혜를 베푸시길,　너희가 대했던 것처럼,　　　죽은 너희 남편과 내게."

with me."

She kissed them, / and they wept / and would not leave her.
나오미가 그들에게 입맞추자,　며느리들은 울면서　　　시어머니를 떠나려 하지 않았다.

---

deal 대하다 | logde 거주하다 | aught 어떤 것(=anything)

"Turn again, / my daughters," / she said, / "why will ye
"돌아가거라,   딸들아."   나오미가 말했다. "어째서 나와 함께

go with me?"
가려 하느냐?"

And Orpah kissed Naomi, / and went back to her own
그러자 오르바는 시어머니에게 입맞춘 후,   친정으로 돌아갔다.

mothers' house, / but Ruth, / whose heart was with
하지만 룻은,   마음이 시어머니에게 있었기에,

Naomi, / would not go back.
돌아가려 하지 않았다.

"Entreat me not to leave thee," / she said, / "or to return
"어머니를 떠나라고 강요하지 마세요."   룻이 말했다.

from following after thee, / for where thou goest / I will
"따라오지 말고 돌아가라 하지도 마세요.   어머니가 가는 곳이면   저도 가겠습

go; / and where thou lodgest / I will lodge; / thy people
니다; 또 어머니가 사시는 곳에서   저도 살겠어요;

shall be my people, / and thy God my God; / where thou
어머니의 백성이 제 백성이며,   어머니의 하나님이 제 하나님이 되실 겁니다; 어머니가 돌아가

diest / I will die, / and there will I be buried; / the Lord
시는 곳에서   저도 죽을 것이고, 그곳에 묻힐 것입니다;   주님께서 저를

do so to me, / and more also, / if aught but death part
데려가신다면.   더 무서운 벌을 내리시길,   죽음 외에 어떤 것이 우리 사이를 갈라

thee and me."
놓는다면."

Key Expression 🎯

here/there 도치구문

장소를 나타내는 부사인 here/there가 문장 맨 앞에 올 경우 뒤따르는 주어
와 동사가 도치됩니다. 단 주어가 대명사일 경우에는 'Here you are.'처럼 도
치가 일어나지 않아요.

▶ Here/There + 동사 + 명사 주어
▶ Here/There + 대명사 주어 + 동사

ex) Where thou diest I will die, and there will I be buried
    당신이 죽는 곳에서 나도 죽을 것이며, 그곳에 묻힐 것입니다.
    Wherever the Ark went among the Philistines, there went also trouble and
    death.
    블레셋 땅 안에서 언약궤가 가는 곳이면 어디든지, 어려움과 죽음 또한 따라
    다녔다.

And so they came to Bethlehem, / and the old friends of
그래서 두 사람은 함께 베들레헴으로 갔다,　　　나오미의 오랜 친구가

Naomi / greeted her tenderly, / and welcomed her back.
　　　　장냥하게 반기며,　　　　친구가 돌아온 것을 환영했다.

It was about the beginning of the barley harvest.
때는 보리 추수가 막 시작될 무렵이었다.

There was a good and great man / in Bethlehem / named
선하고 훌륭한 사람이 있었는데　　　　　베들레헴에는　　　보아스라는

Boaz, / and he was of the family of Naomi's husband. He
이름의,　　그는 나오미 남편의 친척이었다.

had a field of barley / where the reapers were at work, /
보아스에게는 보리밭이 있었는데　일꾼들이 수확 중인,

and Ruth asked Naomi / if she should not go and glean /
룻이 나오미에게 물었다　　　　자신이 주우러 가야 할지

after the reapers, / to get grain, / for they were poor.
일꾼을 따라,　　　　곡식을 얻기 위해,　그들은 가난했기에.

Naomi said, / "Go, / my daughter," / and she went.
나오미가 말하자,　"가거라,　내 딸아,"　룻이 떠났다.

When Boaz came out of the town into his field / and
보아스는 읍내에서 나와 밭으로 가서

greeted his reapers, / he said to his servant / having
일꾼에게 인사하며,　　　　하인에게 말했다

charge of the reapers, /
추수 일꾼을 감독하던,

"What maiden is this?" / and he told him / that she was
"저 여자는 누구냐?"　　　그러자 감독관이 말했다

the Moabitish girl / who had come back with her mother-
그 여자는 모압 여자로　시어머니인 나오미와 돌아왔다고.

in-law Naomi.

barley 보리 | harvest 추수 | reaper 수확하는 사람 | glean 얻다, 모으다 | charge 담당 | mother-in-law
시어머니 | reward 보답 | parch 건조시키다 | reprove 나무라다, 책망하다 | handful 줌, 움큼

Then Boaz spoke very kindly to Ruth, / and told her to
그러자 보아스가 룻에게 친절하게 말을 걸며,　　　　　하녀들과 함께 머물면서,

stay with his maidens, / and freely drink of the water /
자유롭게 물을 마시라고 했다

drawn for them, / and Ruth bowed before him and asked
그녀들을 위해 담겨 있는,　　그러자 룻은 보아스에게 절을 하고 물었다

/ why he should be so kind to a stranger. He told her /
이방인에게 그토록 친절하게 대하는 이유가 무엇인지.　　보아스는 말했다

that he knew / all her kindness to her mother-in-law /
알고 있다고　　룻이 시어머니에게 한 친절한 행동을

since the death of her husband, / and how she had left
남편이 죽은 이후에,

her own family and country / to come among strangers, /
룻이 어떻게 자신의 가족과 조국을 떠나　　이방인들의 땅으로 왔는지,

and he blessed her, / saying, /
보아스는 룻을 축복하며,　　말했다,

"A full reward be given thee / of the Lord God of Israel, /
"당신에게 보답이 있기를　　이스라엘 하나님의,

under whose wings / thou art come to trust."
그분의 날개 아래에서　　당신이 믿고자 하는."

Then he told her to sit down / and eat bread with them,
그리고 나서 보아스는 룻에게 앉으라며　　함께 빵을 먹자고 했고,

/ and he helped her / to the parched corn / with his own
그녀를 도와　　옥수수를 말렸다　　자신의 손으로,

hands, / and when they returned to work / he told his
그리고 사람들이 일하러 돌아가자

young men / to let her glean among the sheaves / and
일꾼들에게 말했다　　룻이 곡식단 사이에서 이삭을 줍게 하고

reprove her not, / and to let some handfuls fall purposely
나무라지 말것이며,　　일부러 이삭을 몇 줌 떨어뜨려

/ for her to glean. When Ruth went home / Naomi said, /
룻이 모을 수 있도록 하라고. 룻이 집으로 돌아오자　　나오미가 말했다,

"Where hast thou gleaned to-day?" / and Ruth told her.
"오늘 어디에서 이삭을 주웠느냐?"　　그러자 룻이 대답했다.

Then Naomi blessed Boaz, / and told Ruth / that he was
나오미는 보아스를 축복하며,   룻에게 말했다

one of their near relatives.
그는 가까운 친척이라고.

And so Ruth gleaned in the fields of Boaz / through all
그렇게 룻은 보아스의 밭에서 이삭을 주웠다

the barley and the wheat harvest. When all the reaping
보리와 밀을 추수하는 기간 내내.   추수가 모두 끝나자,

was done, / the grain was threshed / on a piece of ground
곡식을 타작했고   작은 땅에서

/ made very smooth and level. The sheaves were beaten,
평평하고 부드럽게 만들어 놓은.   곡식단을 두들기고,

/ and then the straw was taken away, / and the grain and
지푸라기를 버린 후,   그 밑에 있던 알곡과 왕겨를

chaff below it / was winnowed. By this / the chaff was
키질로 골라냈다.   이런 과정을 통해

blown away / and only the grain was left.
왕겨는 날아가고   알곡만 남겨졌다.

When Boaz winnowed his barley / Naomi told Ruth / to
보아스가 보리를 키질하고 있을 때   나오미가 룻에게 말했다

go down to his threshing floor / and see him / for he had
보아스가 타작 중인 바닥에 내려가서   그를 보라고

a feast for his friends.
친구를 위한 만찬을 열었기에.

So after the feast / Ruth came near to him and said, /
만찬이 끝난 후   룻은 보아스에게 다가가 말했다,

"Thou art our near kinsman," / and Boaz said, /
"당신은 우리의 가까운 친척입니다."   그러자 보아스가 말했다,

"May the Lord bless thee my daughter," / and with many
"주님께서 축복하시길 내 딸이여,"   그리고 친절하게 이야기

kind words / he gave her six measures of barley / to take
하며   보리 여섯 되를 주고

to Naomi.
나오미에게 가져다 주라고 했다.

relative 친척 | thresh 타작하다 | level 평평한 | chaff 왕겨 | winnow 키질하다 | kinsman 일가, 친척 |
court 궁정, 조정

Boaz remembered / that it was the custom in Israel / for
보아스는 기억하고 있었다   이스라엘의 풍습이라는 사실을

the nearest relative of a man who had died, / to take care
죽은 남편의 가까운 친척이,

of the wife who was left, / and so he went to the gate of
남겨진 부인을 돌보는 것이,   그래서 그는 베들레헴의 문으로 가서

Bethlehem / where the rulers met to hold their court, /
통치자들이 회의를 하기 위해 모여 있던,

and spoke to the elders and chief men about Ruth. He
장로과 지도자에게 룻에 대해 말했다.

also wished them to be witnesses / that he was going to
보아스는 또한 그들이 증인이 되어 주길 바랐다   자신이 룻을 데려가 아내로 삼는

take Ruth to be his wife. Then the rulers all said, /
것에 대해.   그러자 통치자들이 모두 말했다,

"We are witnesses," / and they prayed / that God would
"우리가 증인이요,"   그들은 기도했다   하나님이 룻을 축복시키고

bless Ruth / and make Boaz still richer and greater.
보아스를 더욱 부유하고 큰 사람이 되게 해 달라고.

Key Expression

It ~ for … to 가주어-진주어 구문

명사적 용법으로 쓰인 to 부정사가 너무 길 경우 주어 자리에 it을 놓고 to 부정사를 맨 뒤로 보내는 가주어-진주어 구문으로 사용합니다.
이때 to 부정사의 행위 주체를 표현려면 to 앞에 'for + 목적격'을 삽입하여 의미상 주어를 나타냅니다.
또한 진주어에는 to 부정사 외에 동명사와 that절, 의문사절 등의 명사절도 올 수 있습니다.

ex) It was the custom in Israel for the nearest relative of a man who had died, to take care of the wife who was left.
죽은 남편의 가까운 친척이 남겨진 부인을 돌보는 것이 이스라엘의 풍습이었다.
It was clear that David could not live near the king.
왕의 곁에서 살 수 없다는 것이 분명했다.

171

So Ruth became the honored and beloved wife of Boaz, /
그렇게 룻은 보아스의 명예롭고 사랑스러운 부인이 되었고,

and they had a son named Obed.
오벳이라는 이름의 아들을 낳았다.

Obed grew up / and had a son named Jesse; / and Jesse
오벳은 커서   이새라는 아들을 낳았는데;

was the father of David, King of Israel, / who was first a
이새는 이스라엘의 왕, 다윗의 아버지였다.

shepherd lad of Bethlehem.
베들레헴의 첫 어린 목동이었던.

More than a thousand years after Ruth lived / there was
천 년이 넘게 흐른 후

born in Bethlehem, / of the family of Boaz and Ruth, / a
베들레헴에 태어났다.   보아스와 룻의 혈통을 지닌,

little Child, / who came, to be the Saviour of the world, /
한 아기가,   그는 세상의 구원자가 되기 위해 왔으며,

and the shepherds in the fields, / where, / perhaps, / Ruth
들판의 목동이 되었다.   그 들판에서, 어쩌면, 룻이 이

gleaned, / and David kept his sheep, / heard the angels
삭을 주웠던,   다윗이 양을 지키며,

tell the good news and sing
천사들의 소식과 노래를 들었을지 모른다

"Peace on earth, / good will to men."
"땅에는 평화를,   인간에게 선의를."

Key Expression ♟

once every year : 매년 한 번씩

'모든'이란 의미를 가진 every가 hour, day, week, month, year 등 때를 나타내는 명사와 함께 쓰이면 '매 ~마다'라는 의미의 빈도를 나타내며 every 앞에 once, twice, three times 등을 삽입해 횟수를 표현합니다.

ex) Once every year the tribes came to it to worship and offer sacrifices.
매년 한 번씩 각 지파의 사람이 찾아와 예배를 드리고 제물을 바쳤다.

✠ 17 ✠

SAMUEL — THE CHILD OF THE TEMPLE
사무엘 — 성전의 아이

The Tabernacle / that was built in the wilderness, / and
성막은   황무지에 지었다가,

was brought into Canaan / by the priests / was set up /
가나안으로 가져온   제사장들이   설치됐다

at Shiloh in the very centre of the land of Canaan, / and
가나안 땅 한가운데에 있는 실로에,

once every year / the tribes came to it / to worship and
그리고 매년 한 번씩   각 지파의 사람이 찾아와   예배를 드리고 제물을

offer sacrifices. After it had come to Shiloh to stay / it
바쳤다.   실로에 세워진 후

was called the temple.
성막은 회당이라 불리게 되었다.

When Eli was high priest / a man named Elkanah came
엘리가 대제사장이었을 때   엘가나라는 이름의 사람이 찾아왔고

up / from Ramah / to worship, / and Hannah his wife
라마에서   예배하러,   부인인 한나도

/ went with him. She was a good woman, / and very
남편과 함께 왔다.   한나는 선한 여자로,

sorrowful, / because she saw other wives / with sons and
슬픔이 가득했다.   다른 부인을 보았기 때문에

daughters around them, / and she had none. Her husband
아들과 딸을 데리고 온,   한나에게는 자녀가 없었다.   남편은 사랑스럽고

was loving and kind / and said; /
다정한 사람으로   말했다;

"Am I not better to thee / than ten sons?" / but she
"내가 당신에게 더 낫지 않은가   열 아들보다?"

prayed to God for a son. While she was at Shiloh / she
하지만 한나는 아들을 달라고 기도했다.   실로에 있는 동안

prayed in the temple, / and Eli saw her lips move, /
한나는 회당에서 기도를 드렸고,   엘리는 그녀의 입술이 움직이는 것을 보았다,

honored 명예로운 | temple 성전, 신전, 사원 | high priest 대제사장

though he heard no voice. At first / he spoke harshly to
목소리는 들리지 않았지만.   처음에   엘리는 한나에게 거칠게 말했다,

her, / thinking she had been drinking wine, / but she told
한나가 포도주를 마셨다고 생각하여,   그러나 한나는

him / that she had not taken wine, / but was praying.
말했다   자신은 포도주를 마시지 않았고,   기도 중이었다고.

"I am a woman of sorrowful spirit," / she said, / "and
"저는 슬픔을 가진 여자입니다,"   한나가 말했다.

have poured out my soul / before the Lord." Then Eli
"제 마음을 쏟아냈습니다   주님께."   그러자 엘리는

blessed her / and said; /
한나를 축복하며   말했다:

"Go in peace, / and the God of Israel grant thee the
"평화가 있으리,   이스라엘의 하나님이 당신의 기도에 답하시기를

prayer / that thou hast asked of him." Then Hannah was
그분께 드린 청에."   그러자 한나는 더 이상 슬프지

no longer sad.
않았다.

Her prayer was answered, / and the Lord sent her a little
한나의 기도는 이뤄져서,   주님께서 아들을 보내셨다.

son, / and when he was old enough, / she took him to the
그리고 아들이 충분히 자라자,   한나는 아들을 회당에 데려가,

temple, / for she had promised the Lord / that the child
주님께 약속했기 때문에   아들은 주님의 아이라고.

should be His. So Elkanah came bringing sacrifices, /
그래서 엘가나는 제물을 가져왔고,

and the young child was with them. Hannah told Eli /
아들도 함께 데려왔다.   한나는 엘리에게 말했다

that she was the woman / whom he saw / praying in the
자신이 그 사람이라고   그가 보았던   성전에서 기도하던 모습을.

temple.

pour 쏟다, 따르다 | grant 승인하다, 인정하다

"For the child I prayed," / she said, / "and the Lord
"아이를 달라고 기도를 드렸더니," 한나가 말했다,

has answered my prayer. Therefore I have lent him to
"주님이 기도에 응답하셨습니다. 그래서 주님께 아이를 드리기로 했습니다;

the Lord; / as long as he lives / he shall be lent to the
살아있는 동안 아들은 주님께 드린 사람입니다."

Lord." Eli was very glad / and gave thanks to the Lord,
엘리는 매우 기뻐하며 주님께 감사드리며,

/ and took the little boy to help him / in the service of
아이를 데려가 자신을 돕게 했다 회당의 예배에서.

the temple. Every year / his father and mother came /
매년 아이의 부모가 와서

to bring offerings to the Lord, / and his mother always
주님께 제물을 드렸고, 항상 아이에게 가져왔다

brought him / a little coat which she had made.
자신이 만든 외투를.

Over it / was a linen garment / called an ephod, / such
그 외투 위에 마로 만든 의복을 입었다 에봇이라 불리는,

as the priests wore. Eli was an old man, / and his sons,
제사장이 입었던 것과 같은. 엘리는 나이가 많았고, 그의 아들은,

/ though they were priests, / were not good men, / and
역시 제사장이었지만, 선한 사람이 아니었다,

he believed / the Lord had sent him / one who would be
그래서 그는 믿었고 주님께서 보내셨다고 선한 사람을,

good, / so he loved little Samuel / as if he were his own.
어린 사무엘을 사랑했다 친자식처럼.

One night / when Eli was laid down to sleep, / and
어느 날 밤 엘리가 자려고 누웠을 때,

Samuel also, / while the light was still burning / in the
사무엘도 누웠다, 불이 아직 타고 있을 때

golden candlestick before the Ark, / Samuel heard a
언약궤 앞에 놓인 황금 촛대에서, 사무엘은 자신을 부르는

voice calling him, / and he answered, / "Here am I," /
목소리가 들리자, 대답한 후, "저 여기 있습니다"라고,

and ran to see / what Eli wanted. But Eli said / that he
달려가서 알아보았다　　엘리가 원하는 것이 뭔지.　　하지만 엘리가 말하자　자신은 부르지

had not called, / and Samuel lay down again. When the
않았다고.　　　　　사무엘은 다시 자리에 누웠다.

voice called again, / Samuel went again to Eli's bed, / but
부르는 소리가 다시 들리자.　　사무엘은 또 엘리에게 갔지만.

Eli told him / to lie down again, / for he had not called
엘리는 말했다　　다시 가서 자라고.　　　부른 적이 없으니.

him. When the voice called the third time, / Samuel said;
　　세 번째로 목소리가 부르는 소리가 들리자.　　　　　사무엘이 말했다;

/ "Here am I, / for thou didst call me."
　"여기 왔습니다.　　부르셨기에."

Then Eli told the boy to lie down / once more, / but if he
그러자 엘리는 가서 자라고 하며　　　　또 다시.

heard the voice again / to say, /
다시 한 번 목소리가 들리면　　말하라 했다.

"Speak Lord, / for thy servant heareth."
"주님 말씀하소서.　　당신의 종이 듣겠나이다."라고

And when the voice called again, / "Samuel, Samuel," /
목소리가 다시 들리자.　　　　　"사무엘아, 사무엘아,"라는

the boy answered, /
소년이 대답했다.

"Speak Lord, / for thy servant heareth."
"주님 말씀하소서.　　주의 종이 듣겠나이다."

Then the Lord told Samuel / that the sons of Eli had
그러자 주님이 사무엘에게 말씀하셨다　　엘리의 아들들이 매우 사악해졌고.

become very wicked, / and their father had not kept them
　　　　　　　　　그 아비는 아들을 지키지 못했기에

/ from the evil, / and therefore / He could not accept their
　악으로부터.　　　따라서　　　　그들의 제물을 받아들일 수 없다고.

offerings.

---

lend 빌려 주다 | ephod 에봇, 유대 제사장의 제의(祭衣)

When Eli asked Samuel / what the Lord had said to him,
엘리가 사무엘에게 묻자   주님이 하신 말씀이 무엇인지,

/ the boy told him all / and hid nothing from him, / and
사무엘은 모든 것을 이야기 하며   아무것도 감추지 않았고,

Eli bowed his spirit before the Lord, / and said; /
그러자 엘리는 주님께 절을 하며, 말했다:

"It is the Lord, / let Him do what seemeth Him good."
"주님이시여,   당신께서 좋아 보이는 대로 행하소서."

After this / all the people of Israel knew / that the Lord
이 일이 있은 후   이스라엘의 모든 사람이 알게 되었다

had called Samuel to be a prophet. And as he grew up
주님이 사무엘을 선지자로서 부르셨음을.   사무엘이 성장하자

/ the Lord was with him, / and he was a judge over his
주님은 그와 함께하셨고,   사무엘은 사사가 되었다

people / all his life.
일생 동안.

As for Eli and his sons, / the word of the Lord soon came
엘리와 그의 아들에 대한,   주님의 말씀은 곧 사실이 되었다.

true. When the Philistines came / against the Israelites in
블레셋 사람들이 침입하여   이스라엘에 맞서서 전투가 벌어졌을 때,

battle, / the Elders of Israel said; /
이스라엘의 장로들이 말했다:

"Let us bring the Ark of the Lord / out of Shiloh to us,
"주님의 언약궤를 가져오자   실로에서 우리 쪽으로,

/ that it may save us / out of the hand of our enemies."
그것이 우리를 구할 것이다   적의 손으로부터,"

And so they took it / from the holy place / to the camp
그래서 그들은 언약궤를 가져갔다 거룩한 곳으로부터   이스라엘 진영으로.

of Israel. Then the Philistines fell upon the camp / and
그러자 블레셋 사람들이 진영에 들이닥쳐

scattered the men of Israel. They also took the Ark of
이스라엘 백성을 흩어놓았다.   그들은 하나님의 언약궤도 가져갔고,

God, / and the two sons of Eli were among the thousands
엘리의 두 아들은 수천 명의 시체 속에 있었다.

slain.

Eli, / who trembled for the Ark of God, / sat outside the
엘리는, 언약궤 때문에 떨고 있던, 성문 밖 길가에 앉아

city gate, by the wayside / watching. He was nearly a
지켜보고 있었다. 그는 100세가 다 되어,

hundred years old, / and his eyes were dim, / but when a
눈이 어두웠다,

messenger came with the bad news, / he fell backward in
하지만 나쁜 소식이 도착하자, 그만 의자에서 뒤로 넘어져

his seat / and died. His heart was broken.
죽어버렸다. 그의 마음이 무너져버린 것이다.

Where was Samuel? Perhaps he was praying / in the
사무엘은 어디에 있었을까? 어쩌면 기도하고 있었을지도 모른다

temple / for the return of the Ark of the Covenant.
회당에서 언약궤가 돌아오기를 바라며.

Wherever the Ark went among the Philistines, / there
언약궤가 블레셋 땅 어디에 가든지,

went also trouble and death. When they put it / in the
죽음과 소동 또한 따라다녔다. 언약궤를 놓자

temple of their fish-god Dagon, / the great idol fell down
물고기의 신인 다곤 신전에, 거대한 신상이 무너져

before it / and was broken. And when it was taken to
부서져 버렸다. 또 다른 도시로 가져가자,

another city, / the people were smitten with sickness, /
사람들이 질병으로 고통 받았다.

until at last the Philistines said; /
그리하여 마침내 블레셋 사람들이 말했다;

"Send away the Ark of the God of Israel, / and let it go to
"이스라엘 하나님의 궤를 보내라,

its own place."
원래의 땅으로 보내라."

---

prophet 예언자, 선지자 | as for ~에 대해 말하자면 | fall upon ~에게 덤벼들다 | slay 죽이다, 살인하다 |
smitten 엄습당한, 고통받는

After seven months / they sent it / with gifts of gold / to
7개월 후　　　그들은 궤를 보냈다　선물로 금덩어리도 함께

the Israelites. They placed it / on a new cart drawn by
이스라엘로.　언약궤를 올려놓자　소 두 마리가 끄는 새 수레 위에,

two cows, / and the cows, / guided by the Lord alone, /
소들은,　　　　주님의 인도를 받아,

took a straight way / into the land of Israel. How glad the
곧장 향했다　　이스라엘 땅으로.　　백성들이 얼마나 기뻐

people were / when they looked up from their reaping
했을까　　추수하다가 고개를 들었을 때

/ in the fields, / and saw the Ark coming safely back to
밭에서,　　언약궤가 안전하게 돌아오는 모습을 발견하고.

them. The Philistines watched it from afar to see / if it
블레셋 사람들은 멀리서 지켜본 후

would be guided of God to its own place or not / and
하나님이 언약궤의 땅으로 인도하시는지를

then they returned to their city.
자신들의 도시로 돌아갔다.

Samuel gathered the people to the Lord / after this, / and
사무엘은 백성을 모아 하나님께 갔다　　　　그 후에,

though they had sinned greatly, / and had gone after the
그들은 비록 큰 죄를 지었고,　　　　신을 따랐지만,

gods / of the heathen around them, / they repented / and
주변의 이방인들이 믿는,　　　회개한 후

returned to the faith of their fathers, / and were faithful
선조의 믿음으로 돌아왔고,　　　　믿음을 지켰다

/ all the days of Samuel. He went from year to year on a
사무엘이 다스리는 시기 내내.　사무엘은 매년 여행을 떠나

journey / to three cities of Israel, / and judged the people
이스라엘의 도시 세 곳으로,　　그 땅의 사람들을 다스렸지만,

in those places, / but his home was in Ramah, / the city
그의 집은 라마에 있었다.

where he was born, / and where Hannah had brought
그곳은 자신이 태어난 도시이며,　한나가 그를 기른 곳이었다

him up / for the Lord.
주님을 위해.

cart 수레, 우마차 | bribe 뇌물 | reign 통치하다, 다스리다

18

THE MAKING OF A KING
왕이 만들어지기까지

When Samuel was old / he made his sons judges / in his
사무엘은 나이가 들자   아들들을 사사로 세웠는데   자신을

place, / but they were not holy men / like their father.
대신하여,   그들은 독실한 사람이 아니었다   제 아비처럼.

They loved money, / and would judge unjustly, / if
그들은 돈을 좋아하여,   공정하게 심판하지 않았다,

money were given to them as a bribe. So the people
뇌물로 돈을 받은 경우에는.   그래서 사람들이 사무엘에게

came to Samuel / at Ramah / and said, /
찾아와   라마에 있는   말했다.

"Give us a king to judge us."
"우리를 다스릴 왕을 주옵소서."

And Samuel prayed to the Lord, / and the Lord told him
사무엘이 주님께 기도를 드리자,   주님께서는 하라고 하셨다

to do / as the people had asked him to do, / for they had
백성들이 요구하는 대로,   백성들은 사사로서의

not rejected him as judge, / but the Lord as their King,
사무엘을 거부하는 것이 아니라,   주님을 왕으로 섬기는 것을 거부하는 것이라고,

/ and now they must learn / what kind of a king would
그래서 이제 알아야 한다고   어떤 왕이 백성들을 통치하게 될지.

reign over them. So Samuel told them / what they must
그래서 사무엘은 사람들에게 말했다   무엇을 준비해야 하는지

be ready to do / for their King, / for a king was often
왕을 맞기 위해,   왜냐하면 왕이란 때로는 가혹한

a hard master, / and ruled his people cruelly, / taking
통치차라서,   잔혹하게 백성을 다스리고,

the best of their fields, and their harvests, and their
밭이나 수확물, 가축 중 가장 좋은 것을 취해

flocks / for themselves, / and the finest of their sons and
자신의 것으로 삼고,   훌륭한 아들 딸을 택해

daughters / to be his servants; / but they said, /
종으로 삼을 것이라고;   하지만 사람들은 말했다,

"We will have a king over us, / that we may be like other
"우리를 다스릴 왕을 갖겠습니다, / 다른 나라와 비슷해질 수 있도록,

nations, / and that our king may judge us, / and go out
/ 그러면 왕은 우리를 다스리고, / 우리 앞에서 이끌고

before us / and fight our battles."
/ 전투에서 싸우겠지요."

When Samuel told these things to the Lord / he said, /
사무엘이 이런 백성의 말을 주님께 전하자 / 주님이 말씀하셨다,

"Make them a king," / and Samuel sent the people / to
"그들에게 왕을 세우라," / 그래서 사무엘은 백성들을 보냈다 /

their own cities.
그들 각자의 도시로.

Key Expression

not A but B : A가 아니라 B

not A but B는 'A가 아니라 B'의 의미로 쓰이는 구문입니다. 이처럼 짝을 이루어 쓰이는 접속사를 상관접속사라고 합니다. 이때 A와 B에는 같은 형태의 단어나 구, 절이 와야 합니다.
또한 상관접속사 구문이 주어로 쓰일 경우에는 인칭과 수의 일치에 주의해야 합니다. not A but B는 'A가 아니라 B'라는 뜻이므로 뒤에 오는 B에 인칭 및 수를 일치시켜야 합니다.

▶ both A and B : A와 B 둘 다 (항상 복수)
▶ either A or B : A 또는 B 둘 중의 하나 (단수/B에 일치)
▶ neither A nor B : A도 아니고 B도 아닌 (단수/B에 일치)
▶ not only A but also B : A뿐 아니라 B도(복수/B에 일치)
▶ A as well as B : B뿐 아니라 A도(복수/A에 일치)
▶ not A but B : A가 아니라 B(B에 일치)

ex) Samuel did not choose a king for the people himself, but he waited for the Lord to send him the man He had chosen.
사무엘은 백성을 위해 스스로 왕을 선택하지 않고, 주님께서 선택하신 사람을 보내시길 기다렸다.
He never forgot that his work was not to build the temple of the Lord, but to prepare for it.
다윗은 자신의 일은 성전을 짓는 것이 아니라, 그 일을 준비하는 것임을 결코 잊지 않았다.
Victory over the enemy was not with the many or the few, but with the Lord.
적에 대한 승리는 적의 수가 많고 적음이 아니라, 주님께 달려 있다.

anoint 기름을 붓다(종교 의식에서 머리에 성유를 바르는 행동을 일컫는 말로 주님의 임명을 받음을 의미함) | noble
귀한, 당당한 | seer 예언자, 현인

Samuel did not choose a king / for the people / himself, /
사무엘은 왕을 선택하지 않고　　　　　　백성을 위해　　　　　스스로,

but he waited for the Lord to send him / the man He had
주님을 보내시길 기다렸다　　　　　　　　　　　　　　선택한 사람을,

chosen, / and the Lord said to him / as he went to a city
　　　　그러자 주님이 말씀하셨다　　　　　제프로 가서,

called Zeph, / to hold a sacrifice, /
　　　　　　　제물을 준비하라고,

"To-morrow about this time / I will send thee a man /
"내일 이맘때 쯤　　　　　　　　네게 한 남자를 보낼 것이니

from the land of Benjamin, / and thou shalt anoint him /
베냐민 지파 중에서,　　　　　　　그에게 기름을 부어

to be captain over my people Israel."
이스라엘 백성의 수장으로 삼아라."

On the next day / as Samuel came out to go up / to the
이튿날　　　　　　사무엘이 오르고 있을 때

hill of sacrifice / he met a tall, noble looking young man,
희생에 언덕에　　　　키가 크고 고귀한 외모의 젊은이를 만났다,

/ who, / with his servant, / was looking for the lost asses
　그는,　　종과 함께,　　　잃어버린 아비의 나귀를 찾고 있었다,

of his father, / Kish, the Benjaminite. He had come far, /
베냐민 지파의, 기스였다.　　　그는 멀리까지 왔고

and had heard / that Samuel, / the seer was in that place,
들은 적이 있었기에,　　사무엘이라는,　　선견자가 그곳에 있다는 사실을,

/ and he hoped he would tell him / where to go / for the
　선견자에게 듣고 싶었다　　　　　　어디로 가야 하는지

asses that were lost.
잃어버린 나귀를 찾으려면.

Samuel knew from the Lord / that this was the man God
사무엘은 주님에게 들어 알고 있었고　　　그가 하나님이 선택하신 사람임을,

had chosen, / so he told him to go up with him / to the
　　　　　그래서 함께 올라가자고 했다

sacrifice, / and the next day / he would let him go.
제사를 드리러,　그러면 이튿날에　　　보내 주겠다고.

He told him / that he need not be troubled / about the
사무엘은 말했다   고생할 필요없다고   나귀 때문에,

asses, / for they were found, / but the desire of Israel
찾았기 때문에,   하지만 이스라엘 백성의 바람이

was set upon him. Saul, / for that was his name, / did
그에게 닿았다고.   사울은,   그 사내의 이름인데,

not understand him / until he was invited to feast / with
사무엘의 말을 이해하지 못했다   만찬에 초대되기 전까지는

thirty of the chief men, / and Samuel had talked with
서른 명의 족장과 함께,   그리고 사무엘은 그와 이야기 했다

him / upon the house-top. Early the next morning / they
      지붕 위에서.   이튿날 아침 일찍   두 사람

both rose / and went out of the city, / and while Saul sent
은 일어나서   도시 밖으로 나갔다.   사울이 종을 먼저 보내자,

his servant on before, / Samuel anointed Saul with oil, /
                           사무엘은 사울에게 기름을 붓고,

and kissed him saying, / that the Lord had anointed him /
입을 맞추며 말했다,   주님께서 그에게 기름을 부으셨다고

to be Captain / over his inheritance.
이스라엘의 왕이 되라고 자신의 뒤를 이어.

As a sign that the Lord had done it, / he told Saul three
주님이 직접 하셨다는 증표로,   사무엘은 사울에게 세 가지를

things / that would happen to him / on the way home, /
이야기 한 후 그에게 일어날   집으로 돌아가는 동안,

and charged him to go to Gilgal, / where he would meet
그를 길갈로 보냈다.   그곳에서 사무엘이 그를 만나

him / and sacrifice to the Lord / for seven days. As Saul
      주님께 제사를 드릴 것이라고   7일 동안.

turned to leave the prophet, / God gave him another
사울이 돌아서서 선견자를 떠나자,   하나님은 그에게 또 다른 확신을 주셨고,

heart, / and all the signs came to pass / that day.
          모든 징조가 일어났다   그 날에.

---

desire 욕구, 바람 | house-top 지붕 | inheritance 상속 | body 단체, 소단체가 | kingdom 왕국 | lay up
모으다

At Mizpah / Samuel called all the tribes together, / that
미스바에서는　　사무엘이 모든 지파를 불러 모아 말했다:

the man who was to be their king, / might be chosen /
왕이 될 남자가,　　　　　　　　선택될 것이라고

in their sight, / and when Saul, / the son of Kish, / the
여러분이 보는 앞에서,　　그리고 그때 사울이,　　기스의 아들인,

Benjaminite / was chosen / he could not be found; / he
베냐민 지파의　　선택되었는데　　그를 찾을 수 없었다:

had hidden from the people; / but when they brought him
사울은 백성 뒤에 숨어버린 것이었다:　　사람들이 사울을 앞으로 데리고 나오자,

out before them, / he was taller than any of the people /
그는 그 누구보다 키가 훨씬 커서

from his shoulders up, / and looked a king indeed. For
머리 하나 만큼,　　　　　정말 왕처럼 보였다.

the first time in all their history / they cried, /
역사상 처음으로　　　　　　　백성들은 외쳤다,

"God save the King!"
"왕께 만세!"

Then Saul went home, / and there went with him a body
그리고 사울이 집으로 돌아가자,　　한 무리의 사람들이 함께 돌아갔다

of men / whose hearts God had touched, / while Samuel
하나님께 감동을 받은,　　　　그 동안 사무엘은 책에

wrote in a book / the order of the kingdom / and laid it
기록하여　　　　왕국의 계보를

up before the Lord.
주님 앞에 모아두었다.

 mini test 6

A. 다음 문장을 해석해 보세요.

(1) Entreat me / not to leave thee, / or to return / from following after thee, / for where thou goest / I will go; / and where thou lodgest / I will lodge.
→

(2) He told his young men / to let her glean among the sheaves / and reprove her not, / and to let some handfuls fall purposely / for her to glean.
→

(3) A king was often a hard master, / and ruled his people cruelly, / taking the best of their fields, and their harvests, and their flocks / for themselves, / and the finest of their sons and daughters / to be his servants.
→

(4) Samuel did not choose / a king for the people / himself, / but he waited / for the Lord to send him / the man He had chosen.
→

B. 다음 주어진 문구가 알맞은 문장이 되도록 순서를 맞춰 보세요.

(1) 사무엘은 나이가 들자 자신을 대신하여 아들들을 사사로 세웠다.
(his / in / his sons / made / place / he / judges)
When Samuel was old _____
_____.

(2) 당신이 죽는 곳에서 저도 죽을 것이며, 그리고 그곳에 저도 묻힐 것입니다.
(buried / diest / there / Where / will / thou / I / and / will / I / die, / be)
→

 Answer

A. (1) 어머니를 떠나라고 강요하지 마세요. 따라오지 말고 돌아가라 하지도 마세요. 어머니가 가는 곳이면 저도 가겠습니다; 또 어머니가 사시는 곳에 저도 살겠어요. (2) 그는 일꾼들에게 룻이 곡식 단 사이에서 이삭을 줍게 하고 나무라지 말 것이며, 일부러 이삭을 몇 줌 떨어뜨려 모을 수 있도록 하라고 말했다. (3) 왕이란 때로는 가혹한 통치자

186 The Story of the Bible

(3) 그는 마치 친자식인 것처럼 어린 사무엘을 사랑했다.
(his own / he / little Samuel / He / as if / were / loved)
→

(4) 한나는 <u>자신은 포도주를 마시지 않았고, 기도 중이었다고</u> 말했다.
(had / she / praying / wine, / taken / but / not / was)
She told him that _____

_____.

C. 다음 주어진 문장이 본문의 내용과 맞으면 T, 틀리면 F에 동그라미 하세요.

(1) Naomi's daughter-in-law, Orpah, followed her to her
hometown.
(T / F)

(2) Naomi was married to Boaz.
(T / F)

(3) The Tabernacle was originally built in the land of Canaan.
(T / F)

(4) Hannah's son he grew up to be a judge.
(T / F)

D. 의미가 비슷한 것끼리 서로 연결해 보세요.

(1) smite   ▶   ◀ ① kill
(2) relative   ▶   ◀ ② gather
(3) slay   ▶   ◀ ③ kinsman
(4) glean   ▶   ◀ ④ strike

19

THE SHEPHERD BOY OF BETHLEHEM
베들레헴의 양치기 소년

After Saul had been king of Israel / for a few years, /
사울이 이스라엘의 왕으로 지낸 후　　　　　　　　　몇 년간,

Samuel was deeply troubled about him, / for he had
사무엘은 그로 인해 깊은 근심에 빠졌다,　　　　　　바랐기 때문에

hoped / that he would be as truly a king / as he looked, /
　　　그가 진실된 왕이 되기를　　　　　　　　보이는 대로,

but he had a strange and wilful spirit / that led him / to
하지만 사울에게는 이상하게 고집 센 면이 있어서'　　　　그를 이끌었다

turn away from the counsel of the Lord / and follow his
주님의 조언으로부터 등을 돌리고　　　　　　자신의 길을 따르도록,

own way.

Samuel had been grieved / again and again / by Saul's
사무엘은 비통해 하다가　　　　계속해서　　　사울의 무분별함

rashness, / until at last he said to him / when he had
때문에,　　　마침내 사울에게 말했다

taken the spoil of the enemy / to sacrifice to the Lord, /
그가 적으로부터 빼앗은 전리품으로　　　주님께 번제를 드렸을 때,

"To obey is better than sacrifice; / because thou hast
"번제보다 순종이 우선이오;

rejected the word of the Lord, / He hath also rejected
당신은 주님의 말씀을 거역했으니,　　　주님도 당신을 내치셨소

thee / from being king," / and he went to his house / and
　　　왕의 자리에서,"　　　그리고 사무엘은 집으로 돌아가

mourned over Saul, / for he had loved him.
사울을 생각하며 통곡했다,　　그를 사랑했기 때문에.

---

willful 고집이 센, 의도적인 | grieve 비통해 하다 슬프게하다 | rashness 무분별함, 무모함 | spoil 전리품 |
heifer 어린 암소 | grandson 손자 | doubt 의심

At last / the Lord told Samuel / to cease from mourning
마침내   주님께서 사무엘에게 말씀하셨다   사울을 위해 울지 말라고

for Saul, / for He had rejected him, / but to fill his horn
사울을 버리셨으니,   뿔에 기름을 채워,

with oil, / and go to Bethlehem / where Jesse lived, / for
베들레헴으로 가라고   이새가 살고 있는,

He had chosen / one of the sons of Jesse to be king / in
선택하셨기 때문에   이새의 아들을 왕으로 삼기로

place of Saul.
사울 대신.

Samuel went to Bethlehem / leading a heifer, / as the Lord
사무엘은 베들레헴으로 갔다   어린 암소를 이끌고,

had told him to do, / that he might hold a sacrifice. He told
주님이 시키신 대로,   번제를 드릴 수 있도록.

the elders of the city / to make ready for the sacrifice, /
사무엘은 마을 장로들에게 말했다   번제를 준비하라고,

and when he had found the house of Jesse, / he called him
그리고 이새의 집을 발견하자,   이새와 아들들을

and his sons. Jesse was the grandson of Ruth and Boaz,
불렀다.   이새는 룻과 보아스의 손자였는데,

/ and owned the fields, / no doubt, / where Ruth gleaned.
밭을 소유하고 있었다,   틀림없이,   룻이 이삭을 주웠던 땅에서.

Key Expression 🍀

in place of ∼ : ∼ 대신

in place of∼는 '∼대신'라는 의미로 사람과 사물 모두 사용 가능합니다. 또한
in one's place와 같이 소유격을 이용할 수도 있습니다.

ex) He had chosen one of the sons of Jesse to be king in place of Saul.
그는 사울 대신 이새의 아들을 왕으로 선택했다.
When Samuel was old he made his sons judges in his place
사무엘은 나이가 들자 자신을 대신하여 아들들을 사사로 세웠다.

When Samuel saw Eliab, / the son of Jesse, / he said; /
사무엘은 엘리압을 보자,　　　　이새의 아들인,　　　　말했다;

"Surely the Lord's anointed is before Him," / but the
"주님께서 그에게 기름을 부으실 것이 분명하구나,"　　　　하지만 주님이 말

Lord said; /
씀하셨다;

"Look not on his countenance or on the height of his
"그의 용모나 체격을 보지 말라,

stature, / because I have refused him, / for the Lord
그를 거절했으니,　　　　왜냐하면 주님이 보는

seeth not as man seeth, / for man looketh on the outward
관점은 사람과 다르기에,　　　　사람은 외모를 보지만,

appearance, / but the Lord looketh on the heart."
주님은 마음의 중심을 보느니라."

Then Jesse called Abinidab, / but Samuel said; /
그러자 이새는 아비나답을 불렀고,　　　　사무엘이 말했다;

"The Lord hath not chosen this." Then he made
"주님은 그를 선택하지 않으셨소."　　　　그러자 이새는 삼마를 불러

Shammah / to pass before him, / but Samuel said; /
사무엘 앞을 지나가게 했고,　　　　사무엘이 말했다;

"Neither hath the Lord chosen this."
"그 역시 주님께서 선택하지 않으셨다."

Jesse made seven of his sons to pass / before Samuel, /
이새는 일곱 명의 아들을 지나가게 했으나　　　　사무엘 앞으로,

but Samuel said; /
사무엘은 말했다;

"The Lord hath not chosen these."
"주님은 이들도 선택하지 않으셨다."

"Are here all thy children?" / said Samuel.
"여기 있는 이들이 네 아들 전부이냐?"　　　　사무엘이 말했다.

"There remaineth yet the youngest, / and he keepeth the
"아직 막내가 남았습니다,　　　　양을 돌보고 있습니다,"

sheep," / Jesse replied. Then Samuel said; /
이새가 대답했다.　　그러자 사무엘이 말했다;

countenance 얼굴 | stature 키 | remain 남아 있다 | hither 여기로(=here) | sheepfold 양을 치는 들판

midst 중앙, 한가운데 | ruddy 붉그레한, 혈색이 좋은 | brethren 신도들, 교우들, 형제

"Send and fetch him, / for we will not sit down / till he
"사람을 보내 그 아이를 데려 오라, 우리는 앉지 않을 것이다

come hither."
그 아이가 이곳에 올 때까지."

So Jesse sent out into the sheepfolds / on the hillsides /
그러자 이새는 들판으로 사람을 보내 언덕 위에 있는

outside the city / to bring the lad David in. What did the
도시 밖의 다윗을 데려왔다. 소년이 무슨 생각을

boy think / when he found his father and his brothers
했을까 아버지와 형들이 기다리고 있는 것을 보고,

waiting, / with the old prophet in the midst? What did
나이 많은 선지자와 함께? 무슨 의미였을까

it mean / that the eye of the seer was set upon him, / as
선견자의 눈이 자신에게 향한 것은,

were the eyes of all in the house?
또한 집안 모든 이들의 눈도?

Samuel saw a noble youth, / "ruddy, and of a beautiful
사무엘은 고귀한 소년을 보자, "혈색이 좋고, 용모가 아름다우니,

countenance, / and goodly to look to." He had been told
보기에 좋구나."라고 말했다. 들었기 때문에

/ that he must not look on the outward appearance / "for
외모를 보아서는 안 된다고

the Lord seeth not as man seeth," / and so he waited a
"주님이 보시는 관점은 사람과 다르기에" 그래서 사무엘은 잠시 기다렸고

little / until the Lord said; /
마침내 주님이 말씀이 들렸다;

"Arise, / anoint him, / for this is he." Then he took the
"일어나서, 그에게 기름을 부어라, 선택받은 그 아이다." 그러자 사무엘은 기름 담긴

horn of oil, / and anointed him / in the midst of his
뿔을 가져와서, 아이에게 기름을 부었다 형제 가운데 있던,

brethren, / and the spirit of the Lord came upon David /
그러자 주님의 성령이 다윗에게 임하셨고

from that day forward, / and Samuel went back / to his
그 날 이후로, 사무엘은 돌아갔다

house in Ramah.
라마에 있는 집으로.

It may be / that his father and his brothers did not
어쩌면   그의 아비와 형제는 이해하지 못했을지도 모른다

understand / that the boy had been called / to be king
                        그 소년이 부름을 받았다는 것을

over Israel, / but a new spirit of wisdom, and love, and
이스라엘의 왕으로,   하지만 지혜와 사랑의 강한 성령이

strength / came upon David, / and though he went back
다윗에게 임했기에,   다윗은 양 떼가 있는 곳으로 돌아갔지만

to his father's flocks / with no thought of being greater
                        형제들보다 대단하다는 생각없이,

than his brothers, / he went with a new song / in his heart
                        새로운 노래를 부르며 갔다   마음속으로

/ which he sang to the little harp / he had made / while
수금 가락에 맞춰   자신이 만든

watching the sheep. Long after when he was King of
양을 돌보던 중에.   이스라엘 왕이 되고 한참 후에,

Israel, / he made in memory of these days / the beautiful
다윗은 이 날을 기억하며 만들었다   아름다운 시편을

Psalm / to be sung in the temple / beginning, /
        성전에서 노래하도록   노래는 이렇게 시작한다,

"The Lord is my Shepherd, / I shall not want."
"주님의 나의 목자이시니,   내게 부족함이 없으리."

Key Expression

no longer ~ : 더 이상 ~ 아닌[~ 하지 않는]
no longer는 '더 이상 ~ 아닌' 혹은 '~ 하지 않는'의 의미를 가진 표현입니다.
no longer는 not ~ any longer로 바꾸어 쓸 수 있습니다.

ex) In His sight he was no longer a king.
　주님께서 보시기에 사울은 더 이상 왕이 아니었다.
　There was no longer a famine there.
　그곳에는 더 이상 흉년이 없었다.

---

harp 하프, 수금 | pebble 조약돌 | sullen 뚱한, 시무룩한, 침울한 | depart 떠나다 | gloomy 우울한, 비관적인

THE POWER OF A PEBBLE
조약돌의 위력

Saul the sullen was still king over Israel, / although he
침울해 있는 사울은 여전히 이스라엘을 다스리는 왕이었다

had departed from the Lord, / and in His sight / he was
주님으로부터 멀어지긴 했지만,　　　　　　그러나 주님이 보시기에　　사울은 더 이상

no longer a king. He was very gloomy and dark in his
왕이 아니었다.　　　　그는 마음이 우울하고 어두웠다,

mind, / for he had driven the Lord's spirit away, / and his
　　　주님의 성령을 쫓아냈기에,

light was gone.
그에게 머문 빛은 꺼져버렸다.

His servants tried to amuse him, / and told him of David,
신하들이 왕을 즐겁게 하려고 노력하며,　　　　다윗에 대해 말했다

/ the son of Jesse, / who was a skillful player on the
　　이새의 아들로,　　　수금을 잘 타며,

harp, / and a brave and handsome youth. So Saul sent for
　　용감하고 잘생긴 청년이라고.　　　그러자 사울은 다윗을 데려

David, / and David, / bringing presents from his father, /
오라 했고,　　다윗은,　　　아버지가 보내는 선물을 들고

came to the king's house.
왕궁으로 갔다.

Saul was greatly pleased with David, / and asked Jesse /
사울은 다윗을 보고 매우 기뻐하며,　　　　　이새에게 요청했다

to let his son stay with him, / for when the evil spirit was
다윗을 자신의 곁에 머물게 하라고,　　왜냐하면 악령이 그를 괴롭힐 때,

upon him, / if David played upon his harp / the darkness
　　　다윗이 수금을 타면　　　　어둠이 물러났기

left him. But this did not last, / and after a while / David
때문에.　　하지만 이는 오래가지 않았고,　얼마 후

went back to his flocks, / and Saul forgot him.
다윗이 양 떼에게로 돌아가자,　　사울은 그를 잊어버렸다.

Then the Philistines rose / against Israel / again. Their
그 무렵 블레셋 사람들이 일어났다   이스라엘에 맞서   다시.

camp was on a mountain side, / and Saul gathered his
블레셋 진지는 산 속에 있었기에.   사울은 군사를 불러 모았다

warriors / on the side of another mountain / and there was a
반대쪽 산 위에   그리고 계곡이 있었다

valley / between them.
두 산의 사이에는.

Out of the Philistine camp / a giant came / one day, /
블레셋 진영에서   거인이 나왔다   하루는,

Goliath of Gath. He talked loud / and often in order to
가드 사람 골리앗이었다.   골리앗은 큰 소리를 질러   이스라엘군에게 겁을 주기 위해,

terrify the Israelites, / asking them to send out a man / to
사람을 내보내라고 요구했다

fight with him, / but he was not truly brave, / for he had
자신에게 맞서 싸울,   하지만 그는 진정 용감한 이는 아니었다,

carefully covered his great body / with armor of brass, / so
거대한 몸을 신중히 덮고 있었기에   놋으로 만든 갑옷으로,

that no spear or sword could touch him. He defied Israel /
그래서 창이나 칼이 그의 몸에 닿지 못했다.   그는 이스라엘을 모욕했지만

every morning and evening / for forty days, / and no one
매일 아침 저녁   40일 동안,   아무도 없었다

was found / who would dare to go out alone / to fight him.
감히 홀로 나가   그에게 맞설 이가.

David's elder brothers were in camp, / and Jesse, their
다윗의 형들은 이스라엘 진영에 있었고,   아버지인 이새는,

father, / called David from the flocks / to take food to them.
양 떼와 있던 다윗을 불러   형들에게 음식을 갖다 주라고 했다.

He found / the army of Israel ready to go into battle, / but
다윗은 발견했다   이스라엘의 군대가 전쟁을 준비하는 모습을,

Goliath came out / as he had done each day / and defied the
그러나 골리앗이 나와서   매일 그랬듯이   이스라엘을 모욕하자,

Israelites, / who ran in terror / at the sight of him. The spirit
이스라엘 군은 두려워 도망쳤다   그의 모습만 보고도.   다윗 마음속의

of David / was moved at this, / and he said; /
성령이   이를 보고 감동했고,   그가 말했다;

"Who is this Philistine / that he should defy / the armies
"이 블레셋 사람은 누구입니까   모욕하려 하는

of the living God?" "The man who killeth him," / said
살아계신 하나님의 군대를?"   "그를 죽이는 자는,"   한 사람이

one, / "the King will enrich him, / and, / will give him his
대답했다,   "왕이 큰 재산을 줄 걸세,   그리고,   왕의 딸을 그에게 주고

daughter / and make his father's house free / in Israel."
아비의 집을 자유롭게 만들 것이네   이스라엘 땅에서."

Then Eliab, / David's eldest brother, / spoke sternly to
그러자 엘리압이,   다윗의 큰 형인,   다윗에게 엄하게 말하며

David / asking him / why he had left his sheep / to come
물었고   왜 양 떼를 떠나 산에서 내려와

down and see the battle, / and called him naughty and
전쟁을 보고 있느냐고,   버릇없고 거만하다고 했다,

proud, / but David still talked with the men, / for the
하지만 다윗은 사람들과 이야기를 계속했다,

spirit of the Lord was strong / within him. When Saul
주님의 성령이 강했기 때문에   그 안에 있는.   사울이 다윗의 얘기를

heard of him / and sent for him, / David said; /
듣고   그를 찾아 사람을 보내자,   다윗이 말했다;

"Let no man's heart fail / because of him; / thy servant
"누구도 낙담하게 두지 마십시오   저 자로 인해;   당신의 종이 나아가

will go / and fight with the Philistine."
저 블레셋 사람과 싸우겠습니다."

Saul frowned at David / and said; /
사울이 다윗을 보고 눈을 찌푸리며   말했다;

"Thou art not able to go / against this Philistine; / thou art
"가면 안 된다   이 블레셋 사람에 맞서 싸우러;   넌 어린 아이

but a youth, / and he is a man of war."
일 뿐이고,   저 자는 전장의 장수이다."

---

terrify 무섭게 하다, 겁먹게 하다 | armor 갑옷, 철갑 | spear 창 | defy 저항하다, 모욕하다 | dare 감히 ~ 하다 |
terror 두려움, 공포 | sternly 엄하게, 준엄하게 | naughty 버릇없는, 무례한 | proud 자랑스러운, 오만한 | frown
눈살을 찌푸리다

Then David told the king / how he had killed both a lion
그러자 다윗은 왕에게 이야기 하며   자신이 어떻게 사자와 곰을 죽였는지

and a bear / that had come down upon his father's flocks,
아버지의 양 떼를 습격했던,

/ and that he could also conquer the Philistine.
자신이 블레셋 사람들도 이길 수 있다고 했다.

"The Lord / that delivered me / out of the paw of the
"주님께서   나를 구원하신   사자의 발과,

lion, / and the paw of the bear," / said David, / "He will
곰의 발로부터,"   다윗이 말했다.   "구원하실

deliver me / out of the hand of this Philistine." And
것입니다   이 블레셋 사람이 손에서도."   그러자 사울이

Saul said; / "Go! And the Lord be with thee." Then Saul
말했다;   "가거라! 주님이 함께하시길."

armed David with his own armor, / but David said; /
그러고 나서 사울이 다윗에게 갑옷을 입히려 하자,   다윗이 말했다

"I cannot go with these, / for I have not proved them," /
"이것을 입고 갈 수 없습니다,   입어 본 적이 없으니까요.:

and he put them off.
그리고는 갑옷을 벗었다.

And this was the way / David armed himself / to meet
그리고 이것이 방법이었다   다윗이 자신을 무장한

the giant.
거인을 맞서기 위해.

He took his staff in hand, / and chose five smooth stones
다윗은 손에 막대를 들고,   매끄러운 돌 다섯 개를 골라

/ from the brook / and put them in his shepherd's bag,
개울에서   목자 가방에 넣은 후,

/ and with his sling in his hand, / he drew near to the
물매를 손에 들고,   거인에게 다가갔다.

giant. Goliath came on also, / his armor-bearer carrying
골리앗도 나왔다,   방패 든 사람을 앞세우고,

the shield before him, / but when he saw the youth
하지만 어린 다윗을 보고,

David, / he despised him, / for he was without armor, or
골리앗은 비웃었다,   다윗에게는 갑옷도, 칼이나 창도 없이,

sword or spear, / only his staff.
지팡이뿐이었기 때문에.

paw 발 | sling 투석기, 물매 | despise 경멸하다 | staff 지팡이

"Am I a dog, / that thou comest to me / with a staff," /
"내가 개인가, 내게 오다니 지팡이를 들고,"

said Goliath, / and then he told him / that he would soon
골리앗이 말했다, 그러고 나서 다윗에게 말했다 다윗의 시체를 주겠다고

give his flesh / to the birds and the beasts.
새과 짐승에게.

"Thou comest to me / with a sword, and a spear, and a
"넌 나왔지만 칼과 창과 방패로 무장하고,"

shield," / said David, / "but I come to thee / in the name
다윗이 말했다." 난 네 앞에 나왔다

of the Lord of Hosts, / the God of the armies of Israel /
전능하신 주님의 이름으로, 이스라엘 군대의 하나님이신

whom thou hast despised."
네가 경멸한."

Then the Philistine came down upon little David / to
그러자 골리앗이 다윗에게 다가왔고

destroy him, / and David ran, / not away from him, / as
그를 무너뜨리려, 다윗은 달려갔다, 그에게서 멀리 떨어진 쪽이 아니라,

the men of Israel had done, / but straight toward him,
이스라엘 사람들이 했듯이, 골리앗에게 곧장 다가갔다.

/ taking a pebble from his shepherd's bag / as he ran.
목자의 가방에서 조약돌을 꺼내며 달리는 중에.

Key Expression

in the name of ~ : ~의 이름으로

in the name of ~는 '~의 이름으로'라는 의미입니다. in one's name과 같이 소유격을 사용할 수도 있습니다.
명사 자리에 God, heaven과 같은 명사를 넣으면 다음과 같은 의미의 숙어가 만들어지기도 합니다.

▶ in the name of God[Heaven, Christ, Hell, goodness]
 =in God's[Heaven's, Christ's, Hell's] name
 ① 신의 이름을 걸고, 하늘에 맹세코
 ② 제발, 아무쪼록
 ③ (의문사를 강조하여) 도대체

ex) I come to thee in the name of the Lord of Hosts, the God of the armies of Israel whom thou hast despised.
나는 네가 모독한 이스라엘 군대의 하나님, 전능하신 주님의 이름으로 네 앞에 나왔다.

Quickly putting it in the sling, / he whirled it in the air
재빨리 조약돌을 물매에 걸어서,　　　　　다윗은 물매를 공중에서 빙빙 돌렸고

once, twice, / and then it went swift and straight / to the
한 번, 두 번,　　　그러자 돌은 빠른 속도로 곧장 날아갔다　　　표적을

mark. It sunk into the forehead of the giant, / and he fell
향해.　돌이 거인의 이마에 박히자,　　　　　그는 앞으로

dead upon his face. Then David ran / and stood upon the
고꾸라져서 죽어버렸다.　　　그러자 다윗이 달려가　　골리앗의 시체 위로 올라가

dead Philistine / and cut off his head / with the giant's
　　　　　　그의 머리를 잘라냈다

great sword, / and when the Philistines saw / that their
거인의 거대한 칼로,　　블레셋 사람들은 알게 되자

champion was really dead, / they fled, / pursued by the
자신들의 투사가 진짜 죽었다는 사실을,　　　달아나 버렸고,

shouting hosts of Israel.
이스라엘 군대의 함성이 그 뒤를 따랐다.

Saul had forgotten the youth / who played upon the harp
사울은 그 소년을 잊어버렸었다　　　　　자신의 앞에서 수금을 켰던,

before him, / for when he sent for him / after the battle /
　　　　　사울은 그를 찾아가　　　　전투가 끝난 후

he said, /
말했다,

"Whose son art thou, / thou young man?" and David
"넌 누구의 아들이냐,　　　어린 청년이여?"

answered, /
그러자 다윗이 대답했다,

"I am the son of thy servant Jesse, / the Bethlehemite."
"전 당신의 종 이새의 아들입니다,　　　베들레헴 사람입니다."

And Saul took him to live with him / from that day.
그러자 사울은 그를 곁에 두었다　　　　그 날 이후.

shield 방패 | whirl 빙빙 돌리다 | swift 신속하게 | mark 표적 | forehead 이마 | champion 챔피언, 투사 |
flee 달아나다 | pursue 뒤쫓다

21

FAITHFUL UNTO DEATH
죽을 때까지 지킨 신의

Saul had a son named Jonathan, / and he loved David /
사울에게는 요나단이라는 아들이 있었는데,   그는 다윗을 사랑했다

as his own soul. He took off his princely robes, / even
자신의 영혼처럼.   요나단은 왕자의 예복을 벗어,

to his sword, and his bow, and his girdle, / and made
칼과 활, 허리띠까지,

David wear them; / and David acted wisely / in all that
다윗에게 입혔고;   다윗은 현명하게 행동했다

the king gave him to do. There was great joy and much
왕이 분부한 모든 일에 있어서.   기쁨의 향연이 벌어졌다

feasting / over the Death of Goliath / and the flight of the
골리앗의 죽음과   블레셋 군사의 승리에 대해,

Philistines, / and wherever Saul went, / the women came
그래서 사울이 가는 곳마다.   여자들이 그를 만나러 나와,

out of the cities to meet him, / singing and dancing, / and
노래하고 춤을 추었고,

the song with which they answered one another was, /
그들이 서로 주고 받은 노래의 내용은 다음과 같았다.

"Saul hath slain his thousands,
"사울은 수천 명을 죽였고,

And David his tens of thousands."
다윗은 수만 명을 죽였네."

Saul did not like this, / and an evil spirit of jealousy /
사울은 이 노래를 좋아하지 않았고,   질투의 악령이

came upon him, / and he thought, / "What can he have
그를 찾아왔다.   그래서 사울은 생각했다,   "그가 더 얻을 것이 무엇이랴

more / but the kingdom."
왕국 외에."

The next day / the evil spirit came upon Saul / in the
이튿날   악령이 사울을 찾아왔고   집 안에 있던,

house, / and David played on his harp / to quiet him, / but
다윗은 수금을 연주했지만   그를 진정시키기 위해,

Saul hurled a spear at David, / hoping to fasten him to the
사울은 다윗에게 창을 던져,   벽에 매달려고 했다.

wall with it. This he did twice, / but the Lord guided the
사울은 창을 두 번 던졌지만,   주님이 창을 인도하셔서

spear / away from David, / just as he guided the pebble to
다윗에게서 멀리 떨어지도록,   조약돌을 골리앗에게 인도하셨던 것처럼.

Goliath, / and he was unhurt. Saul was afraid of David.
다윗은 다치지 않았다.   사울은 다윗이 두려웠다.

He was afraid / that God was preparing / him to be king
그는 두려워했다   하나님이 준비하시고 계실까봐   다윗을 이스라엘 왕으로

over Israel, / so he sent him into battle, / hoping he would
그래서 다윗을 전쟁터로 보냈다,   그곳에서 죽게 되길 바라며,

be killed, / but the life of David was in the Lord's hand, /
하지만 다윗의 목숨은 주님 손에 있었기에

and no enemy could destroy it.
적군 중 아무도 그를 해칠 수 없었다.

After a great battle, / in which David had been victorious,
큰 전쟁 후,   다윗이 승리했던,

/ the evil spirit came again upon Saul, / as he sat in his
악령이 사울에게 다시 찾아왔다,   사울이 집에 앉아

house / with his spear in his hand, / while David played
손에 창을 들고 있을 때,   다윗이 수금을 켜고 있는 동안.

on the harp. Again / he tried to kill David, / but the spear
다시 한 번   사울은 다윗을 죽이려 했지만,   창은 벽에 부딪쳤고

struck the wall / and David slipped away.
다윗은 빠져나갔다.

---

girdle 허리 띠 | jealousy 질투, 시샘 | hurl 던지다 | fasten 매다, 고정시키다 | victorious 승리한 | slip away
사라지다, 도망가다

201

It was clear / that David could not live / near the king, /
분명했기에   살 수 없는 것이   왕의 곁에서,

and so he talked with Jonathan, / his friend, / who said, /
다윗은 요나단과 이야기를 나눴고,   그의 친구인,   다윗이 말했다,

"God forbid, / thou shalt not die," / but David said, /
"그럴 리가 없어,   넌 죽지 않을 거야."   하지만 다윗이 말했다,

"Truly / there is but a step / between me and death."
"틀림없이   한 걸음 차이 뿐이야   나와 죽음 사이에는."

Then they made a promise / to each other / before the
그들은 약속했다   서로   주님 앞에서

Lord / that should last while they lived. They promised
주님 / 살아있는 동안 지켜야 할.   그들은 보여 주기로 약속했다

to show / "the kindness of the Lord" / to each other /
보여 주기로 / "주님의 자비를"   서로에게

while life should last.
살아있는 한.

Jonathan told David / that he might go away / for three
요나단이 다윗에게 말했고   떠날 것이라고   사흘 동안,

days, / and they went out into a field together. They
둘을 함께 들판으로 나갔다.

feared the anger of Saul / when he found / that David
그들은 사울이 화낼까 봐 두려웠다   알게 되면

was absent from the feast of the new moon. So Jonathan
다윗이 초하루 축제에 빠졌다는 사실을.   요나단은 다윗에게

told David / to return after three days / and hide behind
말했다   사흘 후 돌아와서   큰 바위 뒤에 숨으라고

a great rock / in the field. Then Jonathan said / he would
큰 바위 / 들판에 있는.   그러고 나서 말하기를

come out / and shoot three arrows from his bow, / as
밖으로 나와   화살 세 개를 쏜 후,

if he were shooting at a mark, / and he would send his
표적을 맞추려는 듯이,   화살 드는 하인을 보내 찾아오도록

arrow-bearer to pick them up. If he should call to the lad,
하겠다고 했다.   요나단이 그 아이에게 외치면,

God forbid 어림도 없는 소리, 천만에, 그럴 리가 없다 | blame ~을 탓하다

/ "The arrows are on this side of thee," / David would
"화살이 이쪽에 있다"라고,   다윗은 알게 될 것이요

know / that Saul was not angry, / and would not hurt him,
사울이 화나지 않았고,   그를 해치지 않을 것이라고,

/ but if he cried, / "The arrows are beyond thee," / David
하지만 외친다면,   "화살이 네 앞에 있다."라고

would know / he was in danger / and must go away.
알게 될 것이라고   위험에 처했으니   도망가야 한다는 것을.

On the second day of the feast, / Saul asked / why David
축제의 둘째 날,   사울이 물어 보자   다윗이 왜 없는지,

was not there, / and Jonathan told him / he had asked
                        요나단이 말했다

permission / to go away / for three days. Then Saul was
허락을 구했다고   멀리 다녀오겠다고   사흘 동안.   그러자 사울은 매우 화를

very angry. He blamed his son / for loving David, / for,
냈다.   사울은 아들을 탓했고   다윗을 사랑하는 것에 대해,   왜냐하면,

/ as Saul's son, / Jonathan should be king / after his
왕의 아들로서,   요나단은 왕이 되어야 했기에   자신이 죽은 후,

death, / but he never would be / if David lived, / and he
하지만 왕이 될 수 없을 거라   다윗이 살아있으면,

commanded Jonathan / to bring him / that he might put
그래서 사울은 요나단에게 명령했다   다윗을 데려오라고   그를 죽이려고.

him to death.

Key Expression

전치사 · 부사의 but

but은 역접의 접속사로 주로 쓰이지만 전치사나 부사로 쓰이는 경우도 있습니다.
전치사로 쓰일 때는 '~외에'(=except), 부사로 쓰일 때는 '단지'(=only)의 의미입니다.

ex) What can he have more but the kingdom.
그가 왕국 외에 무엇을 가질 수 있으랴.
Truly there is but a step between me and death.
틀림없이 나와 죽음 사이에는 한 걸음뿐이다.
No one but the priests and Levites could touch the Ark of God.
제사장과 레위 지파 외에는 누구도 하나님의 궤를 만질 수 없었다.

203

When Jonathan asked / what evil David had done / that
요나단이 묻자   다윗이 무슨 나쁜 일을 했는지

he should be put to death, / Saul cast his spear / at his
죽음을 당해야 할 만큼,   사울은 창을 던졌다

own son. Then Jonathan knew / there was no hope for
친아들에게.   그러자 요나단은 알게 되었고   다윗에게 희망이 없다는 것을,

David, / and left the table / in sorrow.
          식탁을 떠났다   슬픔에 차서.

The next day / he went out to the rock in the field / with
이튿날   요나단은 들판에 있는 큰 바위로 나가

his armor-bearer / and sent him on before. When he shot
갑옷 드는 사람과   그를 앞쪽으로 보냈다.   활을 쏘았을 때,

an arrow, / he cried; /
          요나단이 외쳤다;

"The arrow is beyond thee; / make haste! Stay not!"
"화살이 네 앞에 있다;   서둘러라!   멈추지 말고!"

And David, / in his hiding place / heard it, / and knew /
그러자 다윗은,   숨어있던 곳에서   그 말을 듣고,   알았다

that he must flee / for his life.
도망가야 한다는 것을   목숨을 부지하려면.

swear 맹세하다 | distressed 괴로워하는 |

Then Jonathan gave his bow and arrows to the lad / to
그리고 나서 요나단이 활과 화살을 소년에게 주고

take to the town, / and David came out / from his hiding
마을로 갖고 가라고 하자,　다윗이 숨어있던 곳에서 나왔고,

place, / and they kissed each other / and wept together.
둘은 서로 입맞춘 뒤　함께 울었다.

But at last Jonathan said; /
마침내 요나단이 말했다:

"Go in peace; / as we have sworn both of us / in the
"안심하고 가라;　우리 둘이 맹세하며

name of the Lord, / saying, / The Lord be / between me
주님의 이름으로,　말했듯이,　주님이 계시리니　우리 사이에,

and thee, / and between my children and thy children /
그리고 자녀들 사이에

forever."
영원히."

And David went away to hide from Saul, / and Jonathan
그러자 다윗은 사울을 피해 떠났고,　요나단은 돌아갔다

went back / to the king's house.
왕궁으로.

For seven years / Saul hunted for David / to take his life,
7년 동안　사울은 다윗을 찾아　그를 죽이려 했고,

/ and David, / often hiding / in caves in the wilderness, /
다윗은,　주로 숨어 있었기에　황무지에 있는 동굴에,

could not see his friend Jonathan, / but they were faithful
요나단을 볼 수 없었다,　하지만 두 사람은 자신들의 우정을

in their friendship, / and when at last Saul was slain / in
믿었고,　그래서 끝내 사울이 죽었을 때

battle, / and Jonathan also, / David came to mourn over
전쟁터에서,　요나단도 함께,　다윗은 친구를 애도하기 위해 찾아와,

his friend, / saying; /
말했다:

"I am distressed for thee, / my brother Jonathan; / very
"너로 인해 괴롭구나,　나의 형제인 요나단이여;

pleasant hast thou been unto me; / thy love for me was
넌 내게 큰 즐거움을 주었고;　날 향한 네 사랑은 훌륭했으니,

wonderful, / passing the love of women."
여인의 사랑 이상으로."

205

22

DAVID THE OUTCAST
쫓겨난 자 다윗

For seven years / King Saul hunted David / from one
7년 동안　　　　　사울 왕은 다윗을 찾아 다녔다

end of the land of Israel to the other. The evil spirit of
이스라엘 땅의 끝에서 끝으로.　　　　　　　　질투와 미움의 악령이

jealousy and hate / had full possession of him, / and
　　　　　　　　　그를 완전히 사로잡았고,

David, / with a few faithful men, / was driven from one
다윗은,　　소수의 충직한 사람들과,　　　　여기저기 요새로 내몰리다가,

stronghold to another, / until he cried, / "They gather
　　　　　　　　　　　마침내 외쳤다,

themselves together; / they hide themselves; / they mark
"그들이 함께 모여;　　　　스스로를 숨기며;　　　　내 흔적을 쫓는구나

my steps / when they wait for my soul. What time I am
내 걸음을　　내 영혼을 기다리면서.　　　　　두려워질 때면

afraid / I will trust in thee."
　　　　저는 당신을 믿겠습니다."

He had escaped / again and again / from the hand of
그는 도망쳤고　　여러 차례　　　사울의 손에서,

Saul, / and now / he was down in the desert country /
이제　　　사막 나라에 있었다

by the Dead Sea, / hiding among the cliffs and caves of
사해 근처에 있는,　　엔게디의 절벽과 동굴 사이에 숨은 채.

Engedi. Saul heard of it / and took three thousand men /
사울은 이 소식을 듣자　　3,000명의 부하를 이끌고

to hunt for him / among the rocks of the wild goats. He
그를 찾아 나섰다　　야생 염소의 바위 사이에서.

was very tired / after climbing the rocks, / and seeing a
사울은 매우 지쳐서　　절벽을 오른 후,　　　　　동굴을 보자,

cave, / he went in to lie down / for a little sleep. He did
그 안에 들어가 누웠다　　　　잠시 자려고.

outcast 버림 받는 사람 | possession 소유 | drive 몰다, 몰아붙이다 | stronghold 요새, 근거지 | desert 사막 |
cliff 절벽 | goat 염소 | whisper 속삭이다, 귓속말을 하다 | creep 살금살금 움직이다

not know / that David and his men were / in the cave /
그는 몰랐다   다윗 일행이 숨어있다는 것을   그 동굴의

hiding in the dark sides of it. Then his men whispered to
어두운 쪽에.   그때 다윗의 부하들이 다윗에게 속삭였다;

David; /

"Behold the day / of which the Lord said unto thee; /
"그 날이 왔습니다   주님께서 말씀하신 날이;

'I will deliver thine enemy into thine hand / that thou
'네 적을 네게 이끌 테니

mayest do to him / as it shall seem good to thee.'" Then
그에게 해도 좋다   네가 원하는 대로'라고."

David arose / and crept near to Saul, / and — / did he kill
그러자 다윗이 일어나 조심스럽게 사울에게 다가가더니,   그리고, — 그는 과연 사울을

the man / who had so often tried to kill him?
죽였을까   자신을 여러 번이나 죽이려 했던?

No, / he bent down / and cut off a part of Saul's robe.
아니,   그는 몸을 굽혀   사울의 옷조각을 잘라냈을 뿐이다.

Even this seemed wrong to David.
이 행동마저도 그에게는 잘못인 듯 했다.

"The Lord forbid / that I should do this thing / unto my
"주님께서 금하셨으니   이런 일을 하는 것을   내 주인에게,"

master," / he said / "to stretch forth my hand against
그가 말했다   "그에게 대항하여 손을 뻗는 일을,

him, / seeing he is the anointed of the Lord," / and in this
그는 주님이 기름 부으신 자임을 알기에,"   이렇게 하여

way / he kept his servants from harming Saul, / and after
다윗은 하인들이 사울을 해치는 것을 막았고,   사울은 잠에서

Saul awoke / he went out of the cave.
깨어나자   동굴 밖으로 나갔다.

David also went out of the cave / and cried, /
다윗 또한 동굴 밖으로 나가며   외쳤다,

"My Lord the King!"
"왕이시여!"

And when Saul turned / David bowed down to him / and
사울이 돌아서자   다윗은 절하며

asked him / why he listened to men / who said that he
물었다   왜 사람들의 말을 들었는지

wished to harm the king, / and then he told him / how
자신이 왕을 해치려 한다고 말한,   그리고 말했다

the Lord had given him into his hand / in the cave, / but
주님께서 어떻게 사울을 자신에게 데려오셨는지   동굴 안에 있던,

he would not touch / the Lord's anointed / to harm him.
하지만 자신은 손대지 않았다고   주님이 기름 부으신 사람을   해치려고.

"See, / my father," / he cried / "see the skirt of thy robe
"보소서,   아버지시여,"   다윗이 외쳤다   "당신의 옷자락을 보소서

/ in my hand. I have not sinned against thee, / yet thou
내 손에 있는.   나는 당신에게 죄를 짓지 않았지만,

huntest my soul to take it."
당신은 나를 죽이려고 찾아다녔습니다."

Much more he said, / and asked the Lord to judge
다윗은 또 말했고,   주님께 자신들을 판정해 달라 요청했다,

between them, / and Saul's hard heart was moved / so
그러자 사울의 굳은 마음이 움직여

that he wept aloud.
크게 울었다.

"Is this thy voice, / my son David," / he said, / "Thou art
"이것이 네 목소리냐,   아들 다윗아,"   사울이 말했다,

more righteous than I, / for thou hast rewarded me good,
"네가 나보다 의로운 자구나,   내게 선으로 보답했으니

/ whereas I have rewarded thee evil," / and he made a
내가 악으로 보답했는데도,"   그리고 사울은 다윗에게

covenant with David. For though he made no promise /
서약을 했다.   약속하지는 않았지만

to spare David's life, / he made David promise / to spare
다윗의 목숨을 구해 주겠다고,   다윗에게 약속하게 했다

the life of his children / when he should be made king.
자신의 자녀들 목숨을 구해 주겠다고   다윗이 왕이 되면.

But a year was hardly past before / the evil spirit was
그렇지만 1년이 채 지나기 전에 악령이 다시 한 번 사울에게

again upon Saul, / and he went out with three thousand
찾아왔고, 사울은 3,000명을 이끌고 나갔다

men / to hunt for David. Saul's camp was on a hill, / and
다윗을 찾으러. 사울의 진영은 언덕 위에 있었고,

David saw where it was. At night / he took Abishai, /
다윗에게는 그 위치가 보였다. 밤이 되자 다윗은 아비새를 데리고

one of his warriors, / and went down from the cliffs to
전사 중 한 명인, 절벽에서 내려와 사울의 진영으로 갔다.

Saul's camp, / where Saul lay sleeping in a trench, / and
그곳에서 사울은 참호에 누워서 자고 있었고,

the spear stuck in the ground / by his pillow, / while all
창은 땅에 꽂혀 있었으며 배게 곁에,

his men lay around him. Abishai wished to strike him
모든 사람들은 그의 주변에 누워 있었다. 아비새는 사울을 찔러 죽이려 했지만

through / with the spear, / but David said, /
창으로, 다윗이 말했다,

"Destroy him not, / for who can stretch forth his hand /
"그를 해치지 말라, 누가 손을 대고서,

against the Lord's anointed / and be guiltless? The Lord
주님이 기름 부으신 자에게 죄없다 할 수 있겠느냐?

shall smite him, / or his day shall come to die, / or he
주께서 그를 치실 것이다, 아니면 그의 운명이 다하여 죽거나,

shall fall in battle and perish; / but take thou now the
또는 전쟁터에서 쓰러져 사라지리라; 저 창을 거두고

spear / that is at his pillow, / and the cruse of water, / and
베개 곁에 있는, 물병을 갖고,

let us go."
가자."

skirt 옷자락 | spare 모면하게 하다, 피하게 해 주다 | trench 참호 | guiltless 죄가 없는 | perish 죽다, 소멸하다
| cruse 단지, 병

And they took them / and went away. A deep sleep had
그들은 창과 물병을 가지고   떠났다.   깊은 잠이 내려앉았다

fallen / upon the camp of Saul / from the Lord, / so that
사울의 진영에   주님으로부터,

no one saw them.
누구도 그를 볼 수 없도록.

Then David went up to his stronghold, / and from the
그리고 나서 다윗은 자신의 요새로 올라라,   절벽 끝에서

top of the cliff / he cried to Abner, / the captain of Saul's
아브넬을 불러,   사울의 부하 중 대장인,

men, / and asked / why he had not defended his Master, /
물었다   왜 주인을 지키지 않았는지,

and where was the king's spear, and his cruse of water?
또 왕의 창과 물병이 어디 있는지?

Then Saul cried as before, /
그러자 사울이 지난번처럼 외쳤다,

"Is this thy voice, / my son David?"
"이것이 네 목소리냐,   아들 다윗아?"

"It is my voice, / my lord, O King," / said David, / and
"제 목소리입니다,   왕이시여,"   다윗이 말하며,

again he plead / his cause with his old enemy, / but who
다시 한 번 물었다   오랫동안 적이 된 이유를,

could trust / to the repentance of Saul? He cried, /
하지만 누가 믿으리   사울이 회개했는지?   사울이 외쳤다,

"I have sinned; / return, / my son David, / for I will no
"내가 죄를 지었구나;   돌아오라,   아들 다윗아,

more do thee harm, / because my soul was precious / in
다시는 널 해치지 않겠다,   내 목숨이 중요했구나

thine eyes / this day. I have played the fool, / and erred
네게는   오늘.   내가 미련하게 굴었고,

exceedingly."
대단히 큰 실수를 저질렀구나."

plead 간청하다 | err 실수를 범하다 | exceedingly 극도로, 대단히 | sore 아픈, 화가 난

But David trusted him no more, / and went and made
하지만 다윗은 더 이상 그를 믿지 않았고   블레셋 왕자와 친구가 되어

friends with a Philistine prince / that he might live /
살 수 있게 되었다

within their borders.
블레셋 땅 안에.

Samuel the prophet was dead, / and there was no one /
선지자가 사무엘이 죽었고,   그래서 아무도 없었다

to give counsel / to the darkened soul of the King / when
조언할 사람이   영혼이 어두워진 왕에게

trouble fell upon him. The Philistines had come / with a
곤경에 처했을 때.   블레셋이 쳐들어 왔지만

great army, / but Saul was afraid, / for the Lord's spirit
큰 군사를 이끌고,   사울은 두려워했다.   주님의 성령이 자신 곁에 없었기에.

was not with him. He tried to seek the Lord / through the
사울은 주님을 찾고자 했지만   제사장을 통해,

priests, / and through dreams, / but the Lord answered
또 꿈을 통해,   주님은 응답하지 않으셨다.

him not. Then he went to a witch by night, / and asked
그 후에 사울은 밤에 무당을 찾아가서,

her to bring up the spirit of Samuel. The witch could not
사무엘의 영을 불러 달라고 요청했다.   무당은 사무엘을 부를 수 없었지만,

bring up Samuel, / but the Lord sent him / to speak to
주님이 사무엘을 보내어   사울에게 말하게 하셨고,

Saul, / and the woman cried out with terror / when she
그러자 무당이 두려움에 떨며 외쳤다

saw the prophet of the Lord, / and knew also / that it was
주님의 선지자를 보고,   알게 되자

the King who had called for him.
사무엘을 불러낸 것이 주님이라는 사실을

"I am sore distressed," / said Saul, / "and God is
"전 고통스럽고,"   사울이 말했다,

departed from me. What shall I do?"
"하나님은 나를 떠나셨습니다.   어찌 해야 합니까?"

Then Samuel told him plainly / that the kingdom was
그러자 사무엘이 분명히 말했다   왕국은 사울에게서 빼앗아

taken from him / and given to David, / and that on the
다윗에게 주어질 것이며,   그 다음 날

next day / he and his sons should fall in battle, / and the
사무엘과 아들들은 전쟁에서 죽고

Israelites into the hands of the Philistines.
이스라엘 백성은 블레셋에게 넘어갈 것이라고.

Saul, / forsaken and despairing, / fell to the earth
사울은,   버림받고 절망하여,   쓰러져 기절해 버렸다가,

fainting, / but was revived by the woman, / who gave
무당에 의해 회복됐다.   무당은 사울에게

him food / so that he went away / through the dark / to
음식을 주고   갈 수 있도록 했다   밤 동안

the camp of Israel.
이스라엘 진영으로.

In the battle of the next day / the Philistines conquered.
이튿날 전장에서   블레셋 군사가 승리했다.

The three sons of Saul were slain, / and Saul himself, /
사울의 세 아들은 죽었고,   사울 자신도,

when chased by the Philistines, / fell upon his own sword
블레셋 군사들에게 쫓겨,   자신의 칼 위에 쓰러져 죽었다.

and died.

When a messenger brought news of the battle / to
전령이 전장의 소식을 가져오자

David / he rent his clothes for grief, / and in the chant
다윗에게   그는 슬픔에 옷을 찢으며,   애가를 불렀다

of lamentation / that he made, / he mourned / for his
자신이 만든,   다윗은 애도했다

faithful friend Jonathan, / and had no word of blame / for
신뢰하는 친구 요나단을 위해,   또 사울을 비난하지도 않고

his enemy Saul, / neither did he triumph over him.
적이었던,   승리를 누리지도 않았다.

plainly 분명히 | forsaken 버림받은 | despairing 절망한 | faint 기절하다 | revive 소생시키다, 회복하다 |
chase 뒤쫓다 | grief 비탄, 큰 슬픔 | chant 성가 | lamentation 애통 | triumph 승리하다

 mini test 7

A. 다음 문장을 해석해 보세요.

(1) I come to thee / in the name of the Lord of Hosts, / the God of the armies of Israel / whom thou hast despised.
→

(2) He had hoped / that he would be as truly a king / as he looked, / but he had a strange and wilful spirit that led him to turn away / from the counsel of the Lord / and follow his own way.
→

(3) It may be / that his father and his brothers did not understand / that the boy had been called / to be king over Israel.
→

(4) David ran, / not away from him, / as the men of Israel had done, / but straight toward him.
→

B. 다음 주어진 문장이 되도록 빈칸에 써 넣으세요.

(1) 주님은 나의 목자시니, 내게 부족함이 없으리.

| | this evening. |

(2) 주님이 보시기에 사울은 더 이상 왕이 아니었다.

I feel pretty sure that

(3) 그는 앞으로 고꾸라져서 죽어버렸다.

I was sitting with Peter on his divan,

 Answer

A. (1) 나는 네가 모독한 이스라엘 군대의 하나님, 전능하신 주님의 이름으로 네 앞에 나왔다. (2) 그는 그가 보이는 것처럼 진실된 왕이 되기를 바랐지만, 사울에게는 이상하게 고집 센 면이 있어서 주님의 조언을 따르지 않고 자신의 뜻대로 하려 했다. (3) 어쩌면 그의 아비와 형제는 그 소년이 이스라엘의 왕으로, 부름을 받았다는 것을 이해하지 못

(4) 나와 죽음 사이에는 단 한 걸음이 있을 뿐이야.

→

C. 다음 주어진 문구가 알맞은 문장이 되도록 순서를 맞춰 보세요.

(1) 사울은 이새에게 그의 아들을 자신 곁에 머물게 하라고 요청했다.
(Jesse / stay / Saul / to / his son / asked / with him / let)
→

(2) 감히 홀로 나가 그에게 맞서 싸울 이가 아무도 없었다.
(go out / dare to / no one / who / was found / him / would / alone / to fight)
→

(3) 그는 다윗을 사랑하는 아들을 탓했다.
(for / loving / He / his son / blamed / David)
→

(4) 그는 하인들이 사울을 해치지 못하게 막았다.
(harming / kept / He / from / Saul / his servants)
→

D. 다음 단어에 대한 맞는 설명과 연결해 보세요.

(1) rashness   ▶   ◀ ① to look down on with contempt

(2) defy   ▶   ◀ ② the trait of acting without prudence

(3) despise   ▶   ◀ ③ intensely impetuous, or passionate

(4) hurl   ▶   ◀ ④ to throw down with violence

했을지도 모른다. (4) 다윗은 이스라엘 사람들이 했듯이 그에게서 멀리 떨어진 쪽이 아니라 그에게 곧장 달려갔다. | B. (1) The Lord is my Shepherd, I shall not want. (2) In His sight he was no longer a king. (3) He fell dead upon his face. (4) There is but a step between me and death. | C. (1) Saul asked Jesse to let his son stay with him. (2) No one was found who would dare to go out alone to fight him. (3) He blamed his son for loving David. (4) He kept his servants from harming Saul. | D. (1) ② (2) ④ (3) ① (4) ③

215

23

EVERY INCH A KING
완전한 왕

After Saul's death / David came back to live with his
사울이 죽은 뒤   다윗은 돌아와 자신의 지파 사람들과 살았다.

own people, / for he was of the tribe of Judah. He went
그는 유다 지파의 일원이었기에.   다윗은 헤브론

to Hebron, / the old home of Abraham, Isaac, and Jacob,
으로 갔고,   아브라함과 이삭과 야곱의 고향인,

/ for the Lord had told him to go there, / and the men of
주님께서 가라고 하셨기에,

his tribe came to Hebron / and anointed him king. The
그의 지파의 사람들이 헤브론에 와서   그를 왕으로 기름부었다.

other tribes did not come, / for Saul's son and the captain
다른 지파는 오지 않았다,   사울의 아들과 아브넬 장군이,

of his host, Abner, / were still holding the kingdom. But
아직 왕국을 나스리고 있었기에.

when both were killed by an enemy, / then all the other
하지만 두 사람이 적에게 죽자,

tribes came to Hebron / and made a league with him, / so
모든 지파가 헤브론에 와서   다윗과 연합을 결성했다,

seven years after Saul's death / David became king over
그렇게 하여 사울이 죽고 7년이 흐른 후   다윗은 이스라엘의 왕이 되었다.

all Israel. He was then thirty years old / and his reign
그때 그의 나이는 30세였고

lasted forty years.
통치는 40년 간 계속됐다.

Then David began to establish the kingdom. There was
다윗은 왕국을 확고히 하기 시작했다.

a rocky height / not far from Hebron / with a valley
바위산이 있었는데   헤브론에서 멀지 않은 곳에   주변이 온통 계곡인

all around it / that was still held by the Jebusites, / one
여부스 사람들이 다스리고 있는,

---

every inch a person 어느 모로 보나, 완전히 | league 동맹, 연맹 | establish 수립하다, 확고히 하다 | skilled
숙련된 | workman 직공 | cedar 삼나무

of the tribes of Canaan / that the Lord said / must not
가나안 지파의 사람은   주님에 따르면   그 땅에 남아 있으면

be left in the land. The city was Jerusalem, / and the
안 되었다.   그 도시는 예루살렘이고,

stronghold was Zion, / and close by Zion / was the mount
중심지는 시온이었다,   그리고 시온 근처에는   산이 있었다

/ to which Abraham had once gone / to offer up Isaac.
아브라함이 예전에 갔었던   이삭을 제물로 바치러.

David wanted this / stronghold for the chief city of the
다윗은 시온을 원했고   왕국의 수도로서,

kingdom, / and so he took it, / and it became the city
그래서 그 땅을 얻어,   시온은 다윗 왕국의 수도가 되었다.

of David. He built a beautiful house for himself / there,
다윗은 자신을 위한 아름다운 집을 지었는데   그곳에,

/ and King Hiram of Tyre sent / skilled workmen, and
두로의 히람 왕이 보내어   숙련된 목공과 삼나무를,

cedar trees, / and they built a house of cedar for him.
다윗을 위해 삼나무 집을 지었다.

Key Expression 🔑

부사구 도치 구문

부사나 부사구, 특히 장소나 방향의 의미를 가진 부사구가 문장 맨 앞에 나올 경우 뒤따르는 주어와 동사의 위치가 바뀌는 도치가 일어납니다.

▶ 부사어구(특히 장소나 방향의 부사구) + 동사 + 주어

단 다음의 경우에는 도치가 일어나지 않습니다
① 주어가 대명사인 경우
② 동사가 타동사인 경우
③ 동사가 다른 부사구의 수식을 받는 경우
④ 동사가 조동사를 동반한 경우

ex) Close by Zion was the mount to which Abraham had once gone to offer up Isaac.
시온 근처에는 예전에 아브라함이 이삭을 제물로 바치러 갔었던 산이 있었다.

But stronger than the wish to have a house for himself
하지만 자신을 위한 집을 갖는 것보다 더 큰 바람은

/ was the longing to see / the Ark of God set / within
보는 것이었다　　　하나님의 성궤가 안치되는 것을

the curtains of the Tabernacle / in the city of David. It
회막 안에　　　다윗의 도시 안의.

had been in the house of Abinadab in Kirjath-Jearim /
그 궤는 기럇여아림에 있는 아비나답에 있었고,

for seventy years, / ever since it was sent home / by the
70년 동안,　　　고국으로 돌아온 후 계속　　　블레셋 사람들

Philistines / who captured it. Because the people had
에 의해　　그것을 차지하고 있던.　사람들은 하나님에게 냉담해져서,

grown cold toward God, / they did not wish / to hear
　　　　　원하지 않았다

the reading of the law, / or be led by his counsel. Now
율법을 듣거나,　　　율법의 조언에 인도되는 것을.　　그때

/ David called together the flower of all Israel, / thirty
다윗은 이스라엘의 젊은이들을 불러 모았고,

thousand men, / and they went / to bring the Ark to the
3만 명을,　　　그들은 떠났다　　궤를 다윗의 도시로 가져오려고.

city of David. While on the way / a man who had laid
돌아오는 길에　　　궤에 손을 댔던 한 남자가

his hand upon the Ark / when it was unsteady / was
　　　　궤가 불안정해서

smitten and died, / for no one but the priests and Levites
벌을 받아 죽어 버렸다,　제사장과 레위 지파 외에 누구도

/ could touch the Ark of God. David feared to bring it
하나님의 궤를 만질 수 없었기에.　　다윗은 궤를 더 이상 가져오기 두려워져서,

further, / and so he placed it / in the house of Obededom /
그것을 두었다　　　오벳에돔의 집에

which was near by. It was there three months, / and great
근처에 있던.　　　궤는 그곳에서 3개월 간 머물렀고,

blessing came / to the house / because of it. When David
엄청난 축복이 찾아왔다　그 집에　　궤로 인해.

heard this / he went joyfully down / to bring the Ark to
이 소식을 들리자　다윗은 기쁜 마음으로 자신의 도시로 내려갔고　궤를 가져오기 위해 .

his city, / and it was with sacrifices, and shouting, and
궤는 제물과 환호와, 트럼펫 소리와 함께

the sound of trumpet / that it was brought / and set in
궤를 가져왔음을 알리는

the Tabernacle / that had been made ready for it. And so
회막에 안치했다   예비되어 있던.

the worship of the Lord / was established in Jerusalem,
그렇게 하여 주님을 예배하는 장소가   예루살렘에 세워졌다,

/ which was to be the great altar / for the sacrificial
그곳은 큰 제단이 되었고   제물을 바치는 예배를 위한

worship / until the sacrifice should be taken away, / and
희생 제물이 없어지고,

the kingdom of Christ established on the earth.
그리스도의 왕국이 이 땅에 세워질 때까지.

Key Expression

ever의 의미

부사 ever는 문장에 따라 다양한 의미로 사용됩니다.
① (의문문에서) 언젠가, 일찍이
② (조건문에서) 앞으로, 언젠가, 한번이라도
③ (긍정문에서) 언제나, 항상, 늘, 줄곧
④ 도대체 (의문사와 결합하여 강조의 의미)
⑤ 훨씬 (비교급이나 최상급의 의미 강조)

ex) It had been in the house of Abinadab in Kirjath-Jearim for seventy years,
ever since it was sent home by the Philistines who captured it.
그 궤는 그것을 차지하고 있던 블레셋 사람들에 의해 고국으로 돌아온 후 줄곧
70년 동안 기럇여아림에 있는 아비나답에 있었다.
No child had ever been sent them.
그들에겐 줄곧 자녀가 없었다.
He began to oppress the Israelites more than he had ever done before.
왕은 이전에 일찍이 그랬던 것 보다 더욱 더 이스라엘인을 억압하기 시작했다.

longing 갈망 | capture 포로로 잡다, 차지하다

But David was not satisfied.
하지만 다윗은 만족하지 않았다.

"See," / he said to Nathan the prophet, / "I dwell in a
"보소서," 다윗은 선지자 나단에게 말했다, "나는 삼나무 집에

house of cedar, / but the Ark of God dwelleth within
살고있지만, 하나님의 궤는 장막 안에 놓여 있습니다."

curtains."

That night / the Lord spoke to Nathan / and told him
그날 밤 주님께서 나단에게 말씀하셨고 알려 주셨다

/ what to say to the king. He promised / to establish
왕에게 뭐라고 말할지. 주님은 약속하시며

the royal house of David, / and give final peace to the
다윗의 왕실을 세우고, 백성들에게 완전한 평화를 주시겠다고,

people, / and also to build a house / for the worship of
집을 지으라 하셨다 주님을 예배하기 위한,

the Lord, / but he said / that David's son, / who should
하지만 말씀하셨다 다윗의 아들이,

be king after him, / should build a house to his name, /
그의 뒤를 이어 왕이 될, 주님의 이름으로 집을 지을 것이라고,

and of him the Lord said, / "I will be his Father, / and he
그리고 그에 대해 말씀하셨다, "내가 그의 아비가 되고,

shall be my son."
그는 나의 아들이 되리라."

Then King David went in to the Tabernacle / and
그러자 다윗 왕은 회막에 가서

thanked the Lord for His promise / to him and to his son,
주님의 언약에 감사 드리며 자신과 아들에게 주신,

/ and asked His blessing upon them. Though he reigned
하나님의 축복을 구했다. 40년 간 통치하는 동안,

forty years, / he never forgot / that his work was / not to
다윗은 결코 잊지 않았다 자신의 일은

build the temple of the Lord, / but to prepare for it. So
성전을 짓는 것이 아니라, 그 일을 준비하는 것임을.

dwell 거주하다, 살다 | subdue 진압하다 | choir 합창단, 성가대 | lame 절름발이의

he subdued enemies, / built cities, / made leagues with
그래서 다윗은 적을 진압하고, 도시를 세우며, 우호적인 국가들과 동맹을 맺고,

friendly nations, / gathered much wealth / of wood, and
부를 축적하며 나무와 돌과

stone, / and gold, and silver and precious stones / for the
황금과 은과 보석들로

house of the Lord, / and trained choirs of singers / for the
주님의 성전을 위하여, 또한 성가대를 훈련시켰다

service. He also kept / his heart open toward the Lord,
예배를 위해. 다윗은 또한 지켰다 주님을 향해 마음이 열려 있도록.

/ so that he was able to write / some wonderful poems /
그리하여 쓸 수 있었다 멋진 시를

that were set to music / and sung by the temple choirs.
음악에 맞추어 성가대가 노래하는.

We call them / the Psalms of David.
사람들은 그 시를 불렀다 다윗의 시편이라고.

Though David had grown rich and great, / he did not
비록 다윗은 부유하고 위대해졌지만, 잊지 않았다

forget / his promise to Jonathan. He called Ziba, / who
요나단과 맺은 약속을. 그는 시바를 불러,

had been Saul's servant / and said to him, /
사울의 종이었던 말했다,

"Is there not yet / any of the house of Saul / that I may
"이제 아무도 없느냐 사울의 가족 중 남아있는 자가

show the kindness of God to him?"
내가 하나님의 자비심을 보여 줄 수 있는?"

Then Ziba told him of a man / who was lame in both his
그러자 시바가 한 남자에 대해 말했다 양 다리를 절름거리며,

feet, / who was the son of Jonathan. David sent for him,
요나단의 아들인. 다윗은 그를 데려오도록 하여,

/ and gave him / all the land of Saul, / and a place was
그에게 주고 사울의 모든 땅을, 그를 위해 자리를 만들었다

made for him / at the king's table / among his own sons, /
왕의 식탁에 친아들의 자리 가운데에,

and it was his / while he lived.
그 자리는 그의 것이었다 살아있는 동안.

24

DAVID'S SIN
다윗의 죄

The army of Israel was at war / with the Ammonites, /
이스라엘의 군대는 전쟁 중이었고   암몬 사람들과.

and Joab was the chief captain. David did not go out with
요압은 총사령관이었다.   다윗은 군대와 함께 나가지 않고,

the army, / but stayed in his house / in Jerusalem. One
            자신의 집에 머물러 있었다   이스라엘에 있는.

evening / he was walking on the flat roof of his house, /
어느 날 저녁   다윗은 평평한 지붕 위를 걷고 있었는데,

as the people of that country always do, / and he saw a
그 나라 사람들이 항상 하듯이.

little way off / a very beautiful woman. He sent a servant
가까운 곳에 보였다.   한 아름다운 여성이.   다윗은 하인을 보내

/ to ask who she was, / and found she was the wife of
   그녀가 누구인지 물었고,   우리아의 아내임을 알았다

Uriah / who was in the army with Joab, / fighting the
우리아   요압과 함께 전장에 나가,   암몬 사람들과 싸우고

Ammonites. Then a great temptation was set / before
있는.   그때 큰 유혹이 찾아왔고

David, / and instead of going to the Lord / to be saved
다윗에게,   그래서 주님 앞에 나가지 않고   유혹에서 벗어나기 위해,

from it, / he sent to Joab, / asking him to send him Uriah,
             요압에게 사람을 보내,   헷사람인 우리아를 보내라고 했다.

the Hittite. So Uriah came, / and David talked kindly
그렇게 우리아가 오자,   다윗은 그와 다정하게 이야기를 나눴고,

with him, / and found him a good and faithful man.
             그가 선하고 믿을 만한 사람임을 알았다.

When he went back to Joab / he took a letter from David,
요압에게 돌아갈 때   그는 다윗의 편지를 가지고 왔다

/ who asked that he be set / in the front of the battle. So
   그를 배치하라고 요청하는   최전방에.

Joab placed him there, / and when the two armies met
그래서 요압은 그를 전방에 배치했고,   양국의 군대가 맞섰을 때

/ Uriah was killed, / and Joab sent a messenger / to tell
우리아는 죽고 말았다, 그러자 요압은 전령을 보내 다윗에게 그

David. After her mourning was ended, / Bathsheba,
소식을 알렸다. 애도 기간이 끝난 후,

the wife of Uriah, / became the wife of David, / but the
우리아의 아내인 밧세바는, 다윗의 부인이 되었지만,

Lord was displeased with David. He also knew David's
주님은 기뻐하지 않으셨다. 주님은 다윗의 마음을 알고 계셨고

heart / and how to deal with him, / so he sent Nathan the
어떻게 다뤄야 하는지도 아셨기에, 다윗에게 선지자 나단을 보내 말씀

prophet to him.
하셨다.

"There were two men in one city," / said Nathan, / "one
"한 도시에 두 사람이 있었습니다." 나단이 말했다,

of them rich / and the other poor. The rich man had
"한 사람은 부자였고 다른 사람은 가난했습니다. 부자에게는

many flocks and herds, / but the poor man had nothing,
수많은 양과 소가 있었고, 가난한 사람에게는 아무것도 없었습니다,

/ save one little ewe lamb, / which he had bought and
어린 암양 한 마리 밖에, 그가 사서 키운;

nourished up; / and it grew together / with him and with
양은 함께 자랐습니다 그 사람과 그의 자녀들과;

his children; / it did eat of his own meat / and drink of
사람이 먹는 고기를 먹었고 사람이 먹는 잔으로

his own cup, / and lay in his bosom / and was unto him
마셨으며, 그의 가슴에 눕기도 하며 그에게 있어 마치 딸과 같았습

as a daughter. And there came a traveller / unto the rich
니다. 그러다가 한 여행자가 찾아왔고 부자에게,

man, / and he spared to take of his own flock / to dress
부자는 자신이 양을 내어주지 않고

for the wayfaring man / that was come to him, / but took
여행자에게 옷을 입히려고 자신에게 찾아온,

the poor man's lamb / and dressed it for the man / that
가난한 사람의 양을 가져와 여행자에게 옷을 입혔습니다

was come to him."
그에게 찾아온."

ewe 암양 | nourish 키우다 | bosom 가슴 | spare 할애하다, 내어 주다 | wayfaring 여행을 하는

David was very angry at the man / who could do such a
다윗은 그 자에게 매우 화를 내며   그토록 잔혹한 짓을 한,

cruel thing, / and he said to Nathan, /
나단에게 말했다,

"The man that hath done this thing / shall surely die; /
"그런 일을 한 자는   반드시 죽으리라;

and he shall restore the lamb fourfold, / because he did
또한 양을 4배로 갚아야 하리,   그가 이런 짓을 했고,

this thing, / and because he had no pity."
동정심이 없었기 때문에."

Then Nathan said to David, / "Thou art the man," / and
그러자 나단이 다윗에게 말했다,   "당신이 바로 그 사람입니다,"

he told him / how greatly the Lord had blessed him / in
또 나단은 말했다   주님께서 얼마나 다윗을 축복하셨는지

making him King over Israel, / and in delivering him /
다윗을 이스라엘의 왕으로 세우고,   구해내며

from the hand of Saul, / and how he had slain a faithful
사울의 손에서,   그런데 다윗이 어떻게 충직한 신하를 죽이고

servant / and taken his wife for himself; / therefore evil
그의 부인을 취했는지;   따라서 악이 그에게

would befall him.
닥칠 것이라고 했다.

David said, / "I have sinned against the Lord," / and the
다윗이 말했다,   "제가 주님께 죄를 지었습니다,"   그러자 주님은

Lord saw / that his repentance was real, / and forgave the
아셨고   그가 진심으로 회개하고 있음을,   죄를 용서하셨다.

sin, / but that David might never forget and sin / again, /
하지만 다윗은 결코 잊지 않고 죄를 짓지 않도록   다시는,

the Lord took the little child / that was born to him and
주님께서는 아이를 데려가셨다   다윗과 밧세바 사이에서 태어난,

to Bathsheba. While it was sick / David fasted / and lay
아이가 아픈 동안   다윗은 금식한 채

all night upon the earth, / and would not rise to taste
밤새 땅에 누워 있었고,   일어나 음식을 먹으려 하지 않았다.

food. This he did for seven days / while the little child
다윗은 이렇게 7일을 보냈다   아이가 아픈 동안,

was sick, / but when they told him / that his child was
하지만 사람들이 말하자   아이가 죽었다고

dead / he arose and bathed / and dressed himself / and
그는 일어나 목욕을 하고   옷을 갖춰 입은 후

went to the house of the Lord to worship, / and returned
주님께 예배하러 갔다가,

to take his food. Then his servants wondered at it, / and
돌아와 음식을 먹었다.   신하들이 이를 보고 궁금해하자,

replied, /
다윗이 대답했다.

"While the child was yet alive / I fasted and wept, / for
"아이가 아직 살아있을 동안   나는 금식하고 울었다.

I said, / who can tell / whether God will be gracious
말했기에,   누가 알리요   하나님께서 나를 불쌍히 여기사

unto me / that the child may live. But now he is dead, /
아이를 살리실지.   하지만 이제 아이가 죽었으니,

wherefore should I fast? Can I bring him back again? I
금식해야 할 이유가 무엇인가?   아이를 돌아오게 할 수 있는가?

shall go to him, / but he shall not return to me."
내가 아이에게 갈지언정,   아이는 내게 돌아오지 않으리니."

After this / another child was born to Bathsheba, / and
그 일이 있은 후   밧세바는 또 아이를 낳았고,

they named him Solomon, / which means "Peaceable."
그들은 솔로몬이라는 이름을 붙였다,   "평화를 사랑하는"이란 의미의.

And David wrote a prayer of repentance / for his sin.
그리고 다윗은 회개의 기도문을 적었다   자신의 죄에 대해.

It is the fifty-first Psalm, / and has been the prayer / of
그것이 시편 51편이며,   기도문이 되었다   죄를

penitent souls / for nearly three thousand years.
뉘우치는 영혼들에게   3,000여 년 동안.

---

pity 연민, 동정심 | befall 닥치다 | fast 금식하다 | bathe 씻다 | wherefore 무슨 이유로 | peaceable 평화적인,
평화를 사랑하는 | penitent 뉘우치는

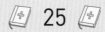

25

DAVID'S SORROW
다윗의 슬픔

David had a very beautiful son / named Absalom. From
다윗에게는 아주 아름다운 아들이 있었다　　　압살롬이라는.

the crown of his head to the soles of his feet / there was
그의 머리에서 발끝까지

no fault to be seen in him. His hair was thick and long,
흠을 찾을 수 없었다.　　　　　머리는 풍성하고 길었으며,

/ and his beauty was much talked of / through all Israel.
그의 아름다움은 회자되었다　　　　이스라엘 전역에서.

But the Lord / who looks upon the heart / saw / that the
하지만 주님은　　마음속을 꿰뚫어 보시는　　알고 계셨다

heart of Absalom was wicked and false. He killed his
압살롬의 마음이 사악하고 거짓되었음.　　　그는 형제인 암논을

brother Amnon, / and then fled to another country / and
죽인 후,　　　　다른 나라로 도망가

stayed three years. When he returned / he tried to see
3년 동안 머물렀다.　　　압살롬은 돌아와서　　아버지를 만나고자 했으나,

his father, / but David would not see him / for two years.
　　　　다윗은 그를 만나지 않았다　　　　2년 동안.

Then Absalom forced Joab to bring him / to the king's
그러자 압살롬은 요압을 시켜　　　　자신을 왕에게 데려가도

house / by setting Joab's barley field on fire. He was false
록 했다　보리밭에 불을 질러서.　　　그는 잘생겼으면서

as well as handsome, / and won his father's heart / by
사악했고,　　　　아버지의 마음을 얻었다

pretending to be humble.
겸손한 척하여.

---

crown 정수리 | sole 발바닥 | pretend ~인 척 하다 | right 권리 | deceive 속이다, 현혹하다 | vow 맹세 서약 |
counselor 상담자, 고문. 모사 | arrange 주선하다, 마련하다

After this / Absalom began to live more like a king /
이 일이 있은 후   압살롬은 왕처럼 살기 시작했다

than a prince. He had fifty men to run / before his chariot
왕자가 아니라.   그는 50명의 사람에게 달리게 했고   그의 마차 앞에서

/ when he rode, / and he stood in the city gates / and
마차를 타고 갈 때,   도시 문 앞에 서서

talked with the men / who came to see the king / about
사람들과 이야기 했다   왕을 만나러 온   자신들의

their rights. He told them / that if he were ruler over the
권리를 주장하려고. 압살롬은 말하면서   만약 자신이 통치자가 된다면

land / every man should have / all that he wanted, / and
모두 가지게 될 것이라고   원하는 모든 것을,

deceived many / by a false show of friendship.
여러 명을 속였다   거짓된 우정을 내보이면서.

Then he asked the king / if he could go to Hebron / to
그러고 나서 압살롬은 왕에게 물었다   자신이 헤브론으로 가서

pay a vow to the Lord / by offering sacrifice there, / and
주님께 서약해도 되는지   그곳에서 제사를 드려.

David told him to go in peace, / and he went. But he had
그러자 다윗은 평안히 가라고 말했고,   압살롬은 떠났다.   하지만 압살롬은

cruelly deceived his father. He had sent spies / through
사악하게도 아버지를 속였다.   그는 첩자를 보내

all the land / to persuade them / to join him at Hebron
나라 곳곳으로   설득했다   헤브론에서 자신과 합류하여

/ and make him king. He also took two hundred men /
자신을 왕으로 만들라고.   그는 또한 200명을 데리고

out of Jerusalem / to help him, / and one of them / was
예루살렘 밖으로 나가   자신을 돕도록 했는데, 그 중 한 명은

David's counsellor. They had arranged / to have all the
다윗의 모사였다.   사람들은 계획했다   모든 사람들이,

people, / as soon as they heard anywhere / the sound of
어디에서든 듣자마자   트럼펫 소리를,

the trumpet, / to cry, /
이렇게 외치라고,

"Absalom is king in Hebron."
"압살롬이 헤브론의 왕이다."

Then it came to the ears of David / that his people had
다윗의 귀에 들려왔다   백성들이 이끌렸다는 소식이

been led away / by deceit / to follow Absalom, / and
속아서   압살롬을 따르도록,   그러자

David, / who had been fearless / before Goliath / and
다윗은,   두려워하지 않았던   골리앗 앞에서도

before great armies of other nations, / was afraid. His
대규모의 군대 앞에서도,   두려워했다.

heart was broken / at the treachery of his son, / and he
그의 마음은 무너져서   아들의 배반을 접하고,

said to his servants, /
신하에게 말했다.

"Arise, / and let us flee; / make haste and go, / for fear
"일어나라,   도망가자;   서둘러 가자,

Absalom may come / and fight against the city / with the
압살롬이 찾아와   싸우게 될 것이 두려우니

sword."
칼을 들고."

His servants were ready to fight for him, / but he fled
신하들은 싸울 준비가 되어 있었지만,   다윗은 서둘러

in haste / over the brook Kedron / and went toward the
도망쳤다   케드론의 시내를 건너   광야로 향했다.

wilderness, / with all of the people of the city with him, /
도시의 모든 사람들이 그를 따랐고,

until there was a great multitude, / and in the midst / the
마침내 거대한 무리를 이뤘다.   그리고 그 중에는

priests and the Levites / bearing the Ark of God, / but
제사장과 레위지파 사람들이 있었다   하나님의 언약궤를 갖고 있는,

when David saw this / he said, /
다윗은 이를 보고   말했다.

"Carry back the Ark of God into the city. If I shall find
"하나님의 언약궤를 다시 도시로 가져가자.   내가 만약 은혜를

favor / in the eyes of the Lord / He will bring me again.
입는다면   주님의 눈 앞에서   그분이 나를 다시 세우시리라.

Let Him do to me / as seemeth good to Him."
그분이 하는 대로 두자   그분이 보시기에 좋은 대로."

deceit 속임수, 사기 | treachery 배반 | favor 호의, 은혜

So the priests and the Levites returned to the city / with
그렇게 제사장들과 레위지파는 도시로 돌아왔다

the Ark of God.
하나님의 언약궤를 갖고.

It was a sad procession / that went over the *Mount of
슬픈 행진이었다   다윗에게 이끌려 감람산을 넘어가는,

Olives led by David, / weeping as he went, / with his
그는 울면서 갔고,

head covered and his feet bare. Some enemies of the
머리가 덥수룩한 채 맨발이었다.   사울 집안의 적들이 나와

house of Saul came out / and troubled him / by the way,
                          그를 괴롭혔지만   가는 길에,

/ but there was no anger / in the heart of David / toward
분노는 없었다   다윗의 마음속에   누군가를 향한.

any. He believed / the hand of the Lord was upon him, /
다윗은 믿었고   주님의 손길이 자신에게 있음을,

and he said, /
말했다,

"It may be the Lord will look on mine affliction."
"주님께서 나의 원통함을 굽어 살피시길."

Key Expression

bring ~ to naught : ~을 무효로 만들다

bring ~ to naught은 '~을 무효로 만들다, 실패로 끝나게 하다'라는 의미를 지닌 숙어입니다. bring은 다양한 숙어를 만들어내는 기본 동사 중 하나인데요. 'bring ~ to + 명사'의 형태로 쓰이는 숙어 몇 가지만 알아볼까요.

▶ bring ~ to naught : ~을 무효로 만들다, 실패로 끝나게 하다
▶ bring ~ to mind : ~을 기억하다
▶ bring ~ to life : ~에 활기를 불어넣다
▶ bring ~ to heel : ~을 굴복시키다
▶ bring ~ to light : ~을 드러내다, 밝히다
▶ bring ~ to one's knees : ~을 무릎 꿇리다, 굴복시키다, 마비시키다
▶ bring ~ to book : ~의 책임을 묻다, 해명을 요구하다
▶ bring ~ to effect : ~을 시행하다, 실행하다
▶ bring ~ to rights : ~을 고치다, 원래 상태로 하다

ex) The Lord was bringing his counsel to naught.
주님께서는 그의 조언을 쓸모 없게 만드셨다.

---

* Mount of Olives 올리브산(예루살렘 동쪽에 위치한 산으로 감람산이라고도 한다)

Absalom came to Jerusalem, / and while he was asking
압살롬은 예루살렘으로 왔고,　　　　　모사에게 물어보는 동안

his chief counselor / what to do, / he was persuaded by
　　　　　　　무엇을 해야 할지,　다윗의 친구에게 설득당했다,

a friend of David, / who had stayed behind, / to wait /
　　　　　　　뒤에 머물러 있던,　　　　　기다리라고

until he had gathered a larger army / before he followed
큰 군대를 모을 때까지　　　　　　　다윗을 쫓기 전에.

after David. This gave him time / to send word to David
　　　　이로 인해 그는 시간을 벌었고　다윗에게 전갈을 보낼

/ to cross over Jordan / before Absalom should overtake
요르단을 건너라는　　압살롬이 그를 따라잡기 전에.

him. The chief counsellor, / when he saw that his advice
모사는,　　　　　　자신의 조언을 따르지 않은 것을 보고,

was not followed, / went to his own house / and hanged
　　　　　　　집으로 돌아가서

himself, / for he knew / that the Lord was bringing his
목을 매달았다,　알았기에　주님께서 자신의 조언을 쓸모없게 만드셨음을.

counsel to naught.

After David had passed over into Gilead / the people of
다윗이 길르앗으로 들어가자

that land brought food, / and dishes, and beds / to the
그곳 사람들이 음식을 가져왔고,　요리와 침구도

sorrowful king and his tired people, / and they were
슬픔에 빠진 왕과 지친 백성들에게,　　　다윗 일행은 대접을 받았다

cared for / in the city of Mahanaim. Then Joab, the
　　　마하나임의 도시에서.　　　그리고 나서 요압 장군은,

captain, / gathered the men together / to go and meet
　　　사람들을 모아

Absalom and his army, / and as they passed out of
압살롬과 그의 군대를 만나러 갔다,　요압 장군 일행이 도시를 빠져나갈 때

the city / David stood in the gate / and charged all the
다윗은 문 앞에 서서　　　　모든 장수들에게 당부했다

captains / as they passed, / saying /
　　사람들이 지나갈 때,　이렇게 말하며

affliction 고통, 원통함 | naught 영, 무가치(=nothing) | charge 책임을 맡기다

"Deal gently, / for my sake, / with the young man, / even
"너그럽게 대하라, 나를 봐서, 젊은이들에게

with Absalom."
압살롬에게도."

So they went out to battle, / and it was in a wood.
그렇게 사람들은 전투에 나섰고, 전투는 숲속에서 치러졌다.

God had given David's army the victory, / and twenty
하나님은 다윗의 군대에게 승리를 안겨 주셨고,

thousand men of Absalom's army / were slain. Absalom,
2만 명의 압살롬 군대가 죽음을 당했다. 압살롬은,

/ who rode on a mule, / was caught by his long thick
노새를 타고 있던, 길고 풍성한 머리가 걸려 버렸고

hair / in the branches of an oak tree, / and the mule went
상수리 나무 가지에, 노새는 달아나 버려

away / and left him hanging there.
나무에 매달린 채 남겨지고 말았다.

A man ran / and told Joab / that he had seen / Absalom
한 남자가 달려와 요압에게 말했다 보았다고 압살롬이 상수리

hanging in an oak.
나무에 매달려 있는 것을.

"Why didst thou not smite him there?" / said Joab.
"어째서 그를 처치하지 않았느냐?" 요압이 물었다.

The man said / he would not have done it / for a thousand
그는 말했다 그런 짓을 하지 않을 거라고 1,000세켈의 은화를

shekels of silver, / because David had charged them all /
주더라도, 다윗이 모두에게 당부했기 때문에

not to touch the young man Absalom.
압살롬을 건드리지 말라고.

But Joab turned away, / and when he had found Absalom
하지만 요압은 돌아섰고, 압살롬을 발견하자

/ in the oak, / he, / with the ten young men / who were
상수리 나무에서, 그는, 열 명의 젊은이와 함께 있던,

with him, / killed Absalom, / and they buried him in the
압살롬을 죽이고, 숲속에 매장했다.

wood.

Then Joab sent two messengers / to carry news of the
그러고 나서 요압은 전령 두 명을 보냈다   승리의 소식을 전하러

victory / to the king, / who sat between the city gates, /
왕에게,   성문에 앉아 있던,

while a watchman stood over the gates / on the city wall.
그때 경비병은 성문 위에 서 있었다   성벽의.

When the watchmen saw the two men running, / one
경비병은 두 명이 달려오는 것을 보자,

after the other, / he cried out and told the king. The first
차례로,   왕에게 외치며 전했다.   첫 번째 전령이

man cried / as he came, / "All is well," / but when the
외쳤다   도착하면서,   "모든 일이 잘 되었습니다." 하지만 왕이 말하자,

king said, / "Is the young man Absalom safe?" / he could
"압살롬이 안전하냐?"라고   그는 대답할

not answer, / and when the second messenger cried, /
수 없었다,   그리고 두 번째 전령이 외치자,

"Tidings, / my lord, the king," / again David asked, /
"소식입니다,   왕이시여."   다윗은 또 다시 물었다,

"Is the young man Absalom safe?"
"압살롬은 안전한가?"

Key Expression

for one's sake : ~를 위해

sake는 동기, 이익, 목적, 원인 등의 뜻을 가진 명사로 for the sake of ~는 '~을 위해'라는 의미를 가진 숙어입니다. for one's sake와 같이 소유격의 형태로 사용할 수도 있습니다.
또한 for Christ's[God's, goodness', heaven's, pity's, mercy's] sake와 같은 단어를 사용하면 '제발, 맙소사, 아무쪼록'의 의미를 가지게 됩니다.

ex) Deal gently, for my sake, with the young man, even with Absalom.
나를 봐서 젊은이들에게, 또한 압살롬에게도 너그럽게 대하라.

gently 다정하게, 너그럽게 | mule 노새 | shekel 셰켈(이스라엘의 통화 단위) | watchman 경비병 | tidings 소식,
기별

"The enemies of my lord the king / and all that rise
"폐하의 적과   폐하에 반대하여 일어선 모든 이는

against thee / to do thee hurt / be as that young man," /
폐하를 해치려고   그 젊은이와 같은 운명이 되었습니다."

said the messenger.
전령이 말했다.

Then the king went up / to the room over the city gate /
그러자 왕은 올라가서   성문 위의 방으로

and wept, / and as he went / he cried, /
울었다,   그는 올라가면서   외쳤다,

"O my son Absalom! My son, / my son Absalom! Would
"오 내 아들 압살롬!   아들아,   내 아들 압살롬!

God I had died for thee, / O Absalom, / my son, / my
내가 너를 대신하여 죽었더라면,   오 압살롬,   내 아들,

son!"
아들아!"

Key Expression 🔑

no more : 그 이상 ~않다

no more는 '그 이상 ~않다, 이젠 ~않다'라는 의미를 가진 구문으로, not ~ any more로 풀어 쓰기도 합니다.

no more는 앞에 설명했던 no longer는 비슷한 의미를 가지고 있는데 의미의 차이가 있으므로 두 숙어의 사용법을 구별할 필요가 있습니다.

no more는 양이나 동작의 재개 여부에 초점을 맞춘 반면, no longer의 경우는 상태의 지속 여부에 초점을 맞춘 표현입니다. 즉, 뒤따르는 동사가 동작을 강조한 동사이거나 양을 나타낼 경우에는 no more를, 상태를 강조한 동사일 경우에는 no longer를 사용하도록 합니다.

ex) Thou shalt go no more out with us to battle.
더 이상 우리와 함께 전쟁터에 나가지 마소서.
Except your youngest brother come down with you, ye shall see my face no more.
막내를 데려오지 않는다면, 너는 더 이상 내 얼굴을 보지 못할 것이다.
She became his wife, so that he was no longer lonely and sad.
그녀는 이삭의 부인이 되었고, 그리하여 그는 더 이상 외롭거나 슬프지 않았다.

The people who had come back joyful / because the
기쁜 마음으로 돌아온 사람들은

enemy had been conquered / were distressed / by the
적에게 승리했기 때문에   고통스러워했다

grief of the king, / so that Joab persuaded David / to
왕이 애통하는 모습을 보고,   그러자 요압이 다윗을 설득하여

come down to the gate / and meet the people.
성문으로 내려와   사람들을 만나도록 했다.

After this / those who were left of the followers of
그 후에   압살롬의 추종자 중 남은 사람들이

Absalom / begged the king / to come back to Jerusalem,
왕에게 애원하자   예루살렘으로 돌아와 달라고,

/ and so he came, / and thousands came to meet him.
다윗은 돌아갔고,   수천 명의 사람들이 그를 만나러 왔다.

He had only forgiving words / for those who had injured
다윗은 용서의 말을 전했다   자신을 상처 입힌 이들에게,

him, / and for Barzillai and the men of Gilead / who had
그리고 바르실래와 길라앗의 사람들에게는

fed them and shown them great kindness / in the darkest
자신을 먹이고 친절을 베풀었으며   왕의 일생에서 가장

hour of the king's life, / and who came a little way on
우울했던 시기에,   자신과 잠시 여행했던,

the journey with them, / he had grateful words and
                감사와 축복의 말을 전했다.

blessings.

And so the king came to his own / again. He was now
그렇게 왕은 그의 자리로 돌아왔다   다시.

getting to be an old man, / and the love of his people /
그는 이제 노인이 되어버렸고,   백성들의 사랑이

made his last days blessed.
그의 남은 여생을 축복했다.

injure 부상을 입히다, 해치다

His warriors said, / "Thou shalt go no more out with us /
다윗의 장수들은 말했다.   "더 이상 우리와 함께 가지 마소서

to battle, / that thou quench not the light of Israel."
전쟁터에,   이스라엘의 등불이 꺼지지 않도록 하소서."

Once / he sinned against the Lord / by numbering his
한 번은   다윗이 주님께 죄를 지었다   백성의 수를 세어봄으로써.

people. He wanted to know / how many men / in his
그는 알고 싶었고   얼마나 많은 남자들이   자신의 왕국에

kingdom / could bear arms in battle, / and he forgot /
있는   전쟁터에서 무기를 들 수 있는지.   잊어버렸다

that victory over the enemy was / not with the many
적에게 승리하는 것은   사람의 수가 많고 적음이 아니라,

or the few, / but with the Lord, / who is the strength
주님께 달려 있다는 것을   그의 민족의 강력한 힘이 되는.

of his people. When he saw that he had done wrong
다윗은 자신이 잘못을 저질렀음을 알게 되자

/ he confessed it / and begged for forgiveness, / but a
죄를 고백하며   용서를 구했지만,

pestilence spread over all the land, / and came near to
온 나라에 역병이 돌아,   예루살렘 근처까지 이르렀다,

Jerusalem, / and the angel was stayed / by the Lord's
천사들은 머물러 있었다   주님의 명령으로

hand / just over the threshing floor of Araunah. This was
아라우나의 타작 마당 바로 앞에서.

the broad flat top of Mount Moriah / where long before /
이곳은 모리아 산 정상에 있는 평원으로   오래 전

Abraham had built an altar / on which to offer Isaac.
아브라함이 제단을 쌓았던 곳이었다   이삭을 제물로 바치기 위해.

When David saw the angel / he said, /
다윗은 천사를 보고   말했다.

"I have done wickedly, / but these sheep, / what have
"제가 악행을 저질렀습니다,   하지만 이 양 떼는,   무슨 짓을 했습니까?

they done? Let Thine hand, / I pray thee, / be against me,
당신의 손으로,   바라옵건대,   저를 치시고,

/ and against my father's house."
제 아비의 집을 치소서."

Then the prophet Gad said, / "Go up, / rear an altar to the
그러자 선지자 갓이 말했다,   "올라가시오,   제단 뒤쪽의 주님께

Lord / in the threshing-floor of Araunah," / and David
아라우나의 타작 마당에 있는,"   그러자 다윗은 갔다

went / as the Lord commanded.
주님이 명하신 대로.

When they reached the mount Araunah / offered David
그들이 아라우나 산에 도착하자   다윗에게 바쳤다

/ the piece of ground with the oxen / for a sacrifice, / but
황소와 땅의 일부를   제사에 사용하도록

he would not take them as a gift.
하지만 다윗은 이를 선물로 받아들이지 않았다.

"But I will surely buy it of thee / at a price," / said David,
"내가 반드시 당신에게서 사겠소   값을 치르고,"   다윗이 말했다,

/ "neither will I offer burnt offerings / to the Lord my
"번제를 드리지도 않겠소   하나님께

God / of that which doth cost me nothing."
거저 얻은 제물로는."

So he bought the piece of ground / and paid for it six
그래서 다윗은 그 땅을 사고   금화 600세켈을 지불했다.

hundred shekels of gold. Twice had the Lord blessed this
주님이 이 땅을 두 번 축복하셨고

spot / with a miracle of salvation, / and twice an altar
구원의 기적을 내리시자,   두 번째 제단이 그곳에 만들어졌다,

had been built there, / and looking upon it, / David said, /
그리고 이를 보며,   다윗이 말했다,

"This is the house of the Lord God, / and this is the altar
"이곳은 하나님의 집이며,   번제를 위한 제단이다

of burnt offering / for Israel," / and he prepared / to build
이스라엘을 위한,"   그리고 나서 다윗은 준비했다

there the temple of Solomon, / — the altar of the world.
그곳에 솔로몬이 성전을 짓도록,   — 바로 세상을 위한 제단이었다.

---

quench 갈증을 풀다, (타는 불을) 끄다 | pestilence 악성 전염병, 역병 | ox 황소

mini test 8

A. 다음 문장을 해석해 보세요.

(1) Absalom, / who rode on a mule, / was caught by his long thick hair / in the branches of an oak tree, / and the mule went away / and left him hanging there.
→

(2) The man said he would not have done it / for a thousand shekels of silver, / because David had charged them all / not to touch the young man Absalom.
→

(3) The enemies of my lord the king / and all that rise against thee to do thee hurt / be as that young man.
→

(4) Neither will I offer burnt offerings / to the Lord my God / of that which doth cost me nothing.
→

B. 다음 주어진 문구가 알맞은 문장이 되도록 순서를 맞춰 보세요.

(1) 제사장과 레위 지파 외에 누구도 하나님의 궤를 만질 수 없었다.
(the Ark of God / touch / but / could / No one / the priests and Levites)
→

(2) 다윗은 또한 그의 마음이 주님을 향해 열려 있도록 지켰다.
(his heart / the Lord / open / kept / He / toward / also)
→

(3) 주님께서 나의 원통함을 굽어 살피시길.
(mine / may be / It / affliction / look on / will / the Lord)
→

A. (1) 노새를 타고 있던 압살롬은 길고 풍성한 머리가 상수리나무 가지에 걸려 버렸고 노새는 달아나 버려 나무에 매달린 채 남겨지고 말았다. (2) 다윗이 모두에게 압살롬을 건드리지 말라고 당부했기 때문에, 그는 1,000세겔의 은화를 주더라도 그런 짓은 하지 않겠다고 했다. (3) 폐하의 적과 폐하에게 반대하여 일어나 해를

(4) 주님께서 그의 조언을 쓸모없게 만드셨다.
(his counsel / naught / was bringing / to / The Lord)
→

C. 다음 주어진 문장이 본문의 내용과 맞으면 T, 틀리면 F에 동그라미 하세요.

(1) David built a beautiful house for the Ark of God after he took
    Zion.
    (T / F)

(2) David didn't forget his promise to Jonathan, so he showed the
    kindness to Jonathan's son.
    (T / F)

(3) David drove Uriah to death to took his wife for himself.
    (T / F)

(4) Absalom, David's Son, could survive in the battle.
    (T / F)

D. 의미가 비슷한 것끼리 서로 연결해 보세요.

(1) subdue   ▶   ◀ ① agony

(2) penitent   ▶   ◀ ② suppress

(3) affliction   ▶   ◀ ③ put out

(4) quench   ▶   ◀ ④ remorseful

Answer

끼치려고 한 모든 이들은 그 젊은이와 같은 운명이 되었습니다. (4) 거저 얻은 제물로는 하나님께 번제
를 드리지도 않겠다. | B. (1) No one but the priests and Levites could touch the Ark of God. (2) He
also kept his heart open toward the Lord. (3) It may be the Lord will look on mine affliction. (4) The
Lord was bringing his counsel to naught. | C. (1) F (2) T (3) T (4) F | D. (1) ② (2) ④ (3) ① (4) ③   239

The Story of the Bible을 다시 읽어 보세요.

THE BEGINNING OF THINGS

Away back in the beginning of things God made the sky and the earth we live upon. At first it was all dark, and the earth had no form, but God was building a home for us, and his work went on through six long days, until it was finished as we see it now.

On the first day God said, "Let there be light," and the black night turned to gray, and light came. God called the light Day, and the darkness Night, and the evening and the morning made the first day.

Then God divided the waters, so that there were clouds above and seas below, and He called the clouds heaven. It was the second day.

Then the seas were gathered together by themselves, and the dry land rose above them, and God saw that it was good. Then He called to the grass, and the plants, and the trees to come out of the ground, and they came bearing their seeds, and He called the third day good.

Then God called to the two great lights, the sun and the moon, to shine clear in the sky, which had been first dark, and then gray, and they rose and set to make day and night, and seasons and years, and the stars came also, and it was the fourth day.

Then God called for all kinds of fishes that swim in the seas, and rivers, and for all kinds of birds that fly in the air, and they came, and it was the fifth day.

And then God called for the animals to live on the green earth, and the cattle and the great beasts, and the creeping things came, and God called them all good.

After this he made the first of the great family of Man. He made them after His own likeness. He made their bodies from the earth, but their souls He breathed into them, so that Man is a spirit, living in an earthly body, and can understand about God and love Him. He blessed them and told them to become many, and to rule over all the earth, with its beasts and birds, and fishes, and it was the sixth day.

The Man's name was Adam, and the woman, who was made from a

piece of Adam's body nearest to his heart, was named Eve.

Then God's world was finished, and on the seventh day there was rest. God was pleased with all that was made, and He made the seventh day holy, by setting it apart from all the others. We keep the Sabbath, or the Lord's day still, in which his children may rest and worship.

Adam and Eve were very happy, for they had never done anything wrong. God gave them a beautiful wide garden, called Eden, full of flowers and all kinds of fruit, and with a river flowing through it, and told Adam to take care of the garden, and He sent all the animals and birds to Adam to be named. God told him also that he might eat the fruit of all the trees of the garden except one — the tree of knowledge of good and evil — but if he ate of the fruit of that tree he should surely die, and Adam and Eve loved God, and had no wish to disobey Him, for He was their Father.

But there was a creeping serpent in the garden, and the evil spirit that puts wrong thoughts in our hearts spoke to Eve through the serpent. "You shall not die," he said, "but you shall be wise like God if you will eat of this fruit," and Eve ate of the fruit, and gave it to her husband.

Then they knew that they had sinned, and when they heard the voice of God in the garden calling them, they hid among the trees, for they were unhappy and afraid. When the Lord had asked Adam if he had eaten of the fruit that was forbidden, Adam laid the sin upon Eve, who gave it to him, and Eve said that the serpent had tempted her to eat of the fruit. God knew that they must suffer for their sin, so He sent them out of the garden to make a garden for themselves, and to work, and suffer pain, as all who came after them have done to this day; but He gave them a great promise, that among their children's children One should be born who would be stronger than sin, and a Savior from it.

After this two little children were sent to comfort Adam and Eve — first Cain, and then Abel. When they grew up Cain was a farmer, but Abel was a shepherd.

They had been taught to worship God by bringing the best of all they had to Him, and so Cain brought fruit and grain to lay upon his altar, but Abel brought a lamb.

God looked into their hearts and saw that Abel wished to do right, but Cain's heart was full of sin. Cain was angry because the Lord was pleased with the worship of Abel, and while they talked in the field Cain killed his brother. When the Lord said to Cain, "Where is thy brother?" he answered, "I know not. Am I my brother's keeper?" And the Lord sent him away from home, to wander from place to place over the earth, and find no rest, but He promised that no one should hurt Cain, or kill him as he had killed his brother, so he went away into another land to live.

Adam lived many years after this and had other children, but at last he died, when his children's children were beginning to spread over the land.

 THE GREAT FLOOD

As the people of the earth grew to be many more and spread over the plains and hills, they also grew very wicked. They forgot God, and all the thoughts of their hearts were evil. Only Noah still worshipped God and tried to do right.

The people had destroyed themselves, and so God said to Noah:

"The end of all flesh is come; make thee an ark of gopher wood."

He told Noah to make it of three stories, with a window in the top, and a door in the side. It was to be a great floating house, more than four hundred feet long and full of rooms, and it was to be covered with tar within and without, so that the water should not creep in.

"I bring a flood of waters upon the earth," said the Lord, "and everything that is in the earth shall die."

This was to be the house of Noah, with his wife, and his three sons and their wives, during the great flood.

Does the house seem large for eight people? God had told Noah to make room for a little family of every kind of bird and beast that lived, and to gather food of all kinds for himself and for them.

So Noah did all that the Lord had told him to do, and seven days before the great storm he heard the Lord calling:

"Come thou and all thy house into the ark," and that very day, Noah with his wife and his sons, Shem, Ham, and Japtheth, and their wives, went into their great black house, and through the window in the top came flying the little families of birds and insects, from the tiny bees and humming birds, to the great eagles, and through the door on the side came the families of animals, two by two, from the little mice to the tall giraffes, and the elephants, and when all had come the Lord shut them in.

It rained forty days and forty nights, and the waters rose higher and higher, covering the hills, and creeping up the mountains, so that every living thing died except Noah, and all that were with him in the ark. But after ten months the tops of the mountains were seen, and Noah sent out a raven and a dove. The raven flew to and fro, but the dove came back into the ark, because she found no place to rest her foot.

After seven days Noah sent her out again, and she returned with an olive leaf in her bill, and then Noah knew that the waters were going away. After seven days again he sent out his good little dove, and she did not come back. So Noah was sure that the earth was getting dry, and that God would soon tell him to go out of the ark.

And so he did.

Think how glad the sheep and cows were to find fresh grass, and the birds to fly to the green trees.

What a silent world it must have been, for there were none but Noah and his family in all the earth. Noah did not forget how God had saved them, and he made an altar of stone, and offered beasts and birds as a sacrifice. When he looked up to the sky there was a beautiful rainbow. It was God's promise that there should be no more floods upon the earth. He still sends the rainbow to show us that He is taking care of this world, and will always do so.

Perhaps the people who lived after this — for Noah's children's children increased very fast — did not believe God's promise, for they began to build a great tower, or temple, on the plain of Shinar; or perhaps they had grown proud and wicked, and wanted a temple for the worship of idols; but the Lord changed their speech, so that they could not understand each other, and they were scattered over other countries; and so each country began to have a language of its own.

ABRAHAM—THE FATHER OF THE FAITHFUL

The people who lived four thousand years ago were very much like children who easily forget. They told their children about the great flood, but nearly all forgot to tell them of the good God who is the Father of us all, whom we should always love and obey. Yet there is always one, if not more, who remembers God, and keeps his name alive in the world. Abram had tried to do right, though there was no Bible in the world then, and no one better than himself to help him but God, and one day He called Abram, and told him to go away from his father's house into another country.

"A land that I will show thee," said the Lord, "and I will make of thee a great nation."

He also made Abram a wonderful promise, —

"In thee shall all the families of the earth be blessed."

He meant that sometime the Savior should be born among Abram's children's children, and that He should be the Savior of all the nations of the earth.

Abram did just what God told him to do. He took Sarai, his wife, and Lot, his nephew, and some servants, and cows, and sheep, and camels, and asses, and went into the land of Canaan. When they rested at night Abram and Lot set some sticks in the ground, and covered them with skins for a tent, and near by they made an altar, where Abram offered a sacrifice, for that was the only way they could worship God when the earth was young.

Abram went down into Egypt when there was a lack of food in Canaan, but he came back to Bethel, where he made the altar before, and worshipped God there.

He was very rich, for his cattle and sheep had grown into great herds and flocks, though he had sold many in Egypt for silver, and gold, and food. Abram and Lot moved often, for their flocks and herds soon ate up the grass. Then they rolled up the tents, and loaded the camels and asses, and went where the grass was thick and fresh.

They could easily live in tents, for the country was warm. But Abram's herdsmen and Lot's herdsmen sometimes quarreled. And so Abram spoke kindly to Lot, and told him to take his servants, and flocks, and herds, and go where the pastures were good, and he would go the other way. So they parted, and Lot went to the low plains of the Jordan, but Abram went to the high plains of Mamre, in Hebron, and there he built another altar to the Lord, who had given him all that country — to him and to his children forever.

There were warlike people in Canaan, and once when they had carried off Lot from Sodom, Abram took his servants and herdsmen and went out to fight. He had more than three hundred men, and they took Lot away from the enemy, and brought him back to Sodom. It was here that Abram met a wonderful man, who was both a king and a priest. His name was Melchisedek, and he brought Abram bread and wine, and blessed him there.

After this, God spoke to Abram one evening, and promised that he should have a son, and then while Abram stood outside his tent, with the great sky thick with stars above him, God promised him that his children's children should grow to be as countless as the stars. That was hard to believe, but Abram believed God always and everywhere.

Still no child came to Abram and Sarai, and Abram was almost a hundred years old, but God spoke to him again, and told him that he should be the father of many nations.

He told Abram that a little boy would be born to them, and his name would be Isaac, and God changed Abram's name to Abraham, which means "Father of many people," and Sarai's to Sarah, which means "Princess."

Abraham was sitting in his tent one hot day, when three men stood by him. They were strangers, and Abraham asked them to rest beneath the tree, and bathe their feet, while he brought them food. So Sarah made cakes, and a tender calf was cooked, and these with butter, and milk, were set before the men. But they were not men of this world; they were angels, and they had come to tell Abraham and Sarah once more that their little child was sure to come. Then the angels went away, but one of them, who must have been the Lord Himself in an angel's form, stopped to tell Abraham that He was going to destroy Sodom and Gomorrah, because the people who lived there were so very wicked, and Abraham prayed Him to spare them if even ten good men could be found in them, for he remembered that Lot lived in Sodom. But the Lord never forgets. The two angels went to Sodom and stayed with Lot until morning, when they took him and all his family outside the city, and then the Lord said to him, "Escape for thy life — look not behind thee, neither stay thou in all the plain."

And the Lord hid them in the little town of Zoar, while a great rain of fire fell upon the wicked cities of the plain, until they became a heap of ashes. Only Lot's wife looked back to see the burning cities, and she became a pillar of salt.

The next morning when Abraham looked from Hebron down toward the cities of the plain, a great smoke was rising from them like the smoke of a furnace.

At last the Lord's promise to Abraham and Sarah came true. A little son was born to them, and they called him Isaac. They were very happy, for though Abraham was a hundred years old, no child had ever been sent them.

When he was about a year old they made a great feast for him, and all brought gifts and good wishes, yet the little lad Ishmael, the son of Hagar, Sarah's servant, mocked at Isaac. Sarah was angry, and told her husband that Hagar and her boy must be sent away. So he sent them out with only a bottle of water and a loaf of bread; for God had told Abraham to do as Sarah wished him to do, and He would take care of little Ishmael, and make him the father of another nation.

When the water was gone, and the sun grew very hot, poor Hagar laid her child under a bush to die, for she was very lonely and sorrowful. While she hid her eyes and wept, saying, "Let me not see the death of the child," she heard a voice out of heaven telling her not to be afraid. "Arise, lift up the lad," said the voice, "for I will make him a great nation."

And God opened her eyes to see a well of water near. Then she filled the empty bottle, and gave the boy a drink, and God took good care of them ever after, though they lived in a wilderness.

Ishmael grew up to be an archer, and became the father of the Arabs, who still live in tents as Ishmael did.

But the Lord let a strange trial come to the little lad Isaac, also. His father loved and obeyed God, but there were heathen people around them, who worshipped idols, and sometimes killed their own children as a sacrifice to these idols. Abraham brought the best of his lambs and cattle to offer to the Lord; but one day the Lord told Abraham to take his only son Isaac and offer him upon a mountain called Moriah as a burnt sacrifice to God. Abraham had always obeyed God, and believed his word, and now, though he could not understand, he rose up early in the morning and took his young son, with two servants, and an ass loaded with wood, to the place of which God had told him.

They were three days on the journey, but at last they came to the high place, where the city of Jerusalem was afterward built, and to the very rock upon which the temple was built long afterward, with its great altar and Holy of Holies.

On Mount Moriah Abraham had left the young men at the foot of the mount, and went with Isaac to the great rock on the top of the mount. "My father," said Isaac, "where is the lamb for a burnt offering?"

"My son, God will provide himself a lamb for a burnt offering," said his father, still obeying God, and believing His word, that Isaac should be the father of many nations.

Abraham made an altar of stones, and bound Isaac and laid him upon it, but when his hand was lifted to offer up the boy, the Lord called to him from heaven. "Lay not thine hand upon the lad," said the voice, "for now I know that thou fearest God, seeing thou hast not withheld thine only son from me."

Then Abraham turned and saw a ram with its twisted horns caught in the bushes, and he offered it to the Lord instead of his son. How glad and grateful Abraham must have been that morning, when he came down the mountain, with Isaac walking beside him, to think that he had still obeyed God when it was hard to do so.

Abraham was an old man when Sarah died. They had lived together a long lifetime, and he mourned for her many days. He bought a field close by the oak-shaded plain of Mamre in Hebron, and there in a rocky cave he buried her. He was called a Prince of God by the Canaanites because he lived a true, faithful life.

A few years after he also went to God, and his body was laid beside Sarah's in the cave-tomb. Ishmael came up from the south country to mourn with Isaac at the burial of their father, the Friend of God, and Father of the faithful.

📖 ISAAC THE SHEPHERD PRINCE 📖

Before Abraham died, he thought much about his dear son Isaac, to whom he was going to leave all that he had. The young man had no mother, no sister, and soon he would have no father. So the old man called his old and faithful servant, and told him to go on a journey into

the land of his fathers, and bring back with him a wife for his son Isaac.
The children of Nahor, Abraham's brother, lived there still, and
Abraham wished for his son Isaac a wife of his own people, who should
be both good and beautiful, and not like the heathen women of Canaan.
So the old servant listened to Abraham and promised to do all that he
commanded.

He loaded ten camels with presents for his master's family away in
Syria, and Abraham said:

"The Lord shall send His angel before thee," and from his tent door he
saw the little caravan of camels and servants, as they set out across the
plain, toward the land beyond the river Jordan.

There was a desert to cross and many dangers to meet, but the old
servant believed in the God his master worshipped, and was not afraid.
When he came to Haran, he stopped outside the town by a well of water.
It was early evening, and the women were coming each with a water-jar
on her shoulder, to draw water.

The old man prayed that the Lord would show him which among these
daughters of the men of the city, was the one who was to be his young
master's wife.

Before his prayer was ended, Rebekah, of the family of Abraham's
brother Nahor, came bearing her pitcher on her shoulder. She looked
very kind and beautiful, and when she had filled her pitcher, the old man
asked her for a drink of water. Then she let down the pitcher upon her
hand saying:

"Drink, my lord," and asked if she should also give water to his camels.
While she was giving him a drink, the man showed her some golden
jewels that he had brought, and when he had asked her name, and knew
that God had sent her to him for his young master, he gave them to her,
and worshipped the Lord who had led him to the house of his master's
brother.

Then Rebekah ran in and told Laban, her brother, and the old servant of
Abraham had a warm welcome at the door of Nahor's house.

"Come in, thou blessed of the Lord," they said.

And after they had cared for the camels and the men, there was a hurrying of servants to prepare a feast, but the old man would not taste food until he had given the message of his master. Then the father and brother of Rebekah, saw that the Lord had sent for her, and they said: "Let her be thy master's son's wife, as the Lord hath spoken."

And the old servant bowed his face to the ground worshipping the Lord who had led him.

Then there was feasting and giving of costly gifts, and preparing to take a long journey, for the old servant was in haste to get back to his master, and Rebekah, who was willing to go, took her maid-servants and rode away into a far country to be the wife of Isaac.

When Isaac was walking in his field at sunset, thinking and praying to God, he looked up and saw that the camels were coming, and he hastened to meet them. When the old servant told Rebekah that it was his young master, she alighted from her camel, and covered herself with a long veil as was the custom of the Syrian women. When the old servant had told the story of his journey, he gave Rebekah to Isaac, and he took her to the tent that had been his mother's, and she became his wife, so that he was no longer lonely and sad.

Isaac lived to a very great age, and had two sons, Jacob and Esau. He was a gentle, quiet man, fond of his family, his flocks, and herds, and at the place where his father and mother were buried, he lived among the fields and oak groves of Hebron until he died.

JACOB, A PRINCE OF GOD

Jacob and Esau were the twin sons of Isaac and Rebekah. They did not look alike as twins often do, and they were very unlike in all their ways. As they grew up, Esau loved the forests and wild places. He made bows and arrows, and was a hunter, and brought home wild birds and deer, for his father was very fond of such food. Jacob helped his father with the flocks, and learned how to cook food from his mother, who loved him more than she loved Esau.

One day Esau came home from hunting tired and hungry, and smelled the delicious soup of red lentils that Jacob was making. He begged Jacob to give him some, and Jacob, who wanted to be eldest, and have the right to the blessing that fathers gave to the first-born in those days, said:

"Sell me this day thy birthright," and Esau gave him all his rights as the first born, for a little food which he might have had as a free gift.

Jacob wanted to be counted in the great promise that God had given to Abraham, but Esau despised it.

Afterward, when Isaac was old and his eyes were dim, he called Esau, and asked him to go out into the fields and shoot a deer, and cook the venison that he loved, so that he might eat it and bless his first born before he died.

Rebekah heard it, and told Jacob to bring kids from the flock, which she cooked and served as venison. Then she dressed Jacob in the clothes of Esau, and told him to say that it was Esau who had brought the venison. Isaac said:

"The voice is the voice of Jacob," but he put his hands on him, and believed it was Esau, and blessed him.

When Esau came home and brought venison to his father, Isaac said:

"Who art thou?" and when Esau said, "I am thy son, thy first-born, Esau," the old man trembled, and told Esau the blessing had been given to another.

Poor Esau cried out with grief, "Hast thou but one blessing?" "Bless me, even me also, O my father."

And so Isaac blessed him, but he could not call back the blessing of the first-born. The Lord knew that Jacob would grow to be a good man, and love the things of God best, and that Esau would always love the things of this world best, yet it was wrong of Jacob and Rebekah to deceive, for we may not do evil that good may come.

After this Esau hated his brother, and said he would kill him.

So Isaac called Jacob, and, blessing him again, sent him away into Syria to the house of Laban, where Rebekah had lived, and where Abraham's servant went to find her for his master's son.

One night, when he was not far on his way, he lay down to sleep, with a stone for his pillow, on a hillside that looked toward his home, and he dreamed a wonderful dream. He saw a ladder reaching from earth to heaven, and a vision of angels who were going up and down upon it. Above it stood the Lord, who spoke to Jacob, and gave to him the promise that He had first given to Abraham, and told him that He would go with him, and bring him again into his own land.

Jacob was afraid when he woke, for he had seen the heavens opened, and had heard God's voice. He made an altar of the pillow of stone, and called it Bethel — the House of God — and then he vowed that the Lord should be his God, and he added, —

"Of all that thou shalt give me, I will surely give a tenth unto thee."

When Jacob came to Haran, he saw the well from which his mother used to draw water. There were three flocks of sheep lying by it, waiting for all the flocks to gather in the cool of the day to be watered. Soon Rachel, the daughter of Laban, came leading her father's flocks, and one of the shepherds told Jacob whose daughter she was.

So Jacob rolled the stone from the well, and watered the flocks of Laban, his mother's brother. Then he kissed Rachel, and told her that he was Rebekah's son, and she ran and told her father.

There was great joy in Laban's house because Jacob had come, and after he had stayed a month with them Laban asked him to stay and take care of his flocks, and he would pay him for his work.

Since the day he had seen Rachel leading her father's flocks he had chosen her in his heart to be his wife. So he said that he would work for Laban seven years, if at the end of that time he would give him Rachel for his wife. Laban was quite willing to do so, and the seven years seemed to Jacob but a few days, for the love he had to Rachel. But, according to the custom of that country, the younger daughter could not be given in marriage before the elder, and so Laban gave his daughter Leah also, and both Leah and Rachel became the wives of Jacob, for Jacob lived in that far away time and country of the early world when men were allowed to take more than one wife, and when each man was both king and priest over his family and tribe, and worshipped God by offering burnt sacrifices upon an altar.

After twenty years of work with Laban, in which he had earned many flocks and herds for himself, Jacob took his wives and the little sons God had sent him, and his flocks and herds, and started on a journey to his old home. Isaac was still alive, and Jacob longed to see him. He had lived long in Haran for fear of his brother Esau, and now he must travel through Edom, Esau's country, on his way to his old home.

As he was on his way some of God's angels met him, and he was strengthened. Still he feared Esau, and sent some of his men to tell his brother that he was coming.

The men came back, saying that Esau, with four hundred men, was coming to meet them.

Poor Jacob! He remembered the sin of his youth, when he had stolen the blessing from Esau, and he was afraid, and prayed God to protect him. He sent his servants again to meet Esau with great presents of flocks, and herds, and camels, and after placing his wives and little ones in the safest place, he sent all that he had over the brook Jabbok, and he stayed on the other side to pray. It was as if he wrestled with a man all night, and when the day began to break the man wished to go, but Jacob said: "I will not let thee go except thou bless me."

So the man blessed him there, and call his name Israel; "for as a prince," he said, "hast thou power with God and with men, and hast prevailed." Then Jacob knew that the Lord Himself, in the form of a man, had been with him, and he had seen Him face to face.

And as the sun rose he passed over the brook. When he looked up he saw Esau and his men coming, and when he had told his family to follow him, he went straight before them, for he was no longer afraid to meet his brother.

Jacob's prayer had been answered, and Esau ran to meet his brother, and throwing his arms around him, wept on his shoulder. Then they talked in a loving and brotherly way, and Esau returned to his home with the presents Jacob had given him, and Jacob went on his way into Canaan full of joy and thankfulness. He stopped a little while in a pleasant place to rest his flocks and cattle, but he longed to see the place where he first saw the angels of God, and heard the voice of the Lord blessing him, so they journeyed on to Beth-el, and there built an altar and worshipped God.

Again the Lord spoke to Jacob at Beth-el, and called him Israel, and blessed him.

After they left Beth-el, they came near to Bethlehem, where many hundred years afterward the Lord Jesus was born, and there another little son was born to Rachel, and there too God sent for her, and took her to Himself, and there her grave was made.

Jacob and Rachel The little boy was named Benjamin, and was the youngest of Jacob's twelve sons, who became the fathers of the twelve tribes of Israel, and the princes of a great nation.

Jacob was almost home. His great family, with all the flocks and herds, had been long on the way, for they often spread their tents by the brooks in the green valleys, that the cattle might rest and find pasture, but at last the long caravan came slowly over the fields of Mamre to Hebron, and Isaac, whom the Lord had kept alive to see his son once more, was there in his tent waiting for him.

But soon after this he died, an hundred and eighty years old, and Esau came, and the two brothers laid their father in the cave that Abraham bought when Sarah died, and where he had buried Rebekah, and Jacob became patriarch in place of his father.

✚ JOSEPH, THE CASTAWAY ✚

Of all the sons of Jacob, Joseph and Benjamin were the dearest to him, because they were the sons of his beloved Rachel, who had died on the journey from Syria into Canaan. They were also the youngest of all the twelve sons. When Joseph was about seventeen years old, he sometimes went with his elder brothers to keep his father's flocks in the fields. He wore a long coat striped with bright colors, which his father had given him, because he was a kind and obedient son, and could always be trusted.

Once he told his father of some wicked thing his brothers had done, and they hated him for it, and could not speak pleasantly to him.

Joseph had many strange and beautiful thoughts when he looked across the fields to the hills, and up into the starry sky at night. He also had some strange dreams that he told to his brothers. He said that he dreamed that they were binding sheaves in the field, and that his sheaf stood up, while the sheaves of his brothers bowed down to it.

Again he dreamed that the sun, and the moon, and eleven stars bowed down to him.

His father wondered that he should have such thoughts, and reproached him saying, "Shall I and thy brethren indeed come and bow down ourselves to thee to the earth?" and his brothers said, "Shalt thou indeed rule over us?" and they hated him.

When they were many miles from home with the flocks their father sent Joseph to see if all was well with them. It was a long journey, and when they saw the boy coming they did not go to meet him, and speak kindly to him, but they said, "Behold this dreamer is cometh. Let us slay him, and cast him into some pit, and we will say some evil beast hath devoured him, and we shall see what will become of his dreams."

But Reuben, the eldest, said, "Let us not kill him; but cast him into this pit," hoping to take him out secretly, and send him to his father.

So when Joseph came near, they robbed him of his coat of many colors, and cruelly cast him into a pit. After this they sat down to eat their bread, and looking up they saw a caravan coming. It was a company of Ishmaelites carrying costly spices down into Egypt to sell them.

Then Judah said, "Why should we kill our brother? Let us sell him to these Ishmaelites."

Then there passed by some Midianite merchants, and who drew Joseph out of the pit and sold him to the Ishmaelites for twenty pieces of silver, and he was carried down into Egypt.

Reuben, when his brothers went back to their flocks, went to the pit to try to save Joseph, but he was not there, and Reuben cried out, "The child is not, and I, whither shall I go?"

The brothers who had been so cruel to Joseph brought his coat to their father, all stained with blood. They had themselves dipped it in the blood of a kid to deceive him, and he mourned long, and would not be comforted, for the beloved child that he believed had been torn in pieces by evil beasts.

JOSEPH, A SERVANT, A PRISONER, AND A SAINT

The king of Egypt, where Joseph was taken by the Ishmaelites, was called Pharaoh, and he had a captain of the guard named Potiphar, who bought Joseph for a house servant. Though he was the son of a Hebrew prince, Joseph did his work faithfully and wisely as a servant, and was soon made steward of the house, and was trusted with all that his master had, and the Lord made all that he did to prosper; but the wife of Potiphar was a wicked woman, who persuaded her husband that Joseph was a bad man, and he was sent to prison.

Even there Joseph won the hearts of all, until the keeper of the prison set him over the other prisoners, and trusted him as Potiphar had done. It was the Lord in Joseph who helped him to win the love and trust of those around him.

Pharaoh sent two of his servants to prison because they had displeased him.

One was his chief cook, and one was the chief butler, who always handed the wine cup to the king, and Joseph had the care of them.

They each had a dream the same night, and were troubled because they could not understand them. Joseph asked them to tell him the dreams, for God knew what they meant.

So the chief butler told Joseph that he saw a vine having three branches, and the branches budded and blossomed, and the blossoms changed into ripe grapes, and he took the grapes and pressed them into Pharaoh's cup, and handed the cup to the king.

Then Joseph said: "The three branches are three days. Within three days the king will take you out of prison, and you shall hand the king's cup to him as you used to do."

Joseph also asked the butler, to think of him when he was again in the king's palace, and speak to the king to bring him out of prison, because he had been stolen from his own land, and he had done nothing wrong that he should be put in prison.

Then the chief cook told his dream. He said that he dreamed that he carried three baskets on his head, one above another.

In the highest one was all kinds of cooked meats for Pharaoh, and the birds flew down and ate from the basket.

"The three baskets are three days," said Joseph as he said to the butler, but he told the cook that in three days he would be put to death, and hanged on a tree, where the birds would eat his flesh.

All this came true, for Pharaoh's birthday came, and he brought out the chief butler to serve at a birthday feast, but he hanged the chief cook.

Yet the chief butler forgot Joseph, and did not speak to the king about him as he might have done.

At the end of two long years, Pharaoh dreamed a dream. He thought he stood by the river of Egypt, and saw seven cows looking well kept and fat, came up out of the river.

Behind them came seven other cows, looking thin and poorly fed, and the thin and poorly fed cows ate up the well-kept and fat ones.

And Pharoah had a second dream. He thought he saw seven heads of wheat growing on one stalk — and they were all full of grain. After them came seven thin heads of wheat with no grain in them; and the seven bad heads of wheat ate up the seven good ones.

In the morning Pharaoh was troubled about these dreams, and called for his wise men who worked magic for him, and they could tell him nothing.

Then the chief butler standing near the king remembered Joseph, and told Pharaoh of the young Hebrew who had told the meaning of his dream, and that of the chief cook, and they had come to pass as he had said, so Pharaoh sent for Joseph and said to him:

"I have heard that thou canst understand a dream to interpret it."

Joseph answered the king humbly and wisely:

"It is not in me," he said, "God shall give Pharaoh an answer of peace."

When the king had told his dream Joseph said:

"The dream is one," and then he showed him that the seven fat cows, and the seven full heads of wheat meant seven good years in the land of Egypt, when the harvests would be great; and the seven lean cows, and the seven empty heads of wheat, meant seven years of famine, when the east winds should spoil the wheat, so there would be nothing to reap in time of harvest and the people would want bread. He told the king that he had better set a wise man over the land, who would attend to saving the grain during the seven good years, so that the people would have bread to eat in the seven years of famine.

The king was greatly pleased with Joseph, and told him that God had taught him to interpret dreams, and had showed him things to come, and there could be no wiser man found to be set over the land.

So he made Joseph a ruler over the whole land, and next to the king in all things.

He put his own ring on his hand, and dressed him in the robes of a prince, and gave him an Egyptian name and an Egyptian wife, so that there was no one in all the land of Egypt so great as Joseph, except the king.

He built storehouses in every city, and stored the grain, until it was like the sand of the sea, and could not be measured.

In the years of plenty two sons were born to Joseph, Manasseh and Ephraim, and then the seven years of dearth began to come. When the people began to cry to the king for bread, he always said, —

"Go to Joseph; what he says to you do."

And Joseph and his helpers began to open the storehouses, and sell wheat to the Egyptians, and to the people of all countries, for the famine was in all lands.

JOSEPH — THE SAVIOR OF HIS PEOPLE

The famine reached even to the fruitful land of Canaan, and Jacob, though rich in flocks and herds, began to need bread for his great family. So he sent his ten sons down into Egypt to buy wheat, keeping Benjamin, the youngest at home.

When they came before the governor they bowed down to him with their faces to the ground. Joseph knew them, though he acted as if he did not, and remembered his dream of his brother's sheaves bowing down to his sheaf. At first, he spoke roughly to them, and called them "spies." But they said that they were all one man's sons, and had come to buy food. Joseph still spoke roughly to them, not because he was angry, but because he did not wish them to know him yet.

His heart was full of love for them, and he was soon going to show them great kindness; but when they told him that they had left an old father and a young brother at home, and one was dead, he still acted as if they did not tell the truth.

He said that to prove themselves true men one of them should go home and bring the youngest brother, and the others should be kept in prison until they returned; and he put them all in prison.

After three days, he said one might stay while the others took the wheat home to their families, but that they must surely come back and bring the boy with them.

Then Reuben, who had tried to save Joseph from the pit long before, told his brothers that all this trouble had come upon them for their wickedness to their brother Joseph, and they said to each other in their own language:

"We are verily guilty concerning our brother; when he besought us, we would not hear, therefore is this distress come upon us."

Joseph understood everything they said though they did not know it, for he had been talking to them through an interpreter, and they thought he was an Egyptian. Now his heart was so full that he had to go out of the room to weep. But he came back and chose Simeon to stay while the others went to Canaan to bring back Benjamin.

They took the wheat that they had bought in bags, and went away; but when they stopped at an inn to rest and feed their asses, one of the brothers opened his bag, and found the money that he had paid for the wheat in the top of his bag. Here was more trouble, and they were afraid. When they came home to their father they told him all that had happened, and as they opened the bags, each one found his money.

Jacob was deeply troubled; for Joseph was gone, and Simeon was gone, and now they wanted to take Benjamin.

Reuben who had two sons said: "Slay my two sons if I bring him not to thee."

But Jacob said Benjamin should not go down to Egypt. But the wheat was gone in a short time, and they were likely to starve so great was the famine, and at last Jacob said they must go to Egypt again for food. Judah said they would go if Benjamin would go with them, but Jacob would not listen to this. He asked them why they told the man that they had a brother, and they replied, that the Governor had asked them if their father was yet living and if they had another brother.

"Send the lad with me," said Judah, "if I bring him not unto thee, let me bear the blame forever."

Then Jacob told them to take him and go, and also to take presents of honey, and spices, and balm, and nuts, and double the money, so as to return that which was put in their bags, and he blessed them, and sent them away.

They went down into Egypt, and stood before Joseph again. When he saw Benjamin with them he told the steward of his house to make ready a fine dinner for them, and bring them to him at noon, and he did so. Then the brothers were afraid that they were all to be put in prison, and at the door of Joseph's house began to tell the steward how they found the money when they opened their bags, and that they had brought it back doubled; but the steward spoke kindly to them, and said that he had placed their money, and that they need not fear, for God had given it back to them.

Then he brought Simeon out, and they made ready to dine with the Governor at noon, and to give him their presents.

When he came they bowed down to him and presented their gifts, and he asked them if they were well, and if the old man of whom they spoke, was still alive, and they replied that he was. When he saw Benjamin, and knew that he was truly his own brother, the son of Rachel, he said: "God be gracious unto thee my son," and he went quickly to his own chamber, lest he should weep before them.

When he came out to them again, and they sat down to dine, he placed the sons of Jacob by themselves, and the Egyptians of his house by themselves, and the brothers were placed according to their ages — Reuben at the head and Benjamin last, and they wondered among themselves at this. Joseph also sent portions from his own table to his brothers, but the portion of Benjamin was five times greater than that of the others.

The next morning their wheat was measured to them, and the asses were loaded with it, and they went on their way, but Joseph had told the steward to put the money of each man in the top of his bag, and in

Benjamin's to put his silver cup.

When they were a little away from the city, the steward overtook them, and charged them with stealing his lord's silver cup.

The men were so sure that no one of them had stolen the silver cup, that they said, "Let him die with whom the cup is found, and the rest of us will be your slaves."

So everybody's bag was opened from the oldest to the youngest, and the cup was found in Benjamin's bag. Then they rent their clothes for grief, and loaded the asses and went back to the city, and when they came to Joseph's house, they fell on their faces before him, Joseph tried to speak sternly and said:

"What deed is this you have done?"

Judah said:

"What shall we say unto my lord, or how shall we clear ourselves? We are my lord's servants."

Then said Joseph:

"The man in whose hand the cup is found he shall be my servant, and as for you, get you up in peace unto your father."

Then Judah came nearer to Joseph, and all his soul came forth into his voice as he said:

"O, my lord, let thy servant speak a word in my lord's ears!"

Then he told the story of their coming down into Egypt, and of the old father and young brother whom he had asked them about; of the love of this father for the little one, for his mother, and his brother now dead. He reminded Joseph that he had told them to bring the boy to him, and that they had said, that if the boy should leave his father, his father would die; but the governor had said "Except your youngest brother come down with you, ye shall see my face no more."

Then Judah told the story of the father's grief when he found that he must let Benjamin go down into Egypt, that they might buy a little food; how he spoke of his two sons, that were the sons of Rachel — that one had been torn in pieces, and now if mischief should befall the other, it would bring his gray hairs in sorrow to the grave. He asked Joseph what he should do when he returned to his father without the lad, seeing that his life was bound up in the lad's life, and Judah begged him, as he had made himself surety for the lad, to take him to be his slave, but to let Benjamin return to his father with his brothers.

"For how shall I go up to my father," said Judah, "and the lad be not with me?"

Then Joseph could bear it no longer. He told all the Egyptians to go out of the room, and then weeping so that the Egyptians and the people in the king's house heard, he made himself known to his brothers.

"I am Joseph, your brother," he said, "whom you sold into Egypt," and he begged them to come near to him.

"Be not grieved nor angry with yourselves," he said, for he saw that they were terrified, "for God sent me before you to save your lives by a great deliverance. It was not you that sent me hither, but God, and he hath made me a ruler throughout all the land of Egypt."

Then he told them to hasten and go to his father and tell him this, and ask him to come down at once, with all his flocks and herds, and dwell in Goshen, the best part of Egypt, for years of famine were yet to come. Then Joseph took little Benjamin in his arms and wept over him, and kissed him, and kissed all his brothers, and after that his brothers talked with him. The king heard the story of Joseph's brothers and was pleased. He told Joseph to send wagons for the wives and little ones of his brothers, and to tell them to bring their father, and all their cattle and sheep, and come to live in Goshen where they should have the best of the land for their flocks and herds.

Joseph did as the king commanded, and also gave them food for the journey, and a suit of clothing to each brother, but to little Benjamin he gave five suits, and three hundred pieces of silver. He also loaded twenty asses with the good things of Egypt as presents to his father, so he sent them all on their journey saying:

"See that ye fall not out by the way."

When they came to Jacob in Hebron, they told him the wonderful story of the finding of Joseph, and his heart was faint, for he did not believe them; but when he had heard all Joseph's messages, and had seen the gifts, and the wagons, he said:

"It is enough: Joseph my son is yet alive: I will go and see him before I die."

So they began the long journey to Egypt, for it took a long time to travel with a great family, and with thousands of cattle and sheep. At Beersheba Jacob stopped and worshiped God, where his father had built an altar years before; and God told him in the night that he need not fear to go down into Egypt, for He would there make him a great nation, and that He would bring him back again to his own land.

So Jacob with all his children and their little ones, and all his flocks and herds came into Egypt. There were sixty-seven souls, and when they had counted Joseph and his two sons, there were seventy.

Jacob sent Judah on before to see Joseph and ask the way to Goshen, so that they might go directly there with the cattle and sheep. And when Joseph knew that his father was coming, he went to meet him in Goshen, and there he wept on his father's neck a long time, and Jacob said:

"Now let me die, since I have seen thy face, because thou art yet alive."

After this Joseph presented five of his brothers to Pharaoh, and the king spoke very kindly to them, and gave them the best of the land for their flocks, and hired some of them to oversee his own shepherds.

Joseph brought his father in also and Jacob blessed Pharaoh.

So the family of Jacob lived in peace, and were cared for by Joseph, just as the Lord had promised Jacob, when in a dream he saw the angels of God at Bethel, and heard above them the voice of the Lord blessing him, and saying:

"Thou shalt spread abroad to the West, and to the East, and to the North, and to the South, and in thee shall all the families of the earth be blessed."

Joseph carried all Egypt through the years of famine, and saved seed for the people to sow their fields in the seventh year so that they said: "Thou hast saved our lives."

He afterwards visited his father, and Jacob made him promise that he would bury him when he died in the tomb of Abraham and Isaac, his father, in his own land.

When Jacob was near his end, Joseph brought his two little sons, Ephraim and Manasseh, to his bedside, and the old man gave them his blessing, laying his right hand upon the head of Ephraim, the youngest, and his left hand on that of Manasseh the first born, even as Isaac had given the birthright blessing to him instead of to Esau, and he said: "The angel which redeemed me from all evil bless the lads."

Then he called all his sons together and told them what should befall them in the last days. To each one he spoke as a prophet speaks who has a vision of things to come, and he blessed them there. When he spoke to Judah, he told him that kings and lawgivers should arise from among his children until the Saviour of the world should come.

Jacob was an hundred and forty-seven years old when he died, and there was great mourning for him.

Joseph had the body of his father embalmed, as the Egyptians had the custom of doing, and after a long mourning in Egypt, Joseph and his brothers and many Egyptians who were Joseph's friends, carried the body of Jacob to Canaan, in a great procession, and buried him in the cave of Machpelah, where his fathers were buried.

After they had returned to Egypt, the brothers of Joseph said: "Perhaps now he will hate us, and bring upon us all the evil we did to him."

So they sent to him to ask his forgiveness for all that was past. Then Joseph wept, for he had nothing but love in his heart toward his brothers, and he wished them to trust him. He comforted them and spoke kindly to them, saying:

"Fear not: ye meant evil unto me, but God meant it unto good. I will nourish you and your little ones."

And so through all Joseph's life, and he lived one hundred and ten years, he was a tender father to all his family, and a wise ruler of the people, and he died after making his family promise to carry his body back into Canaan to be buried with his fathers when they themselves should go. "For God will surely visit you," he said, "and bring you out of this land into the land which he promised to Abraham, to Isaac and to Jacob."

THE CRADLE THAT WAS ROCKED BY A RIVER

After Joseph and all the sons of Jacob had grown old and had passed away, their children's children grew in numbers until they became a great multitude.

The Pharaoh whom Joseph had served also died, and the king who followed him did not like the Hebrews. He feared them because they had grown to be strong, so he set overseers to watch them, and make them work like slaves.

He treated them cruelly, and made them lift the great stones with which they built the tombs of the kings and temples of the gods. He also tried to kill all the little boys as soon as they were born, but the Lord took care of them. Also, the king told his servants, that wherever they found a baby boy among the Hebrews, to throw him into the river Nile, but the little girls, they should save alive.

There was a man named Amrom, who, with his wife Jochebed, had a beautiful little boy whom they tenderly loved. They hid him as long as they could, and then when he was three months old and she could hide him no longer, she made up her mind to give him into the care of God. She made a little boat, or ark of stout rushes, that grew by the river. She wove it closer than a basket, and then covered it with pitch that the water might not enter, just as Noah covered the great ark before the flood. Then she wrapped her baby carefully and laid him in the little boat, and

set it among the reeds at the edge of the river Nile. God and His angels
watched the cradle of the child, and the river gently rocked it. Jochebed
told the baby's sister to wait near by and see what might happen to him,
and this is what happened, or rather what God prepared for the baby in
the boat of rushes.

The king's daughter came down to bathe in the river, and as her maidens
walked up and down by the riverside, she called one of them to bring
to her the little ark that she saw rocking on the river among the reeds.
When she had opened it she saw a beautiful little child, and when it
cried her heart was touched, and she longed to keep it for her own.
"This is one of the Hebrew's children," she said, and as the baby's sister
came near she asked the princess if she should go and get a nurse from
among the Hebrew women to bring it up for her, and the princess said to
her, "Go," and the maid went and called the child's mother. The princess
said: "Take this child away and nurse it for me, and I will give thee thy
wages."

And the mother took her baby joyfully though she hid her joy in her
heart, and carried him home to nurse and bring up for Pharoah's
daughter.

And the child grew, and when he was old enough his mother took him to
the king's palace, and he became the son of the princess. She called his
name Moses, which means "drawn out," because she drew him out of
the water.

MOSES IN MIDIAN

Moses had teachers, and was taught all the learning of the Egyptians,
but his heart was with his own people. He was grieved when he saw
their burdens, and heard their cries when their taskmasters struck them.
Once, when he was a grown man, he saw an Egyptian beating a Hebrew,
and he struck the Egyptian and killed him, for he thought he ought to
defend his people: and when he saw that the man was dead, he buried

him in the sand. In a day or two Moses tried to make peace between two Hebrews who were fighting, and they answered him roughly, and one of them said:

"Who made thee a ruler over us? Wilt thou kill me, as thou didst the Egyptian yesterday?"

Then Moses was afraid, and when the king heard of it, and tried to take his life, Moses fled away out of Egypt, through a desert into Midian. There he found a well and sat down by it to rest. While he sat there the seven daughters of the priest of Midian came to draw water for their father's flocks, and some rough shepherds came and drove them away, but Moses stood up and helped them, and watered their flocks. When their father knew that a noble stranger had been kind to his daughters, he asked him to come into his house, and eat bread with him, and stay as long as he would. So Moses stayed and Zipporah, one of the seven sisters, became his wife.

But Moses did not forget his people. God was preparing him to lead them out of bondage, and he learned many things, during the years that he kept the sheep of his father-in-law in the wilderness.

One day he led his flocks across the desert to Mount Horeb or Sinai. There he saw a bush all bright within as if it burned. He drew nearer to see why the bush was not consumed, and heard the voice of the Lord calling him. The Lord told him to come no nearer, and to put off his shoes, for he stood on holy ground. Then the Lord told him that He was the God of his fathers, and that He had heard the cry of his oppressed people in Egypt.

"I know their sorrows," said the voice from the midst of the fire, "And I am come down to deliver them out of the hand of the Egyptians, and to bring them up out of that land into a good land, and a large — unto a land flowing with milk and honey."

Then the Lord said that Moses must go to the new Pharaoh, for the old king was dead, and bring the children of Israel out of Egypt. Moses was a very humble man, and he could not believe that Pharaoh would listen to him or that the Hebrews would follow him, but the Lord said, "Certainly I will be with thee."

And as a sign that it should be so, He said that after Moses had brought his people out of Egypt, they should serve God in this mountain.

But Moses had many fears. He knew that he had been brought up as an Egyptian, and he feared that his people would not listen to his words. Then the Lord showed signs to Moses to help his faith.

He turned the rod in Moses' hand into a serpent, and then when he was afraid of it, the Lord told him to take it in his hand and it became a rod again.

He also turned his hand white with leprosy, and then changed it again to natural flesh, and told Moses, that these, and other signs he should show in Egypt — to prove that he was sent of God.

But Moses felt himself to be so weak and faithless as a leader of his people, that he still cried out that he was "slow of speech, and of a slow tongue," and when the Lord said, "I will teach thee what thou shalt say," he did not believe, but begged the Lord to send by whom he would, only not by him.

Then the Lord said that Aaron, the brother of Moses could speak well, and that he should go with him to Pharoah and to his people, and should speak for him, but that the wisdom and power of God should be with Moses, and that he should do wonders with the rod in his hand.

THE ROD THAT TROUBLED EGYPT

So Moses took his wife and his sons and returned to Egypt, and the rod of God was in his hand; and Aaron, sent of God, came to meet him in the wilderness, and there Moses told him all that was in his heart, and all that God had sent him to do.

When they came into Egypt they gathered the Israelites together, and Aaron spoke to them, and they believed his words, and the signs that Moses showed them.

Afterward, they went to Pharoah and gave him the message of the Lord, and Pharoah said:

"I know not the Lord, neither will I let Israel go."

And he began to oppress the Israelites more than he had ever done before. They made bricks of clay mixed with straw, that hardened in the sun, and were as lasting as stone, but he forced them to find the straw wherever they could, and make as many bricks as before. This they did until no more straw could be found, and their Egyptian masters beat them cruelly because they failed to make the full number of bricks. Then they turned upon Moses and Aaron and said, that they had put a sword in the king's hand to slay them.

Where could Moses turn except to the Lord who had sent him? The Lord heard him and made to him again the great promise, as he did at the burning bush, and Moses told the people, but they could not believe it, for they were crushed under their cruel burdens.

And now the Lord sent Moses and Aaron again to Pharoah, to show by sign and miracle, that their message was from Him. They took the rod that Moses brought from Mount Horeb, and Moses told Aaron to cast it down before the king, and it became a serpent. Pharoah called his wise men and wizards, and they did the same, only Aaron's rod swallowed up their rods, and Pharoah would not listen to their words.

But in the morning when Pharoah walked by the river the two men stood by him and said again: The Lord God of the Hebrews hath sent me unto thee saying: "Let my people go that they may serve me in the wilderness,"

And then Aaron struck the waters of the river Nile with his rod, and the waters turned to blood.

In all the land, in every stream and pond there was blood, so that the fishes died and no one could drink the water.

But because the wizards could turn water to blood also, Pharoah's heart was hardened toward Moses and Aaron.

While the people were digging wells for water, Aaron stretched forth his rod over the river again, and frogs came up from it, and spread over all the land and filled the houses of the people. This also the magicians did, but so great was the plague that the king said:

"I will let the people go."

"When shall I entreat for thee and for thy people to destroy the frogs from thee and thy houses?" said Moses; and Pharoah told him to do so the next day.

So on the next day Moses prayed to the Lord that the frogs might go out of the land, and the Lord answered his prayer; but when Pharoah saw that the frogs had been destroyed his heart grew hard, and he would not listen to Moses and Aaron.

Then another plague was brought upon the Egyptians. The dust of the land was changed to lice that covered man and beast, and this was followed by swarms of flies that settled upon all the land except Goshen where the Israelites lived.

Then Pharoah said:

"Go, sacrifice to your God in this land," but they would not worship in Egypt, and Pharoah at last told them that they could go into the wilderness, but they must not go very far away. So Moses prayed, and the swarms of flies were swept out of Egypt, but Pharoah did not keep his word.

Then a great sickness fell upon the cattle and sheep of the country, though the flocks and herds of the Israelites were free from it; and this was followed by a breaking out of boils upon men and beasts everywhere, even upon the magicians, but Pharaoh's heart was still too wicked to yield to God.

Then came a great storm of hail over Egypt, such as had never been known in that sunny land. It killed the cattle in the fields, and destroyed the grain that was grown, and broke the trees and herbs. The lightnings fell also and ran upon the ground, and when it was over the heart of Pharaoh was still hard against God.

Then Moses told Pharaoh that the face of the earth would be covered with clouds of locusts that would eat every green thing left by the storm, if he did not let God's people go. This frightened Pharaoh's servants and they begged him to send them away, and though he would not let their wives and little ones go, he said:

"Go now, ye that are men, for that ye did desire," and he drove them out of his presence.

Then at the Lord's word, Moses arose and stretched forth his rod over Egypt, and the plague of locusts came, driven by the East wind, and covered the land until there was no green thing left in Egypt.

Then Pharaoh sent for Moses and Aaron in great haste, and confessing his sin, begged to be forgiven and to be saved from, "this death only," and, at Moses' prayer, a mighty west wind drove the army of locusts into the Red Sea.

But again the heart of Pharaoh turned against God, and the Lord brought thick darkness over the land for three days, only in the homes of the Hebrews there was light. Then Pharaoh was willing to let them take their wives and their little ones, but not their flocks and herds, and because they would not leave them behind, Pharaoh drove Moses and Aaron from him in anger, saying:

"See my face no more."

But the Lord proposed to break the hard heart of Pharaoh. He told Moses to see that every Israelite should take a lamb from the flock and keep it four days. Then, at evening, he was to kill it, and dip a branch of hyssop in its blood, and strike it against the sides of his door, also over it, leaving three marks of blood there. Then he was to close his door and no one was to go out of it until morning.

They were to roast the lamb and eat of it, and be ready for the journey they were to make, and it should be to them forever the feast called the Passover. They were to eat it with unleavened bread, and the feast should be kept forever from the first to the seventh day of the month, a holy feast to the Lord.

And this is why it was called the feast of the Passover. At midnight, after the lamb was killed in each house of the Israelites, and the doors were shut, the Lord passed through the land, and wherever he saw the blood on the side posts and the top of the door, he passed over that house, and it was safe, but in every Egyptian house the first born died, from the child of Pharaoh who sat on the throne, to the child of the captive in the cell, and all the first born of cattle.

The next morning a great cry went up from the land of Egypt, for there was not a house where there was not one dead.

Then Pharaoh was quite ready to let the Israelites go.

"Take all you have and be gone," he said.

They were all ready, and rose up very gladly to join the great procession, led by Moses and Aaron, that gathered in Goshen, and started on its long journey toward the east.

They had heard of the land of their fathers, and now they were going home to be slaves no more. They were a family of seventy souls when they came into Egypt, four hundred and thirty years before, and now they went out a great nation, as the Lord had promised when he blessed their fathers.

The feast of the Passover has been the chief one held by the Israelites, from the time of their coming out of Egypt until now, and since Jesus held the Passover feast with his disciples on the night that he went forth to death, it has become to all Christians the Sacrament of the Lord's Supper.

📖 FOLLOWING THE CLOUD 📖

"God led the people," says the Word, as they came up out of Egypt. He gave them the two leaders by whom He had broken the power of Pharaoh, and set His people free, and He also set a great cloud in the air, just above and before them, to lead them in the right way. It was to them the presence of the Lord. By day it rose white and beautiful against the blue sky, and moved slowly before them. At night it stood still while they rested, and shed light over all the camp, for there seemed to be a fire within the cloud at night. How safe and happy they must have felt away from the cruel taskmasters of Egypt, and the Lord's presence, spreading a wing of cloud over them. They were not led by a straight way to Canaan, for a warlike people lived in the land which they must pass through, but they were led at first through a country without cities or armies, where they would not trouble many people or be troubled by them. They bore with them the embalmed body of Joseph, for they had promised to bury him with his fathers in the cave of Machpelah; and they also had much wealth in herds, and flocks, and gold, and silver. Pharaoh thought of this after they had gone, and his wicked heart grew harder than before, so he ordered his chariots and horsemen to follow them, and they found the Israelites camped by the Red Sea.

Then there was great fear and mourning in the camp when they saw the army of Pharaoh coming, but Moses cried:

"Fear ye not, stand still and see the salvation of the Lord. The Lord shall fight for you, and ye shall hold your peace."

Then the Lord told Moses to speak to the people that they go forward. He also told him to lift up his rod and stretch his hand over the sea and divide it, and the children of Israel should go on dry ground through the midst of the sea. Night was falling, and the waters lay dark before them, but the angel of God, the pillar of cloud and fire, moved from its place before them and went behind them, while Moses and Aaron led them on. Then the presence of the Lord was a cloud and darkness to the Egyptians, but it gave a light by night to the Israelites. A strong east wind drove the waters apart all night, so that there was a way through the sea, and the waters were a wall upon their right hand and on their left. Pharaoh's army saw the broad path through the sea, and followed fast after the Israelites, but as morning dawned the Lord looked from the cloud and troubled the Egyptians. Their chariot wheels came off, and all went wrong with them.

At last the Lord told Moses to stretch his hand forth over the sea, that the waters might come back upon the Egyptians, and he did so; and as the sun rose, the sea swallowed up the Egyptian host, and their bodies were cast upon the shore. There on the other side stood the great host of Israel, and saw the salvation of God, and they believed in Him, and in Moses His servant.

Then a great shout went up from the host of Israel. Moses led them in a song of praise, and Miriam, the sister of Aaron, took a tambourine, and the women followed her in dances as they answered in a chorus of praise: —

"Sing ye to the Lord, for He hath triumphed gloriously; the horse and the rider hath he thrown into the sea."

Soon they took up their journey, the cloudy pillar going before. There was but little water by the way, and after three days of thirst, they came to the waters of Marah, but they were bitter, and the people cried to Moses, "What shall we drink?"

Then the Lord showed him a tree which he cast into the waters, and they were made pure and sweet. Soon after they came to Elim, where there were twelve wells of water, and seventy palm trees, and there they rested.

Again they took up their journey and passed through a desert land, where they could get no food, and again they complained to Moses because he had brought them into the wilderness to die. They did not yet believe that God could supply all their need.

"I will rain bread from heaven for you," said the Lord to Moses. He was ready to provide, if they would only believe in Him and obey Him. Moses called them to come near before the Lord while Aaron should speak his word to them. As they came near and looked toward the wilderness where the cloud stood, the glory of the Lord shone out of it. The Lord had heard them speak harshly to Moses for bringing them into a desert to die, but he said, "At even ye shall eat flesh, and in the morning ye shall be filled with bread."

And his word came true. Great flocks of quails came up and covered the camp at sunset, so that they caught them for food; and in the morning the dew lay around them, and when it had risen, there lay on the ground a small, round, white thing, something like frost, or a little seed, and it tasted like wafers made with honey. The Lord told Moses that the people must gather just enough to eat through the day, and no more. The morning before the Sabbath they must gather enough for two days, for none would fall on the Sabbath. This was the bread that the heavenly Father provided for his children through all the years of their journey from Egypt to Canaan, and they called it "Manna."

There were hard things to bear in the wilderness. Often when they wanted water for their little ones and their cattle, and could not find it, they were like fretful children when they were tired and thirsty. Once, at Horeb, Moses struck a rock with his wonderful rod, and water sprung out in a stream.

There were enemies also in the way. The Amelikites came out to fight with the Israelites. The strong men went to meet the enemy, but Moses stood on a hill with the rod of God in his hand, and Aaron and Hur were with him. While Moses held up the rod, Israel prevailed; but when he let down his hand Amalek prevailed.

But Moses grew tired and they placed a stone for him to sit upon, and Aaron and Hur held up his hands on either side until the going down of the sun, when Amalek was conquered. Moses built an altar there, and called it "*The Lord my Banner."

They were now drawing near the Mount, where Moses saw the burning bush, and heard the Lord calling him to be the leader of his people. They were far out of their way to Canaan, but it was in the Lord's purpose to bring them into obedience and faith before he brought them into the promised land. They had lived long among the Egyptians, and were very far from being like Jacob and Joseph, but there were good and true men like Aaron, and Joshua, and Hur, who helped Moses. It was about three months after the children of Israel left Egypt, that they came into the wilderness of Sinai. There the "Mount of God" still lifts its great granite cliffs toward the sky. There are high valleys midway where it is cooler than below, and there the people encamped and waited to hear what God would say to them, for God talked with Moses on the Mount.

He said He had chosen them, if they would obey his voice, to be a holy nation. He told Moses to tell the people to be ready, and on the third day He would come down in the sight of all the people on Mount Sinai. And so it was, as the people looked there was a thick cloud upon the Mount, from which came thunder and lightning, and the sound of a great trumpet, while the mountain trembled as with an earthquake. Only Moses and Aaron could approach the holy Mount, and from it God gave to Moses the laws that the people were to live by, and Moses wrote them all down that he might read them to the people. A company of the Elders of Israel went up and saw the glory of God afar off, but God called Moses up into the Mount, and the cloud closed him round, while the Lord gave him the laws for a great nation, and the pattern of the tabernacle which He wished him to make for a church in the wilderness. Forty days and forty nights Moses was on the Mount with God, and then God gave him the ten great commandments written with his own hands on tablets of stone, that he might give them to the people. They were to be kept as the rules of life for all people in all times.

Forty days and nights seemed a long time to the people camped around the Mount. Perhaps they thought Moses would never come back to lead them, for they began to think of the gods of Egypt, and asked Aaron to make one for them. So to please them he told them to bring him their gold ornaments, and he melted them and made a golden calf such as the Egyptians worshiped, and before it they made an altar, and they worshiped the calf.

The Lord who sees all things told Moses to go down to the people for they were worshiping an idol. So Moses went down a little way and met Joshua, and they both went down and saw the people feasting, and singing, and dancing, and Moses cast the tablets of stone upon the ground and they were broken. The heart of Moses, too, was almost broken, but he destroyed the golden calf, and punished the people for their great sin, and then went up to the Mount to plead for the life of his people.

"O this people have sinned a great sin," he cried, "and have made them gods of gold, yet now if thou wilt forgive their sin, and if not, blot me, I pray thee, out of the book which thou has written," so great was the love of Moses for his people.

There was a time of repentance among the people after this, and Moses and his servant Joshua reared a tent outside the camp and called it the Tabernacle of the congregation. It was for worship until the true Tabernacle should be built according to the pattern given in the Mount. All who sought the Lord went to worship there, and the pillar of cloud came and stood at the Tabernacle door while Moses talked with God, and all the people saw it and worshiped.

Moses prayed again for the people, and the Lord said:

"My presences shall go with thee, and I will give thee rest."

The Lord called Moses again into the mount, and told him to bring with him two tablets of stone and He would again write the ten commandments upon them.

So Moses hewed them from the rock and took them up into Mount Sinai. Then the Lord came down again in a thick cloud and talked with Moses, and wrote upon the tablets of stone.

After forty days Moses came down to the people bringing the commandments with him, but his face shone with a strange light that the people never saw before, and they were afraid of him. It was something above the light of the sun, for Moses had seen the Glory of the Lord. While they still camped around the mount they began to build the Tabernacle. Moses told the people to bring gold, and silver, and brass, and wood. They also brought precious stones, and oil for the lamp, and fine linen, and they gave so willingly that at last Moses told them that there was more than enough.

These were put in the hands of two wise men whom the Lord had chosen and taught to do the work, and they had willing helpers among the people, for wise hearted women did spin with their own hands, and bring what they had spun, of blue, and purple, and scarlet, and fine linen to make the hangings of the Tabernacle.

If you would know all the beautiful and costly and curious things that were made for this church in the wilderness, you will find them described in the last chapters of Exodus.

The Israelites camped a long time in the high valleys around the Mount of God, and at last set up the Tabernacle. It was so made that it could be taken down and carried with them when they journeyed, for it was a beautiful tent. Over it the pillar of cloud stood. Whenever it moved the people followed, and when it stood still, they rested. Within the Tabernacle they placed a beautiful chest of wood overlaid with gold, which ever after held their most precious things, the tablets of stone written upon by the Lord himself.

This "Ark of Testimony," as it was called, had rings at the sides through which men laid strong rods by which to carry it, and so had the golden table for bread, and the golden altar of incense. There was a beautiful seven-branched candlestick of pure gold in which olive oil was burned for a sacred sign, and there was a brazen altar for burnt offerings, and a great brazen bowl for washing, and other things to be used in the worship of the Sanctuary.

There were beautiful garments, also, for the priests, Aaron and his sons, and for Aaron there was a wonderful breast-plate of gold set with twelve precious stones, bearing the names of the twelve tribes of Israel.

When all was finished, and the Tabernacle was set up, the cloud that veiled the presence of the Lord came and covered it, and the glory of the Lord filled it, so that Moses could not enter; but the Lord spoke to him from the cloud, and told him how the priests should order the worship of the Lord there.

Afterward, Aaron and his sons offered burnt offerings for their sins,

and the sins of the people, in the way the Lord had commanded, and fire
from the Lord came down and consumed the offering.

When the people saw the answer of the Lord they fell on their faces
before him.

In the second month of the second year the cloud rose from over the
Tabernacle, and then the people knew it was time to go on their Journey.
So they took down the tent of the Tabernacle and put all things in order
for the journey. Each of the twelve tribes descended from the twelve
sons of Jacob marched by themselves, carrying banners, and having
captains. In the midst of them all marched the Levites carrying the Ark
and the different parts of the Tabernacle, and when the cloud stood still,
they stopped and set up the Tabernacle, while the people formed their
camp all around it in the order of their tribes.

Still the manna fell with the dew at night, and the people gathered it in
the morning, and when they tired of it, the Lord sent them quails again.
Over and over the people complained and rebelled, but the Angel of
the Lord's Presence still hovered over them, and led them toward the
promised land. Forty years they were on the journey that was so easily
made by the sons of Jacob when they went back and forth to buy wheat
in the time of famine; and forty-two times did they encamp on the way,
yet the mercy of the Lord never failed them, and they were brought into
their own land at last. Then the cloud was no longer needed to go before
them, but long after, when they built a beautiful temple at Jerusalem
in which to put the sacred Ark of Testimony, the cloud came again and
filled the temple with the glory of the Lord.

📖 IN THE BORDERS OF CANAAN 📖

While the host of Israel was in camp at Paran, the Lord told Moses to
send men before them into Canaan to spy out the land.

So he sent twelve men who walked through the land and saw the
people, and the cities and the fields and the fruits. They were forty days

searching the land and they brought from the brook Eschol a cluster of grapes so large that two of them bore it on a staff between them. They also brought some pomegranates and figs.

When they came into the camp they said that the country where they had been was good, and flowing with milk and honey, but the people were strong, and the cities had very high walls. They said they saw giants there.

Caleb, who was one of the twelve, and a good and true man, said: "Let us go up at once and possess it, for we are well able to overcome it," but the men who were with him were afraid of the giants, and said they felt like grasshoppers before them. Then there was great weeping among the people all that night, and they said, "Let us make a captain, and let us return into Egypt." Moses and Aaron were greatly troubled, but the two good men, Caleb and Joshua, stood up and encouraged the people, saying that they need not fear, for the Lord had given them the land, yet they were ready to stone Caleb and Joshua.

Then the Lord spake to Moses from the Tabernacle, and the people saw his glory. He said the people were unbelieving and disobedient, and for this reason they could not enter the promised land. He said, that all who were twenty years old and upward would die in the wilderness, except Caleb and Joshua, who had followed the Lord wholly. He also said that the people would be forty years in the wilderness, and only the youth and the children would live to enter Canaan.

There was mourning and repentance then because of the word of the Lord, and the people promised again to believe and obey, but over and over they lost faith and rebelled, and great storms of trouble fell upon them.

Once the earth opened and many were swallowed up; a sudden sickness destroyed thousands. Near Mount Hor, where Aaron died, fiery serpents ran among the people, and all who were bitten by them died; but there was full forgiveness and cure for those who turned to the Lord. When the fiery serpents entered the camp Moses lifted a brazen image of a serpent up on a pole so high that it could be seen all over the camp, and whoever looked upon it lived. It was a sign of the coming Saviour.

Between the marches and the battles with heathen tribes, some of whom were giants, Moses wrote in a book the laws that God gave him for the government of the people. They were wise laws, the keeping of which would bring health, peace and blessedness to the people. He gave the book to the Levites who carried the Ark, and they were to keep it always beside the Ark, and often read it aloud to the people.

Moses said many things to the people, and as Jacob blessed his twelve sons, so Moses blessed each of the twelve tribes that descended from them, for he was near the end of his long life. The Lord had told him that He should take him to Himself before the people entered Canaan, and that Joshua must lead the people into the promised land. So when they had reached the borders of Canaan, and were encamped near the Jordan, the Lord called his tried servant up into Mount Nebo, that he might see the land beyond the Jordan, where the twelve tribes were to find their promised home. Then the Lord gave him a view of the land, and there he died, as Aaron died on Mount Hor.

No one saw Moses die, and no one knows where he was buried, for the Lord buried him. He was one hundred and twenty years old, and yet as strong as a young man. After his death Joshua became the leader of Israel.

A NATION THAT WAS BORN IN A DAY

The time had come for the people to cross the river Jordan, and enter their own land, and the Lord told Joshua to prepare the people for their last journey before going over Jordan. Joshua first sent two men over the river to see the land.

They went to the walled city of Jericho, and to the house of a woman named Rahab. The king heard that they were there and sent for them, but the woman hid them under the flax that she was drying on the roof of her house. Afterward she let them down by a rope through a window (for her house was built on the town wall), and they escaped. They promised Rahab before they went, that if she would hang a long line of scarlet thread from the window on the wall, that when they came to take the city she should be saved and all her family because of her kindness to them.

After they had returned to the camp they told Joshua that the Lord would surely give them the land, for the people were afraid of them. Then they rose up and marched to the banks of the Jordan and waited for Joshua to lead them over. Some of them remembered how they had passed through the Red Sea, and others had heard it from their parents, and they now waited to see the salvation of God. Joshua told them to follow the priests, and the Levites who would bear the Ark of the Covenant, so when Joshua said:

"Behold the Ark of the Covenant of the Lord of all the earth passeth over before you into Jordan," the people followed.

The Jordan lay spread before them like a lake, for it was the time of year when it overflowed all its banks, but when the feet of the priests who bore the Ark were dipped in the edge of the water, the waters from above stopped and rose like a wall, while the waters below flowed away into the Dead Sea, and left a wide path for the people to walk in, and the Ark stood still in Jordan until everyone had passed over. Then twelve men, one out of every tribe, took a stone from the bed of the river and carried it over for a memorial altar, so that when any should ask in years to come, "What do these stones mean?" someone might tell them how the Lord led Israel through Jordan into their own land.

After the Ark had come up from the bed of Jordan, and there was not one of all the thousands of Israel left behind, the waters came down from the place where they had stayed, and flowed down into the Dead Sea, and overflowed the banks of Jordan as before.

The stones were heaped in Gilgal where they camped, and directly before them rose the walls of Jericho, and here they kept the passover.

For forty years they had been fed with manna from heaven as they camped or journeyed in the wilderness, but now they began to eat the grain and the fruits of the land, and the manna fell no more.

Nearly five hundred years before the family of Jacob left this land to go down into Egypt where Joseph was. They grew to be a great people, but they were slaves. Then the Lord sent Moses to make them free, and they began the long journey, which at last brought them to their own land.

Forty years they were on the journey, and all this time they were pilgrims, but on the day that the Jordan ceased to flow, and parted while they passed over into the land promised to their fathers, they became a nation.

The land was before them, and they had only to obey the Lord and his servant Joshua to conquer and possess it.

As they filled the valley of the Jordan before Jericho, the hearts of the heathen fainted for fear, for they knew that only the Lord could divide a river to let his people pass.

Joshua went out of the camp to look at Jericho, the walled city. It was shut up for fear of the Israelites, and there was no one to be seen.

Suddenly Joshua saw a warrior standing with a drawn sword in his hand.

"Art thou for us," said Joshua, "or for our adversaries?" and the warrior angel answered, "Nay! But as Captain of the host of the Lord, am I now come," and Joshua fell on his face before him.

He knew then that it was the Lord who would conquer Jericho, and he was told how the people were to help him.

So Joshua called the priests, and told them to take up the Ark, and he told seven priests to go before it bearing trumpets of rams'horns. Then the army of Israel, ready for war, followed, half of them marching before the Ark, and half of them coming after, and as the trumpets gave a great sound, they marched once around the city, and then went to camp.

This they did once every day for seven days, but on the seventh day they marched around the city seven times, and as the priests blew the trumpets for the last time, Joshua cried with a mighty voice, "Shout! For the Lord hath given you the city."

Then as a great shout went up from the people, the walls of the city fell down flat, so that the soldiers of Israel went up, every man straight before him, and took Jericho.

And Rahab was not forgotten. The Lord cared for her little house on the wall, and she, with all her family, were brought into the Camp of Israel. And so by the conquest of Jericho the new nation of Israel began to possess its land.

📖 SAMSON THE STRONG 📖

All the days of Joshua — and he lived to be an hundred and ten years old — the Israelites were conquering the people who lived in Canaan, and dividing it among the tribes. Joshua was a father to them, as Moses had been, and when at last they were at rest, each tribe within its own borders, and they had begun to build their houses, and plant their fields, Joshua spoke words of loving counsel to the people, and they set up a stone under an oak tree, as a sign that they would always serve the Lord and keep the law, and then he went to be with God. After his death Israel was ruled by wise men called judges, who helped them to conquer the land little by little. Some of them were good men and brave warriors as Othniel and Gideon and Jephthah and one was a prophetess named Deborah, a noble mother in Israel, and one was a mighty man of strength, Samson, the son of Manoah.

The people of Israel had turned away from the Lord, and could no longer conquer their enemies, but the Philistines had conquered them, and had been their masters for forty years, when the Lord sent Samson to deliver them. He was not a wise man like Moses or Joshua, but he had great strength, and the Lord used him against the Philistines.

Once a young lion came roaring against him, and he caught it and rent it in two, as if it had been a kid. When he passed the same way afterward he saw that the bees had built a nest in the body of the lion, and it was full of honey. At his marriage feast — for he married a Philistine woman — he made a riddle for the young men to guess:

"Out of the eater came forth meat, and out of the strong, came forth sweetness."

They tried for seven days to guess the riddle, but they could not, and then they told Samson's wife to find it out for them, or they would burn her house. She begged him with tears to tell her, and at last he told her of the honey comb in the body of the lion, and she told the young men, so that at the end of the seventh day they said to Samson, "What is sweeter than honey?" and "what is stronger than a lion?"

He saw that he had been betrayed, so he paid his debt, a suit of clothes to each guest, and went home to his father's house. Afterwards when he found that his wife had been given to another he tied firebrands to the tails of three hundred foxes, and sent them among the wheat fields of the Philistines so that the fields were set on fire.

Once the men of Gaza tried to kill him when he was within their city, but he rose at midnight and took the city gates, with its posts and bar, and carried them away on his shoulders to the top of the hill. Again the Philistine lords had promised a great deal of money to a woman, if she would get Samson to tell her what made him so strong, so she begged him to tell her. Three times she thought she knew the secret, and told the Philistines, but they could not bind him. At last he was tired of her questions, and said to her plainly — that from a child no razor had ever touched his hair. If it should be cut he would be as weak as other men. Then she watched and cut his hair while he slept, and the Philistines bound him and carried him to Gaza, where they made him blind, and forced him to grind in the mills of a prison house. The Philistines were glad because Samson was their prisoner at last, and so they came together in a great feast to sacrifice to their god Dagon, for they said, "Our god has delivered Samson into our hands." While they were merry they said:

"Let us send for Samson to make sport for us," and he was brought out of the prison. It was very sad to see the strong judge of Israel, weak and blind, led by a little lad, and making sport for the people in front of their temple. All the lords of the Philistines were there, and upon the broad roof of the temple were about three thousand people watching Samson while he showed his strength, for his hair had grown and his strength was returning. At last as he was standing between two great pillars that held up the roof, he prayed, lifting his sightless eyes to God:

"O Lord God, remember me, I pray thee, and strengthen me only this once."

Then he clasped his arms around the pillars on either side of him, and bowing himself with all his might, saying, "Let me die with the Philistines," he drew the great pillars with him, and the house fell with all that were upon it, on all that were within it. So died Samson who judged Israel twenty years, yet a woman, Deborah, who was also one of the judges in Israel, was stronger than he, for the Lord *looketh on the heart.

📖 RUTH 📖

In the days when the judges ruled in Israel, there was a famine in the land, and an Israelite, who lived in Bethlehem, took his wife and his two sons into Moab where there was food. After a while the Israelite died, and the two sons married women of Moab.

After two years the sons died also, and their mother, Naomi, longed for her home in Bethlehem, for there was no longer a famine there. So she took Ruth and Orpah, her sons' wives, and started on the journey into the land of Israel.

But before they had gone far Naomi said;

"Go! Return each to her mother's house; the Lord deal kindly with you, as ye have dealt with the dead, and with me."

She kissed them, and they wept and would not leave her.

"Turn again, my daughters," she said, "why will ye go with me?"

And Orpah kissed Naomi, and went back to her own mothers' house, but Ruth, whose heart was with Naomi, would not go back.

"Entreat me not to leave thee," she said, "or to return from following after thee, for where thou goest I will go; and where thou lodgest I will lodge; thy people shall be my people, and thy God my God; where thou diest I will die, and there will I be buried; the Lord do so to me, and more also, if aught but death part thee and me."

And so they came to Bethlehem, and the old friends of Naomi greeted her tenderly, and welcomed her back. It was about the beginning of the barley harvest.

There was a good and great man in Bethlehem named Boaz, and he was of the family of Naomi's husband. He had a field of barley where the reapers were at work, and Ruth asked Naomi if she should not go and glean after the reapers, to get grain, for they were poor.

Naomi said, "Go, my daughter," and she went.

When Boaz came out of the town into his field and greeted his reapers, he said to his servant having charge of the reapers, "What maiden is this?" and he told him that she was the Moabitish girl who had come back with her mother-in-law Naomi.

Then Boaz spoke very kindly to Ruth, and told her to stay with his maidens, and freely drink of the water drawn for them, and Ruth bowed before him and asked why he should be so kind to a stranger. He told her that he knew all her kindness to her mother-in-law since the death of her husband, and how she had left her own family and country to come among strangers, and he blessed her, saying, "A full reward be given thee of the Lord God of Israel, under whose wings thou art come to trust."

Then he told her to sit down and eat bread with them, and he helped her to the parched corn with his own hands, and when they returned to work he told his young men to let her glean among the sheaves and reprove her not, and to let some handfuls fall purposely for her to glean. When

Ruth went home Naomi said, "Where hast thou gleaned to-day?" and Ruth told her. Then Naomi blessed Boaz, and told Ruth that he was one of their near relatives.

And so Ruth gleaned in the fields of Boaz through all the barley and the wheat harvest. When all the reaping was done, the grain was threshed on a piece of ground made very smooth and level. The sheaves were beaten, and then the straw was taken away, and the grain and chaff below it was winnowed. By this the chaff was blown away and only the grain was left.

When Boaz winnowed his barley Naomi told Ruth to go down to his threshing floor and see him for he had a feast for his friends.

So after the feast Ruth came near to him and said, "Thou art our near kinsman," and Boaz said, "May the Lord bless thee my daughter," and with many kind words he gave her six measures of barley to take to Naomi.

Boaz remembered that it was the custom in Israel for the nearest relative of a man who had died, to take care of the wife who was left, and so he went to the gate of Bethlehem where the rulers met to hold their court, and spoke to the elders and chief men about Ruth. He also wished them to be witnesses that he was going to take Ruth to be his wife. Then the rulers all said, "We are witnesses," and they prayed that God would bless Ruth and make Boaz still richer and greater.

So Ruth became the honored and beloved wife of Boaz, and they had a son named Obed.

Obed grew up and had a son named Jesse; and Jesse was the father of David, King of Israel, who was first a shepherd lad of Bethlehem.

More than a thousand years after Ruth lived there was born in Bethlehem, of the family of Boaz and Ruth, a little Child, who came, to be the Saviour of the world, and the shepherds in the fields, where, perhaps, Ruth gleaned, and David kept his sheep, heard the angels tell the good news and sing

"Peace on earth, good will to men."

SAMUEL — THE CHILD OF THE TEMPLE

The Tabernacle that was built in the wilderness, and was brought into Canaan by the priests was set up at Shiloh in the very centre of the land of Canaan, and once every year the tribes came to it to worship and offer sacrifices. After it had come to Shiloh to stay it was called the temple. When Eli was high priest a man named Elkanah came up from Ramah to worship, and Hannah his wife went with him. She was a good woman, and very sorrowful, because she saw other wives with sons and daughters around them, and she had none. Her husband was loving and kind and said;

"Am I not better to thee than ten sons?" but she prayed to God for a son. While she was at Shiloh she prayed in the temple, and Eli saw her lips move, though he heard no voice. At first he spoke harshly to her, thinking she had been drinking wine, but she told him that she had not taken wine, but was praying.

"I am a woman of sorrowful spirit," she said, "and have poured out my soul before the Lord." Then Eli blessed her and said;

"Go in peace, and the God of Israel grant thee the prayer that thou hast asked of him." Then Hannah was no longer sad.

Her prayer was answered, and the Lord sent her a little son, and when he was old enough, she took him to the temple, for she had promised the Lord that the child should be His. So Elkanah came bringing sacrifices, and the young child was with them. Hannah told Eli that she was the woman whom he saw praying in the temple.

"For the child I prayed," she said, "and the Lord has answered my prayer. Therefore I have lent him to the Lord; as long as he lives he shall be lent to the Lord." Eli was very glad and gave thanks to the Lord, and took the little boy to help him in the service of the temple. Every year his father and mother came to bring offerings to the Lord, and his mother always brought him a little coat which she had made.

Over it was a linen garment called an ephod, such as the priests wore.

Eli was an old man, and his sons, though they were priests, were not good men, and he believed the Lord had sent him one who would be good, so he loved little Samuel as if he were his own.

One night when Eli was laid down to sleep, and Samuel also, while the light was still burning in the golden candlestick before the Ark, Samuel heard a voice calling him, and he answered, "Here am I," and ran to see what Eli wanted. But Eli said that he had not called, and Samuel lay down again. When the voice called again, Samuel went again to Eli's bed, but Eli told him to lie down again, for he had not called him. When the voice called the third time, Samuel said; "Here am I, for thou didst call me."

Then Eli told the boy to lie down once more, but if he heard the voice again to say, "Speak Lord, for thy servant heareth."

And when the voice called again, "Samuel, Samuel," the boy answered, "Speak Lord, for thy servant heareth."

Then the Lord told Samuel that the sons of Eli had become very wicked, and their father had not kept them from the evil, and therefore He could not accept their offerings.

When Eli asked Samuel what the Lord had said to him, the boy told him all and hid nothing from him, and Eli bowed his spirit before the Lord, and said;

"It is the Lord, let Him do what seemeth Him good."

After this all the people of Israel knew that the Lord had called Samuel to be a prophet. And as he grew up the Lord was with him, and he was a judge over his people all his life.

As for Eli and his sons, the word of the Lord soon came true. When the Philistines came against the Israelites in battle, the Elders of Israel said;

"Let us bring the Ark of the Lord out of Shiloh to us, that it may save us out of the hand of our enemies." And so they took it from the holy place to the camp of Israel. Then the Philistines fell upon the camp and scattered the men of Israel. They also took the Ark of God, and the two sons of Eli were among the thousands slain.

Eli, who trembled for the Ark of God, sat outside the city gate, by the wayside watching. He was nearly a hundred years old, and his eyes were dim, but when a messenger came with the bad news, he fell backward in his seat and died. His heart was broken.

Where was Samuel? Perhaps he was praying in the temple for the return of the Ark of the Covenant.

Wherever the Ark went among the Philistines, there went also trouble and death. When they put it in the temple of their fish-god Dagon, the great idol fell down before it and was broken. And when it was taken to another city, the people were smitten with sickness, until at last the Philistines said;

"Send away the Ark of the God of Israel, and let it go to its own place." After seven months they sent it with gifts of gold to the Israelites. They placed it on a new cart drawn by two cows, and the cows, guided by the Lord alone, took a straight way into the land of Israel. How glad the people were when they looked up from their reaping in the fields, and saw the Ark coming safely back to them. The Philistines watched it from afar to see if it would be guided of God to its own place or not and then they returned to their city.

Samuel gathered the people to the Lord after this, and though they had sinned greatly, and had gone after the gods of the heathen around them, they repented and returned to the faith of their fathers, and were faithful all the days of Samuel. He went from year to year on a journey to three cities of Israel, and judged the people in those places, but his home was in Ramah, the city where he was born, and where Hannah had brought him up for the Lord.

✠ THE MAKING OF A KING ✠

When Samuel was old he made his sons judges in his place, but they were not holy men like their father.

They loved money, and would judge unjustly, if money were given to them as a bribe. So the people came to Samuel at Ramah and said, "Give us a king to judge us."

And Samuel prayed to the Lord, and the Lord told him to do as the people had asked him to do, for they had not rejected him as judge, but the Lord as their King, and now they must learn what kind of a king would reign over them. So Samuel told them what they must be ready to do for their King, for a king was often a hard master, and ruled his people cruelly, taking the best of their fields, and their harvests, and their flocks for themselves, and the finest of their sons and daughters to be his servants; but they said, "We will have a king over us, that we may be like other nations, and that our king may judge us, and go out before us and fight our battles."

When Samuel told these things to the Lord he said, "Make them a king," and Samuel sent the people to their own cities.

Samuel did not choose a king for the people himself, but he waited for the Lord to send him the man He had chosen, and the Lord said to him as he went to a city called Zeph, to hold a sacrifice, "To-morrow about this time I will send thee a man from the land of Benjamin, and thou shalt anoint him to be captain over my people Israel."

On the next day as Samuel came out to go up to the hill of sacrifice he met a tall, noble looking young man, who, with his servant, was looking for the lost asses of his father, Kish, the Benjaminite. He had come far, and had heard that Samuel, the seer was in that place, and he hoped he would tell him where to go for the asses that were lost.

Samuel knew from the Lord that this was the man God had chosen, so he told him to go up with him to the sacrifice, and the next day he would let him go.

He told him that he need not be troubled about the asses, for they were found, but the desire of Israel was set upon him. Saul, for that was his name, did not understand him until he was invited to feast with thirty of the chief men, and Samuel had talked with him upon the house-top. Early the next morning they both rose and went out of the city, and while Saul sent his servant on before, Samuel anointed Saul with oil, and kissed him saying, that the Lord had anointed him to be Captain over his inheritance.

As a sign that the Lord had done it, he told Saul three things that would happen to him on the way home, and charged him to go to Gilgal, where he would meet him and sacrifice to the Lord for seven days. As Saul turned to leave the prophet, God gave him another heart, and all the signs came to pass that day.

At Mizpah Samuel called all the tribes together, that the man who was to be their king, might be chosen in their sight, and when Saul, the son of Kish, the Benjaminite was chosen he could not be found; he had hidden from the people; but when they brought him out before them, he was taller than any of the people from his shoulders up, and looked a king indeed. For the first time in all their history they cried, "God save the King!"

Then Saul went home, and there went with him a body of men whose hearts God had touched, while Samuel wrote in a book the order of the kingdom and laid it up before the Lord.

THE SHEPHERD BOY OF BETHLEHEM

After Saul had been king of Israel for a few years, Samuel was deeply troubled about him, for he had hoped that he would be as truly a king as he looked, but he had a strange and wilful spirit that led him to turn away from the counsel of the Lord and follow his own way.

Samuel had been grieved again and again by Saul's rashness, until at last he said to him when he had taken the spoil of the enemy to sacrifice to the Lord, "To obey is better than sacrifice; because thou hast rejected the word of the Lord, He hath also rejected thee from being king," and he went to his house and mourned over Saul, for he had loved him.

At last the Lord told Samuel to cease from mourning for Saul, for He had rejected him, but to fill his horn with oil, and go to Bethlehem where Jesse lived, for He had chosen one of the sons of Jesse to be king in place of Saul.

Samuel went to Bethlehem leading a heifer, as the Lord had told him to do, that he might hold a sacrifice. He told the elders of the city to make ready for the sacrifice, and when he had found the house of Jesse, he called him and his sons. Jesse was the grandson of Ruth and Boaz, and owned the fields, no doubt, where Ruth gleaned. When Samuel saw Eliab, the son of Jesse, he said;

"Surely the Lord's anointed is before Him," but the Lord said;

"Look not on his countenance or on the height of his stature, because I have refused him, for the Lord seeth not as man seeth, for man looketh on the outward appearance, but the Lord looketh on the heart."

Then Jesse called Abinidab, but Samuel said;

"The Lord hath not chosen this." Then he made Shammah to pass before him, but Samuel said;

"Neither hath the Lord chosen this."

Jesse made seven of his sons to pass before Samuel, but Samuel said;

"The Lord hath not chosen these."

"Are here all thy children?" said Samuel.

"There remaineth yet the youngest, and he keepeth the sheep," Jesse replied. Then Samuel said;

"Send and fetch him, for we will not sit down till he come hither."

So Jesse sent out into the sheepfolds on the hillsides outside the city to bring the lad David in. What did the boy think when he found his father and his brothers waiting, with the old prophet in the midst? What did it mean that the eye of the seer was set upon him, as were the eyes of all in the house?

Samuel saw a noble youth, "ruddy, and of a beautiful countenance, and goodly to look to." He had been told that he must not look on the outward appearance "for the Lord seeth not as man seeth," and so he waited a little until the Lord said;

"Arise, anoint him, for this is he." Then he took the horn of oil, and anointed him in the midst of his brethren, and the spirit of the Lord came upon David from that day forward, and Samuel went back to his house in Ramah.

It may be that his father and his brothers did not understand that the boy had been called to be king over Israel, but a new spirit of wisdom, and love, and strength came upon David, and though he went back to his father's flocks with no thought of being greater than his brothers, he went with a new song in his heart which he sang to the little harp he had made while watching the sheep. Long after when he was King of Israel, he made in memory of these days the beautiful Psalm to be sung in the temple beginning, "The Lord is my Shepherd, I shall not want."

THE POWER OF A PEBBLE

Saul the sullen was still king over Israel, although he had departed from the Lord, and in His sight he was no longer a king. He was very gloomy and dark in his mind, for he had driven the Lord's spirit away, and his light was gone.

His servants tried to amuse him, and told him of David, the son of Jesse, who was a skillful player on the harp, and a brave and handsome youth. So Saul sent for David, and David, bringing presents from his father, came to the king's house.

Saul was greatly pleased with David, and asked Jesse to let his son stay with him, for when the evil spirit was upon him, if David played upon his harp the darkness left him. But this did not last, and after a while David went back to his flocks, and Saul forgot him.

Then the Philistines rose against Israel again. Their camp was on a mountain side, and Saul gathered his warriors on the side of another mountain and there was a valley between them.

Out of the Philistine camp a giant came one day, Goliath of Gath. He talked loud and often in order to terrify the Israelites, asking them to send out a man to fight with him, but he was not truly brave, for he had carefully covered his great body with armor of brass, so that no spear or sword could touch him. He defied Israel every morning and evening for forty days, and no one was found who would dare to go out alone to fight him. David's elder brothers were in camp, and Jesse, their father, called David from the flocks to take food to them. He found the army of Israel ready to go into battle, but Goliath came out as he had done each day and defied the Israelites, who ran in terror at the sight of him. The spirit of David was moved at this, and he said;

"Who is this Philistine that he should defy the armies of the living God?" "The man who killeth him," said one, "the King will enrich him, and, will give him his daughter and make his father's house free in Israel."

Then Eliab, David's eldest brother, spoke sternly to David asking him why he had left his sheep to come down and see the battle, and called him naughty and proud, but David still talked with the men, for the spirit of the Lord was strong within him. When Saul heard of him and sent for him, David said;

"Let no man's heart fail because of him; thy servant will go and fight with the Philistine."

Saul frowned at David and said;

"Thou art not able to go against this Philistine; thou art but a youth, and he is a man of war."

Then David told the king how he had killed both a lion and a bear that had come down upon his father's flocks, and that he could also conquer the Philistine.

"The Lord that delivered me out of the paw of the lion, and the paw of the bear," said David, "He will deliver me out of the hand of this Philistine." And Saul said; "Go! And the Lord be with thee." Then Saul armed David with his own armor, but David said;

"I cannot go with these, for I have not proved them," and he put them off.

And this was the way David armed himself to meet the giant.

He took his staff in hand, and chose five smooth stones from the brook and put them in his shepherd's bag, and with his sling in his hand, he drew near to the giant. Goliath came on also, his armor-bearer carrying the shield before him, but when he saw the youth David, he despised him, for he was without armor, or sword or spear, only his staff.

"Am I a dog, that thou comest to me with a staff," said Goliath, and then he told him that he would soon give his flesh to the birds and the beasts. "Thou comest to me with a sword, and a spear, and a shield," said David, "but I come to thee in the name of the Lord of Hosts, the God of the armies of Israel whom thou hast despised."

Then the Philistine came down upon little David to destroy him, and David ran, not away from him, as the men of Israel had done, but straight toward him, taking a pebble from his shepherd's bag as he ran. Quickly putting it in the sling, he whirled it in the air once, twice, and then it went swift and straight to the mark. It sunk into the forehead of the giant, and he fell dead upon his face. Then David ran and stood upon the dead Philistine and cut off his head with the giant's great sword, and when the Philistines saw that their champion was really dead, they fled, pursued by the shouting hosts of Israel.

Saul had forgotten the youth who played upon the harp before him, for when he sent for him after the battle he said, "Whose son art thou, thou young man?" and David answered, "I am the son of thy servant Jesse, the Bethlehemite."

And Saul took him to live with him from that day.

📖 FAITHFUL UNTO DEATH 📖

Saul had a son named Jonathan, and he loved David as his own soul. He took off his princely robes, even to his sword, and his bow, and his girdle, and made David wear them; and David acted wisely in all that the king gave him to do. There was great joy and much feasting over the Death of Goliath and the flight of the Philistines, and wherever

Saul went, the women came out of the cities to meet him, singing and dancing, and the song with which they answered one another was, "Saul hath slain his thousands, and David his tens of thousands."

Saul did not like this, and an evil spirit of jealousy came upon him, and he thought, "What can he have more but the kingdom."

The next day the evil spirit came upon Saul in the house, and David played on his harp to quiet him, but Saul hurled a spear at David, hoping to fasten him to the wall with it. This he did twice, but the Lord guided the spear away from David, just as he guided the pebble to Goliath, and he was unhurt. Saul was afraid of David. He was afraid that God was preparing him to be king over Israel, so he sent him into battle, hoping he would be killed, but the life of David was in the Lord's hand, and no enemy could destroy it.

After a great battle, in which David had been victorious, the evil spirit came again upon Saul, as he sat in his house with his spear in his hand, while David played on the harp. Again he tried to kill David, but the spear struck the wall and David slipped away.

It was clear that David could not live near the king, and so he talked with Jonathan, his friend, who said, "God forbid, thou shalt not die," but David said, "Truly there is but a step between me and death."

Then they made a promise to each other before the Lord that should last while they lived. They promised to show "the kindness of the Lord" to each other while life should last.

Jonathan told David that he might go away for three days, and they went out into a field together. They feared the anger of Saul when he found that David was absent from the feast of the new moon. So Jonathan told David to return after three days and hide behind a great rock in the field. Then Jonathan said he would come out and shoot three arrows from his bow, as if he were shooting at a mark, and he would send his arrow-bearer to pick them up. If he should call to the lad, "The arrows are on this side of thee," David would know that Saul was not angry, and would not hurt him, but if he cried, "The arrows are beyond thee," David would know he was in danger and must go away.

On the second day of the feast, Saul asked why David was not there, and Jonathan told him he had asked permission to go away for three days.

Then Saul was very angry. He blamed his son for loving David, for, as Saul's son, Jonathan should be king after his death, but he never would be if David lived, and he commanded Jonathan to bring him that he might put him to death.

When Jonathan asked what evil David had done that he should be put to death, Saul cast his spear at his own son. Then Jonathan knew there was no hope for David, and left the table in sorrow.

The next day he went out to the rock in the field with his armor-bearer and sent him on before. When he shot an arrow, he cried;

"The arrow is beyond thee; make haste! Stay not!"

And David, in his hiding place heard it, and knew that he must flee for his life.

Then Jonathan gave his bow and arrows to the lad to take to the town, and David came out from his hiding place, and they kissed each other and wept together. But at last Jonathan said;

"Go in peace; as we have sworn both of us in the name of the Lord, saying, The Lord be between me and thee, and between my children and thy children forever."

And David went away to hide from Saul, and Jonathan went back to the king's house.

For seven years Saul hunted for David to take his life, and David, often hiding in caves in the wilderness, could not see his friend Jonathan, but they were faithful in their friendship, and when at last Saul was slain in battle, and Jonathan also, David came to mourn over his friend, saying;

"I am distressed for thee, my brother Jonathan; very pleasant hast thou been unto me; thy love for me was wonderful, passing the love of women."

DAVID THE OUTCAST

For seven years King Saul hunted David from one end of the land of Israel to the other. The evil spirit of jealousy and hate had full possession of him, and David, with a few faithful men, was driven from one stronghold to another, until he cried, "They gather themselves together; they hide themselves; they mark my steps when they wait for my soul. What time I am afraid I will trust in thee."

He had escaped again and again from the hand of Saul, and now he was down in the desert country by the Dead Sea, hiding among the cliffs and caves of Engedi. Saul heard of it and took three thousand men to hunt for him among the rocks of the wild goats. He was very tired after climbing the rocks, and seeing a cave, he went in to lie down for a little sleep. He did not know that David and his men were in the cave hiding in the dark sides of it. Then his men whispered to David;

"Behold the day of which the Lord said unto thee; 'I will deliver thine enemy into thine hand that thou mayest do to him as it shall seem good to thee.'" Then David arose and crept near to Saul, and — did he kill the man who had so often tried to kill him?

No, he bent down and cut off a part of Saul's robe. Even this seemed wrong to David.

"The Lord forbid that I should do this thing unto my master," he said "to stretch forth my hand against him, seeing he is the anointed of the Lord," and in this way he kept his servants from harming Saul, and after Saul awoke he went out of the cave.

David also went out of the cave and cried, "My Lord the King!"

And when Saul turned David bowed down to him and asked him why he listened to men who said that he wished to harm the king, and then he told him how the Lord had given him into his hand in the cave, but he would not touch the Lord's anointed to harm him. "See, my father," he cried "see the skirt of thy robe in my hand. I have not sinned against thee, yet thou huntest my soul to take it."

Much more he said, and asked the Lord to judge between them, and Saul's hard heart was moved so that he wept aloud.

"Is this thy voice, my son David," he said, "Thou art more righteous than I, for thou hast rewarded me good, whereas I have rewarded thee evil," and he made a covenant with David. For though he made no promise to spare David's life, he made David promise to spare the life of his children when he should be made king.

But a year was hardly past before the evil spirit was again upon Saul, and he went out with three thousand men to hunt for David. Saul's camp was on a hill, and David saw where it was. At night he took Abishai, one of his warriors, and went down from the cliffs to Saul's camp, where Saul lay sleeping in a trench, and the spear stuck in the ground by his pillow, while all his men lay around him. Abishai wished to strike him through with the spear, but David said, "Destroy him not, for who can stretch forth his hand against the Lord's anointed and be guiltless? The Lord shall smite him, or his day shall come to die, or he shall fall in battle and perish; but take thou now the spear that is at his pillow, and the cruse of water, and let us go."

And they took them and went away. A deep sleep had fallen upon the camp of Saul from the Lord, so that no one saw them.

Then David went up to his stronghold, and from the top of the cliff he cried to Abner, the captain of Saul's men, and asked why he had not defended his Master, and where was the king's spear, and his cruse of water?

Then Saul cried as before, "Is this thy voice, my son David?"

"It is my voice, my lord, O King," said David, and again he plead his cause with his old enemy, but who could trust to the repentance of Saul? He cried, "I have sinned; return, my son David, for I will no more do thee harm, because my soul was precious in thine eyes this day. I have played the fool, and erred exceedingly."

But David trusted him no more, and went and made friends with a Philistine prince that he might live within their borders.

Samuel the prophet was dead, and there was no one to give counsel to the darkened soul of the King when trouble fell upon him. The Philistines had come with a great army, but Saul was afraid, for the Lord's spirit was not with him. He tried to seek the Lord through the priests, and through dreams, but the Lord answered him not. Then he went to a witch by night, and asked her to bring up the spirit of Samuel. The witch could not bring up Samuel, but the Lord sent him to speak to Saul, and the woman cried out with terror when she saw the prophet of the Lord, and knew also that it was the King who had called for him. "I am sore distressed," said Saul, "and God is departed from me. What shall I do?"

Then Samuel told him plainly that the kingdom was taken from him and given to David, and that on the next day he and his sons should fall in battle, and the Israelites into the hands of the Philistines.

Saul, forsaken and despairing, fell to the earth fainting, but was revived by the woman, who gave him food so that he went away through the dark to the camp of Israel.

In the battle of the next day the Philistines conquered. The three sons of Saul were slain, and Saul himself, when chased by the Philistines, fell upon his own sword and died.

When a messenger brought news of the battle to David he rent his clothes for grief, and in the chant of lamentation that he made, he mourned for his faithful friend Jonathan, and had no word of blame for his enemy Saul, neither did he triumph over him.

EVERY INCH A KING

After Saul's death David came back to live with his own people, for he was of the tribe of Judah. He went to Hebron, the old home of Abraham, Isaac, and Jacob, for the Lord had told him to go there, and the men of his tribe came to Hebron and anointed him king. The other tribes did not come, for Saul's son and the captain of his host, Abner, were still holding the kingdom. But when both were killed by an enemy, then all the other tribes came to Hebron and made a league with him, so seven years after Saul's death David became king over all Israel. He was then thirty years old and his reign lasted forty years.

Then David began to establish the kingdom. There was a rocky height not far from Hebron with a valley all around it that was still held by the Jebusites, one of the tribes of Canaan that the Lord said must not be left in the land. The city was Jerusalem, and the stronghold was Zion, and close by Zion was the mount to which Abraham had once gone to offer up Isaac. David wanted this stronghold for the chief city of the kingdom, and so he took it, and it became the city of David. He built a beautiful house for himself there, and King Hiram of Tyre sent skilled workmen, and cedar trees, and they built a house of cedar for him.

But stronger than the wish to have a house for himself was the longing to see the Ark of God set within the curtains of the Tabernacle in the city of David. It had been in the house of Abinadab in Kirjath-Jearim for seventy years, ever since it was sent home by the Philistines who captured it. Because the people had grown cold toward God, they did not wish to hear the reading of the law, or be led by his counsel. Now David called together the flower of all Israel, thirty thousand men, and they went to bring the Ark to the city of David. While on the way a man who had laid his hand upon the Ark when it was unsteady was smitten and died, for no one but the priests and Levites could touch the Ark of God. David feared to bring it further, and so he placed it in the house of Obededom which was near by. It was there three months, and great blessing came to the house because of it. When David heard this he went joyfully down to bring the Ark to his city, and it was with sacrifices, and shouting, and the sound of trumpet that it was brought and set in the Tabernacle that had been made ready for it. And so the worship of the Lord was established in Jerusalem, which was to be the great altar for the sacrificial worship until the sacrifice should be taken away, and the kingdom of Christ established on the earth.

But David was not satisfied.

"See," he said to Nathan the prophet, "I dwell in a house of cedar, but the Ark of God dwelleth within curtains."

That night the Lord spoke to Nathan and told him what to say to the king. He promised to establish the royal house of David, and give final peace to the people, and also to build a house for the worship of the Lord, but he said that David's son, who should be king after him, should build a house to his name, and of him the Lord said, "I will be his Father, and he shall be my son."

Then King David went in to the Tabernacle and thanked the Lord for His promise to him and to his son, and asked His blessing upon them. Though he reigned forty years, he never forgot that his work was not to build the temple of the Lord, but to prepare for it. So he subdued enemies, built cities, made leagues with friendly nations, gathered much wealth of wood, and stone, and gold, and silver and precious stones for the house of the Lord, and trained choirs of singers for the service. He also kept his heart open toward the Lord, so that he was able to write some wonderful poems that were set to music and sung by the temple choirs. We call them the Psalms of David.

Though David had grown rich and great, he did not forget his promise to Jonathan. He called Ziba, who had been Saul's servant and said to him, "Is there not yet any of the house of Saul that I may show the kindness of God to him?"

Then Ziba told him of a man who was lame in both his feet, who was the son of Jonathan. David sent for him, and gave him all the land of Saul, and a place was made for him at the king's table among his own sons, and it was his while he lived.

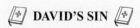

DAVID'S SIN

The army of Israel was at war with the Ammonites, and Joab was the chief captain. David did not go out with the army, but stayed in his house in Jerusalem. One evening he was walking on the flat roof of his house, as the people of that country always do, and he saw a little way off a very beautiful woman. He sent a servant to ask who she was, and found she was the wife of Uriah who was in the army with Joab, fighting the Ammonites. Then a great temptation was set before David, and instead of going to the Lord to be saved from it, he sent to Joab, asking him to send him Uriah, the Hittite. So Uriah came, and David talked kindly with him, and found him a good and faithful man. When he went back to Joab he took a letter from David, who asked that he be set in the front of the battle. So Joab placed him there, and when the two armies met Uriah was killed, and Joab sent a messenger to tell David. After her mourning was ended, Bathsheba, the wife of Uriah, became the wife of David, but the Lord was displeased with David. He also knew David's heart and how to deal with him, so he sent Nathan the prophet to him.

"There were two men in one city," said Nathan, "one of them rich and the other poor. The rich man had many flocks and herds, but the poor man had nothing, save one little ewe lamb, which he had bought and nourished up; and it grew together with him and with his children; it did eat of his own meat and drink of his own cup, and lay in his bosom and was unto him as a daughter. And there came a traveller unto the rich man, and he spared to take of his own flock to dress for the wayfaring man that was come to him, but took the poor man's lamb and dressed it for the man that was come to him."

David was very angry at the man who could do such a cruel thing, and he said to Nathan, "The man that hath done this thing shall surely die; and he shall restore the lamb fourfold, because he did this thing, and because he had no pity."

Then Nathan said to David, "Thou art the man," and he told him how greatly the Lord had blessed him in making him King over Israel, and in delivering him from the hand of Saul, and how he had slain a faithful servant and taken his wife for himself; therefore evil would befall him. David said, "I have sinned against the Lord," and the Lord saw that his repentance was real, and forgave the sin, but that David might never forget and sin again, the Lord took the little child that was born to him and to Bathsheba. While it was sick David fasted and lay all night upon the earth, and would not rise to taste food. This he did for seven days while the little child was sick, but when they told him that his child was dead he arose and bathed and dressed himself and went to the house of the Lord to worship, and returned to take his food. Then his servants wondered at it, and replied, "While the child was yet alive I fasted and wept, for I said, who can tell whether God will be gracious unto me that the child may live. But now he is dead, wherefore should I fast? Can I bring him back again? I shall go to him, but he shall not return to me." After this another child was born to Bathsheba, and they named him Solomon, which means "Peaceable."

And David wrote a prayer of repentance for his sin. It is the fifty-first Psalm, and has been the prayer of penitent souls for nearly three thousand years.

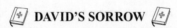 DAVID'S SORROW

David had a very beautiful son named Absalom. From the crown of his head to the soles of his feet there was no fault to be seen in him. His hair was thick and long, and his beauty was much talked of through all Israel. But the Lord who looks upon the heart saw that the heart of Absalom was wicked and false. He killed his brother Amnon, and then fled to another country and stayed three years. When he returned he tried to see his father, but David would not see him for two years. Then Absalom forced Joab to bring him to the king's house by setting Joab's barley field on fire. He was false as well as handsome, and won his father's heart by pretending to be humble.

After this Absalom began to live more like a king than a prince. He had fifty men to run before his chariot when he rode, and he stood in the city gates and talked with the men who came to see the king about their rights. He told them that if he were ruler over the land every man should have all that he wanted, and deceived many by a false show of friendship.

Then he asked the king if he could go to Hebron to pay a vow to the Lord by offering sacrifice there, and David told him to go in peace, and he went. But he had cruelly deceived his father. He had sent spies through all the land to persuade them to join him at Hebron and make him king. He also took two hundred men out of Jerusalem to help him, and one of them was David's counsellor. They had arranged to have all the people, as soon as they heard anywhere the sound of the trumpet, to cry, "Absalom is king in Hebron."

Then it came to the ears of David that his people had been led away by deceit to follow Absalom, and David, who had been fearless before Goliath and before great armies of other nations, was afraid. His heart was broken at the treachery of his son, and he said to his servants, "Arise, and let us flee; make haste and go, for fear Absalom may come and fight against the city with the sword."

His servants were ready to fight for him, but he fled in haste over the brook Kedron and went toward the wilderness, with all of the people of the city with him, until there was a great multitude, and in the midst the priests and the Levites bearing the Ark of God, but when David saw this he said, "Carry back the Ark of God into the city. If I shall find favor in the eyes of the Lord He will bring me again. Let Him do to me as seemeth good to Him."

So the priests and the Levites returned to the city with the Ark of God. It was a sad procession that went over the *Mount of Olives led by David, weeping as he went, with his head covered and his feet bare. Some enemies of the house of Saul came out and troubled him by the way, but there was no anger in the heart of David toward any. He believed the hand of the Lord was upon him, and he said, "It may be the Lord will look on mine affliction."

Absalom came to Jerusalem, and while he was asking his chief counselor what to do, he was persuaded by a friend of David, who had stayed behind, to wait until he had gathered a larger army before he followed after David. This gave him time to send word to David to cross over Jordan before Absalom should overtake him. The chief counsellor, when he saw that his advice was not followed, went to his own house and hanged himself, for he knew that the Lord was bringing his counsel to naught.

After David had passed over into Gilead the people of that land brought food, and dishes, and beds to the sorrowful king and his tired people, and they were cared for in the city of Mahanaim. Then Joab, the captain, gathered the men together to go and meet Absalom and his army, and as they passed out of the city David stood in the gate and charged all the captains as they passed, saying,

"Deal gently, for my sake, with the young man, even with Absalom." So they went out to battle, and it was in a wood. God had given David's army the victory, and twenty thousand men of Absalom's army were slain. Absalom, who rode on a mule, was caught by his long thick hair in the branches of an oak tree, and the mule went away and left him hanging there.

A man ran and told Joab that he had seen Absalom hanging in an oak. "Why didst thou not smite him there?" said Joab.

The man said he would not have done it for a thousand shekels of silver, because David had charged them all not to touch the young man Absalom.

But Joab turned away, and when he had found Absalom in the oak, he, with the ten young men who were with him, killed Absalom, and they buried him in the wood.

Then Joab sent two messengers to carry news of the victory to the king, who sat between the city gates, while a watchman stood over the gates on the city wall. When the watchmen saw the two men running, one after the other, he cried out and told the king. The first man cried as he came, "All is well," but when the king said, "Is the young man Absalom safe?" he could not answer, and when the second messenger cried, "Tidings, my lord, the king," again David asked, "Is the young man Absalom safe?"

"The enemies of my lord the king and all that rise against thee to do thee hurt be as that young man," said the messenger.

Then the king went up to the room over the city gate and wept, and as he went he cried, "O my son Absalom! My son, my son Absalom! Would God I had died for thee, O Absalom, my son, my son!"

The people who had come back joyful because the enemy had been conquered were distressed by the grief of the king, so that Joab persuaded David to come down to the gate and meet the people.

After this those who were left of the followers of Absalom begged the king to come back to Jerusalem, and so he came, and thousands came to meet him.

He had only forgiving words for those who had injured him, and for Barzillai and the men of Gilead who had fed them and shown them great kindness in the darkest hour of the king's life, and who came a little way on the journey with them, he had grateful words and blessings.

And so the king came to his own again. He was now getting to be an old man, and the love of his people made his last days blessed.

His warriors said, "Thou shalt go no more out with us to battle, that thou quench not the light of Israel."

Once he sinned against the Lord by numbering his people. He wanted to know how many men in his kingdom could bear arms in battle, and he forgot that victory over the enemy was not with the many or the few, but with the Lord, who is the strength of his people. When he saw that he had done wrong he confessed it and begged for forgiveness, but a pestilence spread over all the land, and came near to Jerusalem, and the angel was stayed by the Lord's hand just over the threshing floor of Araunah. This was the broad flat top of Mount Moriah where long before Abraham had built an altar on which to offer Isaac.

When David saw the angel he said, "I have done wickedly, but these sheep, what have they done? Let Thine hand, I pray thee, be against me, and against my father's house."

Then the prophet Gad said, "Go up, rear an altar to the Lord in the threshing-floor of Araunah," and David went as the Lord commanded. When they reached the mount Araunah offered David the piece of ground with the oxen for a sacrifice, but he would not take them as a gift.

"But I will surely buy it of thee at a price," said David, "neither will I offer burnt offerings to the Lord my God of that which doth cost me nothing."

So he bought the piece of ground and paid for it six hundred shekels of gold. Twice had the Lord blessed this spot with a miracle of salvation, and twice an altar had been built there, and looking upon it, David said, "This is the house of the Lord God, and this is the altar of burnt offering for Israel," and he prepared to build there the temple of Solomon, — the altar of the world.